The Poetry and Paintings
of the First Bible
of Charles the Bald

RECENTIORES: LATER LATIN TEXTS AND CONTEXTS
James J. O'Donnell, Series Editor

Editorial Board

Poetry and the Cult of the Martyrs: The Liber Peristephanon *of Prudentius*
by Michael Roberts

Dante's Epistle to Cangrande
by Robert Hollander

Macaronic Sermons: Bilingualism and Preaching in Late-Medieval England
by Siegfried Wenzel

Writing Ravenna: The Liber Pontificalis *of Andreas Agnellus*
by Joaquín Martínez Pizarro

Anacreon redivivus: *A Study of Anacreontic Translation in Mid-Sixteenth-Century France*
by John O'Brien

The Whole Book: Cultural Perspectives on the Medieval Miscellany
edited by Stephen G. Nichols and Siegfried Wenzel

Parody in the Middle Ages: The Latin Tradition
by Martha Bayless

A Comedy Called Susenbrotus
edited and translated by Connie McQuillen

The Poetry and Paintings of the First Bible of Charles the Bald
by Paul Edward Dutton and Herbert L. Kessler

The opening poem (lines 51–100), with medallion portraits of DAVID REX IMPERATOR +, *top,* and KAROLVS REX FRANCO\<RVM\>, *bottom;* Paris, BN lat. 1, fol. 1v

The Poetry and Paintings
of the First Bible
of Charles the Bald

Paul Edward Dutton and Herbert L. Kessler

Ann Arbor

THE UNIVERSITY OF MICHIGAN PRESS

2000   1999   1998   1997   4   3   2   1

A CIP catalog record for this book is available from the British Library.

Library of Congress Cataloging-in-Publication Data

Dutton, Paul Edward, 1952–
    The poetry and paintings of the First Bible of Charles the Bald /
Paul Edward Dutton and Herbert L. Kessler.
        p.   cm. — (Recentiores)
    Includes bibliographical references and index.
    ISBN 0-472-10815-8 (alk. paper)
    1. Christian poetry, Latin (Medieval and modern)—France—Tours—
History and criticism.   2. Christian poetry, Latin (Medieval and
modern)—Translations into English.   3. Christian poetry, Latin
(Medieval and modern)—Illustrations.   4. Illumination of books and
manuscripts, Carolingian—France—Tours.   5. Art and literature—
France—Tours—History.   6. Charles II, King of France, 823–877.
7. Manuscripts, Medieval—France—Tours.   8. Scriptoria—France—
Tours.   I. Kessler, Herbert L., 1941–   . II. Title.
III. Series.
PA8056.D88   1997
871'.3093823—dc21   97-4833
                                                                            CIP

In memory of Robert Deshman (1941–1995)
who loved medieval poetry and painting
and their intricate entwinings

Preface

The two authors began work on this monograph in 1994. Though at first we imagined that we would produce only a long article, the many mysteries of the First Bible of Charles the Bald, upon which we had separately written, would not let us so lightly move on. In 1991, at the invitation of Guglielmo Cavallo, Herbert Kessler had delivered a paper in Spoleto entitled, "A Lay Abbot as Patron: Count Vivian and the First Bible of Charles the Bald," in which he suggested that the manuscript conveyed a message of humility and royal rectitude that actually subverted the interests of the lay abbot and promoted those of the canons. In *The Politics of Dreaming in the Carolingian Empire* in 1994 Paul Dutton advanced some new hypotheses about the Bible's poetry and Presentation miniature. In the fall of 1994, though we had not yet met, we decided to pool our skills and knowledge of history, philology, art history, and Carolingian studies in an attempt to unlock some of the persistent puzzles bound up in the fascinating First Bible.

What followed was a voluminous and invigorating e-mail and fax correspondence over the next year, as pieces of the puzzle were slowly put together, discoveries made, and hypotheses tested. We carried out the research on all aspects of this book together and in full collaboration, jointly composed it, and take full responsibility for it in its entirety.

In the spring of 1995, Herbert Kessler traveled to Paris as a guest of the École des Hautes Études en Sciences Sociales. Through the good graces of M. François Avril, Conservateur-en-chef of the Bibliothèque Nationale, he was able to reexamine the First Bible during his visit, check its faded *tituli,* and study the codicology and illuminations of the volume. Paul Dutton, with the support of the Social Sciences and Humanities Research Council of Canada, made computer-generated concordances of various Carolingian verses and traveled to Baltimore and Toronto. We would also like to thank a number of individuals who generously commented on aspects of our work in progress: Édouard Jeauneau, Maurizio Bettini, Michael McCormick, Lawrin Armstrong, Jean-Claude Bonne, Dominique Alibert, Barbara Rosenwein, Mildred Budny, Giles Constable, Johannes Fried, Lawrence Nees, and James O'Donnell.

In June 1995 we met in Baltimore and worked intensely to resolve some of the outstanding problems posed by the First Bible. The meeting in Baltimore also transformed a scholarly project, first facilitated by modern technology and the instantaneous exchange of electronic mail, into a rich and rewarding human experience and friendship. We can only hope that other medievalists will enter into similar collaborations as a way of bringing down their own often hard, but frangible, disciplinary walls.

Contents

Illustrations

Frontispiece

The opening poem (lines 51–100) of the First Bible, with medallion portraits of David and Charles

Text Figure

Color Plates   *following page 50*

Plates   139

Except for fig. 22, which is copied from André Wilmart's 1926 article, all photographs are reproduced with permission of the owners of the objects.

Introduction

Few illuminated manuscripts of the early Middle Ages present as much information about the purpose and circumstances of their creation as the First
Bible of Charles the Bald (Paris, Bibliothèque Nationale, MS lat. 1).[1] The 353
lines of verse found in the First Bible establish that the great codex was made
at the monastery of Saint-Martin in Tours and was presented to Charles the
Bald by the canons as an expression of their gratitude and in order to promote
the monastery's special interests. Two poems and a painting at the end of the
volume imagine the event, portraying Count Vivian of Tours and the canons
assembled before the king (fols. 422r–423r, figs. 15–17 and IV). Flanked by
courtiers and arms-bearers, Charles is about to receive the enormous volume
from the veiled hands of two canons, while others pray for, and seem to sing
the praises of, the young king.

Though the First Bible has been much admired and its art frequently reproduced,[2] the relationship between its poetry and paintings has never been

---

1. See Herbert L. Kessler, *The Illustrated Bibles from Tours* (Princeton, N.J., 1977); Charles Samaran and
Robert Marichal, *Catalogue des manuscrits en écriture latine portant des indications de date, de lieu ou de
copiste,* vol. 2 (under the direction of M-T. d'Alverny, with entries by M. Garand, M. Mabille, and J. Met-
man): *Bibliothèque Nationale, Fonds Latin (Nos. 1 à 8,000)* (Paris, 1962), p. 3; Percy Ernst Schramm and
Florentine Mütherich, *Denkmale der deutschen Könige und Kaiser. Ein Beitrag zur Herrschergeschichte von
Karl dem Grossen bis Friederich II, 768–1250,* Veröffentlichungen des Zentralinstituts für Kunstgeschichte in
München, 2 (Munich, 1962), pp. 129–30; Wilhelm Koehler, *Die karolingischen Miniaturen,* vol. 1: *Die Schule
von Tours,* part 1: *Die Ornamentik* (Berlin, 1930; rpt. 1963), pp. 250–55, 396–401, part 2: *Die Bilder* (Berlin,
1933; rpt. 1963), pp. 27–64, 220–31, and Tafeln (Berlin, 1933; rpt. 1963), plates 69–89; Edward K. Rand, *A
Survey of the Manuscripts of Tours,* vol. 1, Studies in the Script of Tours, 1 (Cambridge, Mass., 1929), pp.
155–56.

The First Bible has also been known as the Vivian Bible and the Bible of Count Vivian: see Wilma
Fitzgerald, *Ocelli nominum: Names and Shelf Marks of Famous/Familiar Manuscripts* (Toronto, 1992), p. 30.
The reasons for now abandoning those popular names will become apparent below.

2. See *Metz enluminée* (Metz, 1989), plates A–F [color]; Robert G. Calkins, *Illuminated Books of the
Middle Ages* (Ithaca, N.Y., 1983), pp. 96–118, which contains black and white reproductions of all the major
illuminations as well as five *incipit* pages; Florentine Mütherich and Joachim E. Gaehde (provenance and
commentaries), *Carolingian Painting* (New York, 1976), plates 21–23; Wilhelm Koehler, *Die karolingischen
Miniaturen,* plates 69–89.

deeply or systematically examined.[3] The reasons for this neglect are not hard to find. While the paintings have been widely regarded as among the finest achievements of Carolingian art and are easily accessible in reproductions, the Latin poetry accompanying them is difficult and, at points, obscure, and has been effectively inaccessible to students of the First Bible. No complete translation of the poems has, for instance, been available. Moreover, some scholars have simply disregarded the poems as inferior and not worthy of sustained study. Samuel Berger, a great authority on the history of the medieval Bible, dismissed the dedicatory verses as "détestables";[4] but along with many others he too was forced to turn to the verses for invaluable information about the provenance of the codex.[5] Yet, in selectively reading a few lines of poetry and ignoring the rest, scholars may have undermined the very integrity and overall design of the First Bible. We would do well to bear in mind that the first and last words in this magnificent Bible are those of the "modest author of the execrable verses,"[6] that the verses and some of the *tituli* not only accompany but drive the essential design of the volume and its paintings, and that the poet, who has been so neglected and dismissed, may in the end prove to have been the architect of the much admired volume.

To separate pictures and poems, to study one intensely and overlook the other almost completely, does violence to the shape and context of many medieval manuscripts. No archaeologist would, for instance, describe an Attic vase and neglect its Homeric inscription, but that is what we have too often done in the case of the First Bible and other illuminated manuscripts. The separation of words and paintings produced together may more closely reflect the divided enterprises of modern scholarship than it does the character of a medieval entity as singularly complex as the First Bible of Charles the Bald.

The complete corpus of poems in the First Bible has only been widely avail-

---

3. For background material on poetry and painting in the Carolingian world, see Peter Godman, *Poets and Emperors: Frankish Politics and Poetry* (Oxford, 1987), pp. 173–75; Rosamond McKitterick, "Text and Image in the Carolingian World," in *The Uses of Literacy in Early Medieval Europe,* ed. Rosamond McKitterick (Cambridge, 1990), pp. 297–318, rpt. in McKitterick, *The Frankish Kings and Culture in the Early Middle Ages,* Variorum Collected Studies, 477 (Aldershot, 1995), item 8; David Ganz, "'Pando quod Ignoro': In Search of Carolingian Artistic Experience," in *Intellectual Life in the Middle Ages: Essays Presented to Margaret Gibson,* ed. L. Smith and B. Ward (London, 1992), p. 27; and John Lowden, "The Royal/Imperial Book and the Image or Self-Image of the Medieval Ruler," in *Kings and Kingship in Medieval Europe,* ed. Anne J. Duggan (London, 1993), pp. 216–26.

4. Samuel Berger, *Histoire de la Vulgate pendant les premiers siècles du Moyen Age* (Paris, 1893), pp. 215–19.

5. Du Cange in 1688 was one of the first to begin mining the verses for historical information. For his important and fundamental reading, see the entry on *Armigerii* in Charles Du Fresne Du Cange, *Glossarium mediae et infimae Latinitatis conditum a Carolo du Fresne domino Du Cange . . . ,* 9th ed., revised by D. P. Carpentier, G. A. L. Henschel, and L. Favre, 10 vols. (Paris, 1937–38), 1:392–94.

6. Edward K. Rand and George Howe, "The Vatican Livy and the Script of Tours," *Memoirs of the American Academy in Rome,* (1918), p. 30 n. 9.

able in an edition Ludwig Traube first published in 1886.[7] Though Traube was a superior Latinist and a pioneering paleographer, his edition contains numerous misreadings, some of them quite serious and bound to confuse readers.[8] In fact, Traube did not consult the manuscript itself when making his edition for the *Monumenta Germaniae Historica,* but relied upon earlier editions of the poems and asked Auguste Molinier in Paris to reexamine the manuscript on his behalf.[9] Unfortunately those scholars who have employed Traube's edition have been forced to reprint his errors,[10] so that it seemed imperative for us to reedit the verses. Moreover, given the importance of respecting a unique and

---

7. The standard edition of Ludwig Traube is printed in "Bibliothecarum et Psalteriorum Versus," 3, in *Monumenta Germaniae Historica: Poetae Latini Aevi Carolini* (hereafter abbreviated as *MGH PLAC*), vol. 3 (Berlin, 1896; rpt. 1964), pp. 243–52. The first part of the volume, that is, pp. 1–264, was first published in 1886 and later reprinted in 1896 along with the second part of the volume, pp. 265–823. The *carmina* or portions of them had been edited many times before: see E. Baluze, *Capitularia regum Francorum,* vol. 2 (Paris, 1677), p. 1572; M. Bouquet, *Recueil des historiens des Gaules et de la France,* vol. 7 (Paris, 1749), p. 316; Auguste Comte de Bastard d'Estang, *Peintures, ornements, écritures et lettres initiales de la Bible de Charles le Chauve conservée à Paris* (Paris, 1883); and Léopold Delisle in "Mémoire sur l'École calligraphique de Tours au IXe siècle," *Mémoires de l'Academie des Inscriptions et Belles Lettres* 32.1 (1885), p. 40. See also Henri Auguste Omont, *Peintures et initiales de la première Bible de Charles le Chauve* (Paris, 1911), pp. 5–9.

8. All references in this note and throughout the study are to the poem and line numbers found in the appendix to this book. Traube's misreadings are the following:

Poem	Manuscript	Traube
I.20	GEMITVS	genitus
I.40	EFFERT	offert
I.105	QVOS	quod
I.155	QVOSDAM	quodam
I.168	MONET	movet
I.170	CVPIT	capit
I.182	PRAEPOSVIT	proposuit
II.5	SVI	sibi
IX.2	IVRA	iussa
XI.4	SVMMVS	primus
XI.23	FIAT	fiet

In another three cases, Traube introduced orthographical changes:

I.58	ERI	heri
I.162	EXPOLIANS	exspolians
II.6	CONPOSVIT	composuit

At X.16 he emended "Aut" to "Haut" and so noted the change in his critical apparatus at *MGH PLAC* 3:250. At II.5, he printed "sibi," which he later corrected to "sui" in his "Praeterita" in *MGH PLAC* 3:752. The other misreadings all went unremarked by Traube in the "Praeterita" and should not, therefore, be taken as editorial interventions or misprints.

9. See Traube, *MGH PLAC* 3:242.

10. To give but a few examples, Godman, *Poets and Emperors,* p. 174 n. 117, received "primus Aregarius" from Traube's edition rather than the manuscript reading at XI.3 of "summus Aregarius"; Bernice M. Kaczynski, "Edition, Translation, and Exegesis: The Carolingians and the Bible," in *"The Gentle Voices of Teachers": Aspects of Learning in the Carolingian Age,* ed. Richard E. Sullivan (Columbus, Ohio, 1995), p. 184 n. 31 repeated Traube's original reading at II.5 of "translata sibi" rather than the manuscript's "trans-

original manuscript on its own terms, we have attempted to restore the poetry to the state of its original inscription with little editorial intervention. In fact, we have introduced only one new emendation, though others might be called for and justified.[11]

We have also supplied a translation of the poetry, though we warn the reader that it should be considered preliminary and in want of improvement. Many obscurities and difficulties persist in our understanding of the poems. Indeed, since the reader has recourse to the Latin text on the facing pages of the appendix, an attempt has been made in the translation and the commentary and notes that accompany it to try to express what we take to be the meaning of the poetry.

Many readers may wish to start with the reedited verses, translation, commentary, and plates before turning to the analysis and arguments made in the study itself. The coauthors are acutely aware how problematic some of these arguments are, but we have tried to state them as directly as possible, given the evidence at hand, in the hope that they will lead others to further study and refinement of our understanding of the majestic First Bible. The proper function of a monograph such as this one, we believe, is to put forward a consistent and reasonable interpretation of an issue or problem, which readers can then test. We also harbor the hope that our study will stimulate new study of one of the Western world's great books, for this deluxe manuscript may have become almost too familiar and our thinking about it at times too conventional.

The underlying assumption that has for too long governed the investigation of the First Bible has been that its paintings could be examined in splendid isolation as objects without a larger political and cultural context. This supposition, we think, plays false with the very nature of the First Bible, which cannot be fully understood without taking into account its connected character and a set of political preoccupations that occasioned its very creation and invested the book with meaning. We believe that in 845 at Saint-Martin a poet and several painters worked together and with deliberation to send a special message to young Charles the Bald. The First Bible was, if we are right, a kind of painted Trojan Horse, out of which were to pour ideas and images that the canons hoped would steal into, capture, and transform the heart of a Christian king.

Our monograph, then, properly addresses the problems of who wrote the

---

lata sui." In two cases Traube's reading, "proposuit," at I.182 was printed instead of the manuscript's "praeposuit": see Hans Hubert Anton, *Fürstenspiegel und Herrscherethos in der Karolingerzeit,* Bonner historische Forschungen, 32 (Bonn, 1968), p. 255; and Nikolaus Staubach, *Rex Christianus: Hofkultur und Herrschaftspropaganda im Reich Karls des Kahlen,* vol. 2: *Die Grundlegung der "religion royale"* (Cologne, 1993), p. 94.

11. See VI.11 and II.5 in the edition and commentary found in the appendix.

poems, when and why the codex was constructed and presented, how the poems and paintings physically and intellectually relate to each other, and what they attempted to say to the king. This study of the First Bible is not, however, intended to be comprehensive, and many issues and themes arising from the poetry and paintings have been left aside.[12] Here we intend to explore, as best we can, the complicated, layered, and intertwined communication of written and painted images in an attempt to recover some small measure of the fuller message and meaning of the First Bible of Charles the Bald.

12. The language of love found throughout the verses, particularly in the first long dedicatory poem (at I.13, 17, 124, 128, 175, 198), is, for instance, in want of study, as are the subtle variations in the imagery of the four core illuminations of the First Bible and the sources and date of their *tituli*.

CHAPTER 1

The Poetry

A distinction should be drawn between the verses and *tituli* found in the First Bible. There are four sets of dedicatory verses: I (fols. 1r–2v, see figs. 1–4, frontispiece, and I), which stands at the start of the codex; VI, which occupies the recto of folio 329 (fig. 9) and which has the Majestas Domini illumination on the verso (fig. 10); and X (fol. 422r, fig. 15) and XI (fol. 422v, fig. 16), which precede the Presentation miniature on folio 423r (fig. 17). Verses I, X, and XI are not found on illuminated folios, but were inscribed in rustic-capital letters written in gold on purple pages placed at the head and back of the codex. Verse VI was written in alternating lines of red and gold ink on the unpainted side of an illuminated folio. Each of the dedicatory verses speaks directly to King Charles the Bald.[1]

There are also seven sets of *tituli* in the First Bible, all of which are found on illuminated pages. Four of these are also found in the so-called Moutier-Grandval Bible (London, British Library, Add. MS 10546; see figs. 23–26), which was produced at Tours about a decade before the First Bible:[2] III on the Genesis frontispiece on folio 10v (fig. 6); IV on the Exodus frontispiece on folio 27v (fig. 7); VII on the Majestas Domini illumination on folio 329r (fig. 10); and IX on the Apocalypse frontispiece on folio 415v (figs. 13 and III). Three sets of *tituli* are unique to the First Bible: II on the frontispiece to Jerome's preface to the Vulgate on folio 3v (fig. 5); V on the frontispiece to the Psalms on folio 215v (figs. 8 and II); and VIII on the Epistles frontispiece on folio 386v (fig. 11).

Though there has been some scholarly speculation about the relation of the two sets of *tituli* to the First Bible and its artistic sources,[3] there has been no systematic attempt to sort out the origins of the various poems and their rela-

---

1. I.1 and 190; VI.3 and 28; X.2; XI.7, 35, and 42 as David and at line 15 as Caesar.
2. For a facsimile, see Johannes Duft et al., *Die Bibel von Moutier-Grandval, British Museum Add. MS. 10546* (Bern, 1971).
3. See the review of this question in Kessler, *Illustrated Bibles,* pp. 10–11.

tionship to each other, to the miniatures, or to the poetry of the time. There is, however, evidence to suggest that one author wrote the four dedicatory verses and the three new *tituli* and that he chose to retain or incorporate the four older *tituli* in the First Bible.

For one thing, both the style and substance of the four dedicatory verses are consistent. The poet played from first to last with the theme of Charles as David.[4] Not only does he assert that the king has the power of David (I.195) but also that David is another name for Charles (VI.1–4, X.1–2, XI.7) and that the Carolingian ruler is one to whom songs should be sung just as they were for the psalmist himself (XI.35–38). In three of the verses (I.193, VI.28, and X.2) the king is called "alme" and, in two others, (VI.27 and XI.42) "rex bone." Moreover, in all four poems, the poet refers to Charles as the "decus" or adornment of the kingdom (I.199, VI.3, X.1, XI.25). Twice (I.190 and VI.1) he praises the king as "inclite." At VI.4 he calls the king the "eclesiae fautor" and at X.17 the "eclesiae fotor," the latter being merely an orthographical variant. In all four verses, the poet concludes with a valediction, with *Amen* at VI.30 and X.44, with *Vale* at I.200, and with *Ave* at XI.42.

But it is not just the repeated royal and panegyrical vocabulary that argues for a single author of the dedicatory verses, it is also the shared language throughout the *carmina*. Twice "paradise" is invoked in the vocative (I.119 and XI.18); "clare primordia" occurs in two different poems (I.157 and VI.7); "verumque fidesque" ends lines of verse in two poems (VI.23 and XI.5); "in sensu parili" begins lines in two different poems (I.92 and VI.16); "actio" appears in three poems (I.185, VI.21, X.16); and "nova rite" is repeated once (I.113 and VI.6). The poet also liked to list attributes and substantives in almost uninterrupted and dizzying sequence. At I.44 and X.25 he employed the same half line: "pauper egenus inops." At X.13 he slightly altered a line used earlier at I.137, "Iusta iubens, iniusta vetans, mala cuncta repellens."

So intertwined, in fact, are the various themes, phrases, and vocabulary of the four dedicatory verses that it would be almost impossible to treat them separately as the work of different authors. Moreover, the poems have historical referents supplied in X and XI that securely place the contemporaneous creation of all four dedicatory verses in the 840s at Saint-Martin in Tours.

The four sets of *tituli* shared by the Moutier-Grandval Bible and the First Bible, in contrast, probably existed in an exemplar that was at Tours in the 830s and 840s. The *tituli* in this copy may have been composed or assembled at Tours when Fridugis was abbot (804–34), but there is not enough evidence at

---

4. See *carmina* I.195; VI.1; X.1, 9; XI.7, 35, and 42.

present to allow us either to date them or to determine their origin.[5] Moreover, the shared *tituli* may not have been the work of a single poet. While all the dedicatory verses are composed in elegiac couplets, only one of the shared *tituli* is (VII). The other three *tituli* are made up of a variety of complex and remarkable metrical schemes, which even contain unusual metrical shifts within individual poems.[6] Whereas the assemblers of the First Bible did not alter or adapt the *tituli* they took from their exemplar, the illuminators did introduce changes to the accompanying art, a subject to which we shall return. More work still remains to be done on the shared *tituli,* not only on their origins, but also on their distinctive metrical characters. The different style and vocabulary of these older verses set them sharply apart from the other poems in the First Bible.[7]

The fact that poems II, V, and VIII are standard elegiac distichs may suggest that they were not taken from the exemplar containing the metrically more complicated and varied *tituli* common to the Moutier-Grandval Bible and the First Bible. Indeed, poems II and VIII have exactly the same form as one another, that of three elegiac distichs. Poem V, however, is a single couplet, like VII. The three sets of *tituli* unique to the First Bible also share common vocabulary and phrases with the dedicatory verses. For instance, in II.4 Jerome is described as "altithrono fultus ubique deo," while in VI.10 the evangelist Mark's voice is said to be "suo fulta perenne deo." If "altithronus" seems a relatively rare word in the *titulus,* a similar compound, "alticanorus," can be found in the dedicatory verses at I.63. And whereas one *titulus* (VIII.6) refers to the Old Testament as the *series prisca* and the New Testament as the *series nova,* dedicatory verse I.113 calls the New Testament the *nova series* and VI.5 calls the Old Testament the *series vetusta.* Indeed, the phrase "ire queat,"

---

5. Though Ludwig Traube had printed the four sets of *tituli* common to the Moutier-Grandval and First Bible in his edition of the poetry of the First Bible in *MGH PLAC* 3:248–50 in 1886, he later reached the conclusion that they had been taken from a much older Italian Bible: see Traube, "Paläographische Anzeigen III," *Neues Archiv der Gesellschaft für ältere deutsche Geschichtskunde* 27 (1901): 264–65, rpt. in Traube, *Vorlesungen und Abhandlungen von Ludwig Traube,* vol. 3: *Kleine Schriften,* ed. S. Brandt (Munich, 1920), pp. 244–45. Wilhelm Koehler, following the opinion of Karl Strecker, separated the sets of *tituli* common to the two codices from the *tituli* unique to the First Bible, and dated the former to late antiquity: see Koehler, *Die karolingische Miniaturen* 1:2, p. 109. Carl Nordenfalk, "Beiträge zur Geschichte der Turonischen Buchmalerei," *Acta Archaeologica* 7 (1936): 297, argued that all the *tituli* belonged together as an earlier product, but that the evidence of the art suggested that the sixth century was too late a date for the model. Alfred A. Schmid, "Die Kanontafeln und die Miniaturen," in Duft et al., *Die Bibel von Moutier-Grandval,* p. 184, argued that the common *tituli* are Carolingian in origin.

6. *MGH PLAC* 3:815–18. Traube classified III.1–2 as an asclepiadic stanza ending with an adonic verse; III.3–6 as a trochaic tetrameter catalectic; III.7–10 as an iambic dimeter catalectic; III.11–12 as an alcaic stanza at the start, but finishing with a pentameter; IV as a sapphic stanza; and IX as an iambic trimeter at the start, with phalaecian elements (IX.3: "Leges e veteris").

7. This view is at variance, therefore, with that of Nordenfalk, "Beiträge zur Geschichte," p. 297.

which is used at VIII.2 in the new *titulus* to describe why blinded Paul needed to be led forward, has parallels in the dedicatory verses in "obire queat" (XI.28) and "obire queunt" (I.140). Of perhaps greatest interest are the two datives "olli" (VIII.4) and "ollis" (II.6), which match similar uses in the dedicatory verses at I.102 and I.17. We shall return to the importance of these unusual forms of *ille* below.

While poems II and VIII seem of a piece with the dedicatory verses in terms of style and vocabulary, the origin of poem V, the elegiac couplet that serves as the *titulus* for the frontispiece to Psalms on folio 215v (figs. 8 and II), is less certain. Even here, however, one feature is striking. The poet of the dedicatory verses had a fondness for adjectives formed with the suffix *-ficus*. Thus, at I.81 he used the familiar epithet "pacificus" for Solomon and at I.188 referred to the height of poetry as the "versificalis apex." Indeed, the new *titulus* at II.2 speaks of the "legis honorificae." Most striking of all, the first dedicatory poem calls David "hymnificus" (I.76), while the new *titulus* (V.1) calls him "psalmificus." These words can be considered synonyms and, therefore, might suggest that poem V, like poems II and VIII, was written by the poet who composed the dedicatory verses. Moreover, XI.35–36 contains a specific evocation of both poem V and the painting of David surrounded by his musicians.

Thus, a case can be made that not only did one poet compose the four dedicatory verses (I, VI, X, and XI), but that he also composed two of the *tituli* (II and VIII) and most probably the other new *titulus* (V) as well. Moreover, even if a *titulus* such as poem V once existed in a lost Turonian record that supplied information for the composition of the illuminations in the Moutier-Grandval Bible and the First Bible of Charles the Bald, it might still be argued that the poet who wrote 328 out of the 353 lines of poetry in the First Bible chose or kept that *titulus* because it suited his purpose and larger design. Indeed, he had doubtless examined the older *tituli* before he began, since the use of "nectare sancto" in the shared *titulus* (IV.4) is paralleled by his own use of "nectare perpetuo" at I.118. One of his recurrent themes, after all, was that the Bible was holy food. In addition, the theme of the Testaments as law, which is also evident in the common *tituli* IV and IX, recurs throughout the new *tituli* and the four dedicatory verses. Thus, the common *titulus* IX.3 refers to the New Testament as "leges novellae" and the first dedicatory verse speaks of the "testamenti praecepta novelli" (I.89).

But who was this poet? Misunderstanding the reference to Charles as David at XI.7, Léopold Delisle assumed the poet was someone named David.[8] E. K. Rand and George Howe speculated that he might have been Amalricus, the

8. "Mémoire sur l'École calligraphique," p. 40 and n. 4.

magister scholarum of Saint-Martin and a later archbishop of Tours, or Milo, one of his successors as master,[9] but there is no evidence that either Amalricus or Milo was an active poet.

The one prominent and productive poet of Saint-Martin in the mid 840s was Audradus Modicus,[10] and it was recently suggested that he may have been the author of the verses of the First Bible.[11] Audradus wrote eleven sets of poems, which he collected together in a thirteen-part work that he presented to Pope Leo IV in Rome on 29 June 849. He must have later revised the whole collection, since the twelfth book, the prose *Liber revelationum* or *Book of Revelations,* was added to and revised in the early 850s. Audradus had been a priest[12] and canon of the monastery of Saint-Martin during the abbacy of Fridugis, for his name is to be found as the fifty-fourth on the list of 219 canons of Saint-Martin.[13] Moreover, he participated in the production of other manuscripts in the scriptorium, and his name was inscribed in the angles of the geometrical design of the opening page of the *Liber comitis* of Saint-Père of Chartres, an elegant lectionary that contained the Epistles and Gospels (fig. 22).[14] André Wilmart, who studied the manuscript and published plates of it before the manuscript was destroyed in the Second World War, thought that Audradus had designed, written, and decorated the manuscript early in his career at Tours.[15] In 847, Audradus became the suffragan bishop of

9. "Vatican Livy," p. 30 n. 9. See also Rand, *Survey of Manuscripts,* p. 156.

10. On Audradus Modicus, see Traube, *MGH PLAC* 3:67–72; Walter Mohr, "Audradus von Sens, Prophet und Kirchenpolitiker (um 850)," *Archivium Latinitatis Medii Aevi* 29 (1959): 239–67; Ursula Penndorf, *Das Problem der "Reichseinheitsidee" nach der Teilung von Verdun (843): Untersuchungen zu den späten Karolingern,* Münchener Beiträge zur Mediävistik und Renaissance-Forschung, 20 (Munich, 1974), pp. 94–116; Franz Brunhölzl, *Histoire de la littérature du Moyen Âge,* vol. 1, pt. 2: *L'époque carolingienne,* trans. H. Rochais (Turnhout, 1991), pp. 197–98; and Paul Edward Dutton, *The Politics of Dreaming in the Carolingian Empire* (Lincoln, Nebr., 1994), pp. 128–56.

11. *Politics of Dreaming,* pp. 139, 148. See also Herbert L. Kessler, "A Lay Abbot as Patron: Count Vivian and the First Bible of Charles the Bald," in *Committenti e produzione artistico-letteraria nell'alto medioevo occidentale, 4–10 aprile 1991,* Settimane di studio del Centro Italiano di Studi sull'alto medioevo, 39 (Spoleto, 1992), pp. 665–68.

12. This is evident from the fact that he became a suffragan bishop and that he once called himself a *sacerdos* in his *Liber revelationum.*

13. *Libri confraternitatum sancti Galli, Augiensis, Fabariensis,* ed. P. Piper, in *Monumenta Germaniae Historica: Necrologiae Germaniae, Supplementband* (Berlin, 1884), p. 13, col. 14.15 and p. 77, col. 235.22. On the list and the order of the canons' appearance, see Rand and Howe, "Vatican Livy," pp. 25–34. On the number of canons at Saint-Martin, which was limited to two hundred in the 840s, see Charles the Bald, charter 113 (from 16 April 849), ed. G. Tessier, *Recueil des actes de Charles II le Chauve, roi de France,* 3 vols. (Paris, 1943–55), 1:301–3.

14. For a detailed analysis of the contents of this lectionary (listed as "Aud"), see Emil J. Lengeling, "Pericopes," in *New Catholic Encyclopedia,* vol. 11 (New York, 1967), p. 133. See also Klaus Gamber, *Codices liturgici latini antiquiores,* Spicilegium friburgense, subsidia 1 (Freiburg, 1963), item 1214, pp. 223–24.

15. André Wilmart, "Le lectionnaire de Saint-Père," *Speculum* 1 (1926): 269–78, and "Errata in 'Lectionnaire de Saint-Père,'" *Speculum* 1 (1926): 450. See also Yves Delaporte, *Les manuscrits enluminés de la*

Sens under Archbishop Wenilo, but was deposed in late 849 along with the other suffragans of west Francia. Beginning in the 840s, he began to receive visions of things mostly political, which he recorded in his *Book of Revelations* and on occasion tried to communicate to the king. It is not known when he died, though he seems to have fallen silent by 855.

Traube, the editor of Audradus's poems,[16] probably ignored him as a possible author of the unique poetry of the First Bible of Charles the Bald because he believed that that volume had been produced and presented to Charles the Bald in 850,[17] and he knew that Audradus had departed Tours in 847 to become the suffragan bishop of Sens. Traube himself had, oddly enough, identified the most telling characteristics of Audradus's poetry and had used these as proofs of his authorship of the other poems edited under his name. "Audradus loved," he wrote, "to insert the datives *olli* and *ollis,* [and] not just at the beginning of a line of verse as do those who imitate Virgil."[18] In his extant poetry Audradus used *olli* for *illi* on five occasions and *ollis* for *illis* once.[19] It constituted, as Traube noted, a distinctive feature of his *carmina,* one doubtless influenced by his close reading of Virgil.[20] In the new poems of the First Bible of Charles the Bald the poet employed *olli* twice, once in the first

---

bibliothèque de Chartres (Chartres, 1929), pp. 1–2 and plate 1; Rand, *Survey of Manuscripts,* pp. 133–34; Koehler, *Die karolingischen Miniaturen,* 1:1, pp. 408–9; and *Catalogue général des manuscrits des bibliothèques publiques de France,* vol. 53: *Manuscrits des bibliothèques sinistrées de 1940 à 1944* (Paris, 1962), pp. 2, 5, 15.

16. *MGH PLAC* 3:76–121 and, in a supplement, at 3:739–45. Despite Audradus's own specific numbering of the parts of his collection, Traube assigned new numbers, perhaps because when he began he lacked books 1 to 4 of the collection. He edited the twelfth book, the *Liber revelationum,* separately in Ludwig Traube, "'O Roma nobilis.' Philologische Untersuchungen aus dem Mittelalter," in *Abhandlungen der philosophischen-philologischen Classe der königlich bayerischen Akademie der Wissenschaften* 19 (Munich, 1892), pp. 374–91.

Here the numbers of Audradus's works are cited according to Audradus's own numbering system (not Traube's), followed by the line number of the poem. Page references to Traube's edition are also given.

On the poetry of Audradus, with partial editions, see also Augusto Gaudenzi, "Un ignoto poema di Audrado di Sens," *Bulletino dell'Istituto Storico Italiano* 7 (1889): 39–45 and *Audrado di Sens, Il fonte della vita: Con testo a fronte,* ed. and trans. Francesco Stella (Florence, 1991).

17. *MGH PLAC* 3:241. On flyleaf A of the First Bible Étienne Baluze noted that he had acquired the codex in 1675 from the canons of Metz for inclusion in the library of Colbert. Below that another note in an early-modern cursive script gives a date for the Bible's creation: "Hunc ipsum codicem Vivianus Comes Rector Ecclesiae S. Martini Turonensis et quidem monachi undecim obtulerunt Carolo Calvo Francorum regi anno 850 dum Turonis in dicta Ecclesia versaretur." See also Rosamond McKitterick, "The Study of Frankish History in France and Germany in the Sixteenth and Seventeenth Centuries," *Francia* 8 (1991): 570–71, rpt. in *Frankish Kings and Culture,* item 14.

18. *MGH PLAC* 3:71 n. 1.

19. For *olli,* see Audradus 5.54, ed. Traube, *MGH PLAC* 3:74; 5.84, p. 75; 7.31, p. 87; 11.322, p. 117; and 11.435, p. 120. For *ollis,* see Audradus 11.335, p. 117. See also chapter 4 n. 11 below for the Turonian understanding of this usage.

20. For Virgil's use of *olli,* see *Aeneid* 1.254, 4.105, 5.10, 5.197, 5.284, 5.358, 5.580, 6.321, 7.458, 7.505, 8.94, 8.594, 9.740, 10.745, 11.236, 12.18, 12.300, 12.309, 12.537, 12.788, 12.829. For his use of *ollis,* see *Aeneid* 6.730, 8.659.

dedicatory verse (I.102) and once in the last of the new *tituli* (VIII.4). He used *ollis* in the first dedicatory verse (I.17) and in the first of the new *tituli* that immediately follows it (II.6).

Traube also noted that Audradus liked to use forms of the word *misellus*.[21] This word expressed his characterization of himself as one of the small, wretched, and humble of the world. At the end of the poem in honor of Saint Peter, Audradus gave thanks, for instance, that the saint had loosened the chains that bind humans and joyfully asked him to open up a land of light for the small and wretched *(miselli)*.[22] Indeed, the epithetic name *Modicus,* which Audradus took for himself, was also designed to express his personal sense of smallness and humility.[23] On occasion he characterized his writing in the same terms. In the first book of his poems, the one dedicated to the Trinity, he called on God to accept his "modica verba."[24] Once again, in his account of his meeting with the pope, he drew attention to his own smallness and insignificance *(minimus)*.[25] This cultivated and self-conscious humility on Audradus's part was not simply a plea for mercy, of course, but a strategy for securing special privilege and charitable attention. In introducing the proem to his collected works, he called on God to have pity on him: "Audradi miserere tui."[26]

Some of the same suggestive language appears in the verses of the First Bible of Charles the Bald. Early in the first dedicatory verse, the poet called on King Charles to be merciful toward the defenseless poor and to let every little wretch *(misellus)* thrive and praise the merciful king (I.43–46). Mercy was presented as one of the king's defining characteristics (X.3). In perhaps the most self-reflective of all his lines, the poet described his own work in the First Bible as a meager *(modicus)* and rather rustic *(rusticulus)* composition (I.88). If other evidence of Audradus's authorship can be found, this line might almost prove, in the end, to be the revealing signature of Audradus's composition of the new poetry of the First Bible of Charles the Bald, the equivalent of the tiny and unobtrusive signature he left behind in the *Liber comitis* (fig. 22).

---

21. See 5.47, ed. Traube, *MGH PLAC* 3:74, "miselle"; 6.66, p. 86, "misellis"; and 9.126–27, p. 94, "misellam . . . animam."

22. See Audradus 6.64–66, ed. Traube, *MGH PLAC* 3:85–86.

23. All of these usages of AVDRADVS MODICVS, it should be noted, belong to the set of poems in honor of Julian and his friends (Audradus 8–11), and all occur in the *incipits* or *explicits.* See the title of book 8, ed. Traube, *MGH PLAC* 3:90; the *explicit* of the same, p. 90; the *explicit* of book 9, p. 100; and the *explicit* of book 10, p. 108. The lack of *incipits* and *explicits* in the other books of poems devoted to Julian may testify to the corruption of the manuscript tradition. On the name Audradus, see Traube, "O Roma nobilis," p. 390.

24. Audradus 1.37, ed. Traube, *MGH PLAC* 3:742. See also the similar reference to his unworthiness as a poet at 8.*prol.*23–25, p. 89.

25. *Praefatio.*2, ed. Traube, *MGH PLAC* 3:740 and "O Roma nobilis," p. 375.

26. *Proemium.*1, ed. Traube, *MGH PLAC* 3:741 and "O Roma nobilis," p. 377.

Ironically, for all his deliberate cultivation of humility, Audradus talked about himself a great deal, "jusqu'à la fatuité," as Franz Brunhölzl observed.[27] Not only did he print his name with care and some measure of pride on the opening page of his lectionary, but his *De fonte vitae* is a familiar and at times intimate dialogue between himself and Hincmar.[28] In his writing, Audradus frequently breaks into the first person, refers to his own books and poems, and once even dreamed of a doctor of the Church praising the fine poetry found in his venerable *De fonte vitae.*[29] He took special pride in the fact that he had met Pope Leo IV and introduced himself in his description of the event as "ego Audradus omnium servorum dei minimus."[30] Here again we encounter that particular Audradan mixture of personalized humility and individual pride, in which he both debased himself as "the least" and yet still drew particular attention to himself as "ego Audradus." In the same account, which later served as the introduction to his collected works, the poet described how the pope in the presence of his bishops and wise Roman clerics had accepted and sanctioned Audradus's gift book and, then, ordered it to be placed in the archives *(in scrinio)* of the Church of Rome.[31]

The poet of the First Bible also liked to talk about himself and his verses. He may have spoken of the meager and plain style of his poetry (I.88), but he also seems to have believed that only God himself was beyond the reach of his verse making (I.188). Throughout the verses he gave stage directions and direct commands to the king and the people assembled in the Presentation miniature. He personally called on the king to read the Bible carefully (I.59) and invited the whole world to pray with him (*mecum,* X.38) for Charles. The poet, again speaking in the first person, also suggested that he would only be completely satisfied when the king had become a dedicated reader of the Bible (I.127–28). In the last of the dedicatory verses, he identified himself as the fourth monk and specifically pointed out who he was, the fourth brother following the named three, in the facing illumination (XI.7; figs. 16–17 and IV).[32]

---

27. *Histoire de la littérature,* vol. 1.2, p. 197: "Cet homme . . . avait une haute estime de lui-même jusqu'à la fatuité."

28. See the thoughtful analysis of the poem provided by Stella, in *Audrado di Sens, Il fonte della vita,* pp. 13–59.

29. 12 *(Liber revelationum).*13, ed. Traube, "O Roma nobilis," p. 388.

30. *Praefatio.*2, ed. Traube, *MGH PLAC* 3:740 and "O Roma nobilis," p. 375.

31. *Praefatio.*7–12, ed. Traube, *MGH PLAC* 3:740 and "O Roma nobilis," p. 375: "quos [titulos] ille reverenter excepit et cum episcopis qui aderant—nam ad sollemnitatem apostolorum omnes illius patriae ex more convenerant—et cum ceteris sapientibus Romanis clericis ad purum examinatos auctoritate suae cathedrae catholico canone roboravit et provida utilitate legendos fidelibus adnotavit et ad honorem suae sedis in scrinio sanctae matris ecclesiae Romanae servare decrevit."

32. Du Cange in his entry on *Armigerii* in *Glossarium mediae et infimae Latinitatis* 1:393 already assumed that the *quartus* was the poet. Kessler, "A Lay Abbot as Patron," in *Committenti e produzione,* p. 650 suggested that the poet was probably "the prominent grey-beard" and Dutton, *Politics of Dreaming,* p. 148, suggested that outline no. 12 in his fig. 18 represented Audradus. For different identifications now, see chapter 5 below.

Once again he personally praised the king (XI.8). The attempt to call attention
to himself as the *quartus*[33] without naming himself was typical of Audradus,
who had tried both to announce and hide his name in the tiny rustic-capital
letters on the opening page of the *Liber comitis*. A more self-effacing poet
might have depersonalized his voice in the First Bible, which was supposed to
be a sublime gift given to a great king by the whole monastery; this one could
not.

Audradus, who had been deeply influenced by Virgil,[34] generally preferred
to compose his poems in dactylic hexameters, but did write the eighth book,
the first part of the four-part set of poems on Saint Julian and his friends, in
elegiac couplets. The new poems of the First Bible are, moreover, shot through
with Virgilian influence.[35] The most revealing indications of that influence are
the examples of the datives *olli* and *ollis*, but there are others, many of which
are noted in the appendix. One might be tempted, for instance, to introduce a
benign emendation such as *scrutari exoro* as a way of making sense of the
unusual "scrutarier oro" at I.59, but this would be to choose an easier reading
over the correct one. For the poet of the dedicatory verses was one who was
familiar with even rare Virgilian usages and may have remembered that Virgil,
in a rare example of paragoge, had once employed the form "farier" (*Aeneid*
11.242) in order to fill out a line of verse. Thus, the First Bible poet may have
aped his master even in his creative expansions. Given that the unique First
Bible poems are elegiac distichs, it should not be too surprising to discover
stock Ovidian phrases in them.[36]

There are a number of specific correspondences between the unique poems
of the First Bible and Audradus's verses. Audradus was, for instance, fond of
the verb *tono*, particularly in its participial forms,[37] and to pseudoclassical references to God as the Thunderer. The verb is also to be found twice in the first
dedicatory verse of the First Bible (I.85 and I.92). Even the compound word

---

33. There were other famous 'fours'. Socrates opens the *Timaeus* (17a) by asking where the fourth person was, the one who had been present at the previous day's discussion, and Ovid in the self-reflective *Tristia* 4.10.51–54 named himself as the fourth in a line of Augustan poets.

34. For sympathetic readings of Audradus's poetry, see Brunhölzl, *Histoire de la littérature,* vol. 1.2, p.
198; and Stella, *Audrado di Sens,* pp. 25, 37–40, 47–53.

35. "Tela inimica" (I.164), for instance, was a Virgilian phrase (*Aeneid* 11.809), as were "O decus" (X.1
and *Georgics* 2.40 and *Aeneid* 11.508), "rex bone" (VI.27 and XI.42 with "bone rex" at *Aeneid* 11.344), "terraeque marisque" (I.159 and *Aeneid* 1.598), "summa dies" (I.48 and *Aeneid* 2.324), "Insuper his" (X.43 and
Aeneid 9.274), and "super aethera" (VI.13 and *Aeneid* 1.379).

36. Among these are "plusve minusve" (VI.17 and *Fasti* 5.110 and 6.274), "mystica sacra" (VI.11 and
Heroides 2.42), "nobilitate potens" (I.138 and *Metamorphoses* 13.22), "mihi crede" (I.37 and *Ars Amatoria*
2.259, 3.653), and "regale decus" (XI.25 and *Metamorphoses* 9.690). Audradus himself used "immortale
decus" on several occasions: see 5.102, ed. Traube, *MGH PLAC* 3:76 and 7.1, p. 86.

37. See Audradus 2.10, ed. Traube, *MGH PLAC* 3:743; 2.25, p. 744; 2.48, p. 744; 5.319, p. 81; 6.57, p. 85;
7.9, p. 86; 8 *prol.*1, p. 89; 9.87, p. 93; 9.99, p. 94; 10.57, p. 102; 11.173, p. 113; 11.233, p. 114; 11.348, p. 118;
11.356, p. 118; 11.382, p. 119.

altithronus applied to God (II.4), to which we drew attention before, was used several times in a similar way by Audradus.[38] Moreover, Audradus used the phrase "pietatis opus" twice,[39] while the First Bible has the same at X.30 and the related construction "pietatis ope" at VI.28. Audradus ended the first hexameter line of the first book of his work with the phrase "summo deitatis honore,"[40] which is similar to the First Bible's completion of a line with "merito deitatis honores" (X.21). Indeed, both Audradus and the First Bible poet used similar formulaic phrases of valediction, "et sine fine vale(to),"[41] and employed another combination of the variable, liturgical valediction "(felix) per saecula (vivat)."[42] Audradus also favored the use of future imperatives ending in *-to,*[43] and we find two such in the first dedicatory verse: "esto" at I.47 and the rare form "fito" at I.43.[44] The intensified form "iam iam" or "iamiam," which both Virgil (*Aeneid* 2.701) and Ovid (*Metamorphoses* 12.588) used, is also found twice in Audradus's poems[45] and once in the First Bible (X.37). The other intensified word, *meme,* which Audradus liked to employ[46] and which he also knew from reading Virgil (*Aeneid* 9.427), is not to be found in the First Bible, though, as already noted, the poet once employed "mecum" (X.38), a composite word used seven times in the *De fonte vitae* as part of the refrain.

Both Audradus and the First Bible poet employed variations of *genus humanum* to describe humankind.[47] Traube noted that Audradus would also on occasion employ *populus* in the plural in the sense of "humans," and the First Bible poet does the same.[48] But the most striking parallels are to be found

---

38. Audradus 9.118, ed. Traube, *MGH PLAC* 3:94, "altithronique dei vox." See also Audradus 10.134, ed. Traube, *MGH PLAC* 3:105, "spiritus altithroni."

39. Audradus 3.8, ed. Traube, *MGH PLAC* 3:745 and 11.468, p. 121.

40. Audradus 1.1, ed. Traube, *MGH PLAC* 3:741.

41. Audradus 5.61, ed. Traube, *MGH PLAC* 3:75 and First Bible I.200.

42. Audradus 5.374, ed. Traube, *MGH PLAC* 3:83 and First Bible X.39. See also Audradus 5.14, p. 73, "ut vivas felix," and 5.240, p. 79, "felix sed vivet in aevum." On this formula in Audradus's poetry, see Stella, *Audrado di Sens,* p. 154 at line 374.

43. "Esto" is to be found at Audradus 5.99, ed. Traube, *MGH PLAC* 3:76; 5.162, p. 77; 5.402, p. 84; and 5.403, p. 84; "faveto" at 7.64, p. 88; "iubeto" at 5.313, p. 81; and "valeto" at 5.61, p. 75; and 6.48, p. 85.

44. See the commentary at I.43 in the appendix below.

45. Audradus 9.214, ed. Traube, *MGH PLAC* 3:97 and 10.130, p. 104.

46. Audradus 6.28, ed. Traube, *MGH PLAC* 3:85 and 9.261, p. 98. See Traube, *MGH PLAC* 3:71 n. 1.

47. See Audradus, 5.247, ed. Traube, *MGH PLAC* 3:79, "Humano generi"; 5.320, ed. Traube, *MGH PLAC* 3:81, "genus humanum"; 11.192, p. 113, "Humani generis"; and 12 *(Liber revelationum)*.2, ed. Traube, "O Roma Nobilis," p. 379.4 and 10, p. 383.2.

48. Thus, X.17, "cleris populisque levamen," has parallels in Audradus 9.55, ed. Traube, *MGH PLAC* 3:92, "omnes cives populique coacti"; 10.12, p. 101, "At populi dudum nimio terrore fugati"; 10.28, p. 101, "Ne pereant populi praesentes"; 11.209, p. 114, "hi populi pereant"; 11.391–92, p. 119, "tollunt/ Praesbiteri et populi"; 11.156, p. 112, "Omnibus his populis"; and 11.23, p. 109, "populos . . . cunctos." For Traube's opinion, see *MGH PLAC* 3:71 n. 2.

in his talk of the divine. The poet spoke of the Bible as the true source of divine wisdom:

Hic fons, hic doctrina potens, hic flumina opima
    Eclesiae sanctae candidiora nive.

(I.61–62)

This recalls the imagery Audradus himself used when speaking of the flowing rivers of the *fons vitae*. For both poets, the Creator was the "spiritus auctor."[49] In this case, Audradus supplied a variant expression, "auctor vitae," in a later poem that helps us to understand the precise meaning of the phrase found in both the First Bible and his own first book.[50] The mysterious phrase, "dulcis amor," that begins I.17 was expanded to "dulcis amor patris" by Audradus, in imitation of Alcuin, in the second of the Julian poems.[51] Indeed, the First Bible poet began one line of verse (I.96) with a phrase, "A patre descendens natus," very like a phrase used by Audradus in his first book, "A patre procedens et nato."[52] Both the First Bible poet and Audradus also referred to the Trinity as "in nomine trino,"[53] and heaven for both was an *arx*.[54] The First Bible's phrase, "caeli terraeque marisque creator" (I. 159), has three almost identical formulations in Audradus's poems.[55]

Considerable repetition occurs in the unique poems of the First Bible.[56] Despite this, there are few specific phrases of more than three words shared by the First Bible poet and Audradus, and this despite the fact that Audradus was also a repetitive poet. But we need to note that aside from the refrain in the *De fonte vitae,* Audradus rarely repeated more than half a line and virtually always in the same poem.[57] It should not be assumed that, when he used the

---

49. First Bible I.26 and Audradus 1.36, ed. Traube, *MGH PLAC* 3:742.

50. Audradus 10.31, ed. Traube, *MGH PLAC* 3:101. Audradus may have been influenced by Juvencus 3.503: "Huic auctor vitae," that is, Christ.

51. Audradus 9.234, ed. Traube, *MGH PLAC* 3:97.

52. Audradus 1.38, ed. Traube, *MGH PLAC* 3:742.

53. Cf. I.57 and Audradus, *Proemium.* 3, ed. Traube, *MGH PLAC* 3:741.

54. See VI.12 and X.42 and Audradus 8.11, ed. Traube, *MGH PLAC* 3:90; 10.235, p. 108; 11.317, p. 117; and 11.441, p. 120.

55. Audradus 11.187, ed. Traube, *MGH PLAC* 3:113, "imperium caeli terraeque marisque"; 9.204, p. 97, "deum caeli terraeque marisque"; 10.148, p. 105, "Spiritus omnipotens, caeli terraeque creator." Cf. also Audradus 6.56, p. 85; 9.328, p. 100; 10.158, p. 105; and 11.234, p. 115.

56. See "verumque fidesque" at VI.23 and XI.5; "pauper egenus inops" at I.44 and X.25; "opere ore (arte) fide" at I.60, I.194, and X.22; "te miserante boet" at I.44 and 45; "rex Carole alme" at VI.28 and X.2; "clare primordia" at I.157 and VI.7; "extat ea en homini" at I.146 and 147; "iusta iube(n)s, iniusta veta(n)s mala cuncta" at I.137 and X.13; and "in sensu parili" at I.92 and VI.16.

57. See "docuit sermone paterno" at Audradus 5.46, ed. Traube, *MGH PLAC* 3:74 and 5.135, p. 77; "quod deus omnipotens" at 11.56, p. 109, and 11.417, p. 120; "spiritus (est) persona deus" at 1.52 and 1.61, p. 743; "spiritus alm(us)" at 1.38, 1.43, and 1.47, p. 742.

same line in the same poem,[58] he did so to fill space or through a lack of poetic ingenuity, but rather that he may have employed repetition for specific poetic effect. Audradus repeated lines and phrases within a poem in order to teach, to reinforce central themes, and to repeat pleasing metrical effects. Hence, if he is the author of the new poems in the First Bible, it should not be surprising to find little exact repetition from his other verses, for he was only locally and purposely repetitive.

The poet of the First Bible had special reasons for employing repetition as one of his chief tools. He probably did not imagine that the king or, in fact, any reader would turn to the magnificent Bible to separate out his poems and read them independently, as we are doing. The first dedicatory verse, for instance, is separated from the second (VI) by 327 folios and the second from the third and fourth (X and XI) by another 93 folios. Hence, the poet needed to return to his main themes and reinforce his emphasis upon the law and the king's duty to look after the world's wretched. Repetition was, therefore, a deliberate attempt to connect themes and, in so doing, to overcome the vast fields of parchment that lay between distant poems. The poet also repeated material and themes because his verses were didactic and propaedeutic to the proper reading of the Bible. The king, after all, was young and needed careful instruction in reading the Bible and paying attention to his spiritual betters.

This need may well explain certain other features of the poetry of the First Bible. There are many more lists of things in the *carmina* of the First Bible than there are in Audradus's books.[59] These lists betray the poet's panegyrical purpose, as for example when he runs off a sequence of royal virtues and praises;[60] but they also reflect his opinion of the king's general interests and attention span. One of these lists of precious objects, "argentum, aurum, gemmae, vascula, vestes" (I.133), is not unlike a similar list found in Audradus's poem on Saint Julian, "aurum aut argentum, vestes vitesque domusque."[61] In his poetry Audradus had, on occasion, inserted examples of homespun wisdom involving metals,[62] as the poet also does in the First Bible (I.37–38, X.31–34). Both poets also liked to employ alliteration and polyptoton, that is, playing with the different forms of words sharing the same root: "corda canet" (XI.36), "magno magnis" (I.189), "monet sive monendo iubet" (I.168) are a

---

58. See Audradus 5.86, ed. Traube, *MGH PLAC* 3:75 and 5.342, p. 82; 5.96, p. 76 and 5.365, p. 83; 5.94, p. 76 and 5.363, p. 83; 9.284, p. 99 and 9.285, p. 99 with variations; and 11.284, p. 116 and 11.399, p. 119 with slight variation.

59. See Audradus 9.332, ed. Traube, *MGH PLAC* 3:100: "Sidera cum caelo, sol, luna vel ignis et aer" and 9.142, p. 95: "Plebs, omnis sexus populosque, senex iuvenisque." For some lists in the First Bible, see I.7–8; I.47; I.55; I.133; I.139; I.150–52; I.199; VI.20; X.25; X.33–34; XI.22.

60. See I.191; I.199; VI.3–4; VI.27; X.22; XI.41–42.

61. Audradus 11.50, ed. Traube, *MGH PLAC* 3:109.

62. Audradus 5.62–77, ed. Traube, *MGH PLAC* 3:75.

few examples in the First Bible, and "genitus genitor," "membra regit membris et mentes mente resolvit," and "caelorum claves curamque" a few in Audradus's verse.[63]

Given the thematic and stylistic correspondences between Audradus's poetry and that of the First Bible, it does not seem implausible that Audradus Modicus was the author of the unique poems found in the First Bible of Charles the Bald and that he composed this poetry specifically for that deluxe volume. Moreover, the context and circumstances of Audradus's life and times lends support to this attribution, since he was a prominent and senior canon, truly a *primus,* at Saint-Martin around 845 when the First Bible of Charles the Bald was being prepared; since he was the most conspicuous and productive poet of the monastery during that period; since he had worked in the scriptorium preparing precious books before; and since he held, according to his *Book of Revelations,* strong opinions about Vivian and the material fortunes of Saint-Martin.[64] As he would later when he became the suffragan bishop of Sens, Audradus styled himself the protector, an inspired, almost saintly advocate of his brothers and their causes.[65] If Audradus Modicus was the author of the verses in the First Bible of Charles the Bald, as the poetry itself suggests, then that magnificent pandect provided a special opportunity for the poet and soon-to-be suffragan bishop to employ his "modest means" to remind the young king of the need for humility, justice, and royal patronage.

If, however, Audradus was not the poet of the First Bible, which remains a very real possibility given our lack of information about the other canons of Saint-Martin, then we would have to imagine or invent someone almost identical to him in attitude, capacities, and circumstances. It seems more efficient and reasonable in this light to refer, from this point on in our study, to the poet of all the new poetry of the First Bible as Audradus Modicus. But the reader should bear in mind, as the authors themselves are acutely aware, that this attribution is not a matter of fact, but one of argument and will doubtless remain so. It is, however, an attribution that accords with and helps to elucidate the circumstances, context, and history of the First Bible.

---

63. Audradus 10.169, ed. Traube, *MGH PLAC* 3:106; 6.15, p. 84; and 6.22, p. 84.
64. See Franz Felten, *Äbte und Laienäbte im Frankenreich: Studien zum Verhältnis von Staat und Kirche im früheren Mittelalter,* Monographien zur Geschichte des Mittelalters, 20 (Stuttgart, 1980), p. 50; Kessler, "Lay Abbot as Patron," pp. 665–68; and Dutton, *Politics of Dreaming,* pp. 145–49.
65. See chapter 2 n. 54 below.

CHAPTER 2

Context

To understand the context of the creation of the First Bible, one needs to know the date of its production and the issues touching Saint-Martin at the time. A great deal hinges on Charles the Bald's itinerary and the monastery's struggle to preserve its autonomy.

The young king's world was an uneasy one in the years after the Treaty of Verdun in 843. The reconfiguration of the kingdoms resulting from the treaty forced some nobles to choose a single kingdom in which to consolidate their properties. Count Adalard of Tours was apparently one of the powerful men who changed his loyalties after Verdun. He had been a distinguished warrior on Charles the Bald's side at the Battle of Fontenoy in 841, served as the lay abbot of Saint-Martin, and was the uncle of Charles's wife Ermintrude. Although he had played a critical role in the king's very survival after the death of Louis the Pious, he left Charles's service in 844. Adalard probably surrendered his offices to the king in the latter half of 844; he almost disappears from west Frankish records and annals at that point.[1] In a letter written around September 844, Lupus of Ferrières spoke of Adalard as being on the point of leaving at some point earlier that year, which Janet Nelson reasonably took to be a reference to Adalard's imminent departure from west Francia.[2] Indeed, in this letter Lupus seems to suggest that in the summer of that year Adalard was tidying up his business before departing. The count promised that before he

---

1. See Ferdinand Lot, "Note sur le sénéchal Alard," *Le Moyen Age,* 2d series, 21 (1908): 189–90, rpt. in Lot, *Recueil des travaux historiques de Ferdinand Lot,* 3 vols. (Geneva, 1968–73), 2:595–96, and Janet L. Nelson, *The Frankish World, 750–900* (London, 1996), pp. 156–58.

2. *Epistola* 36, ed. Léon Levillain, *Loup de Ferrières, Correspondance,* 2 vols. (Paris, 1964), 1:158. See also *Sevati Lupi epistulae,* ed. Peter K. Marshall (Leipzig, 1994), p. 90, and *The Letters of Lupus of Ferrières,* trans. G. R. Regenos (The Hague, 1966), pp. 60–61. The letter in question here must have been written after 5 July when Lupus returned from the disastrous battle in Aquitaine at which he had been captured. See Janet L. Nelson, *Charles the Bald* (London, 1992), p. 142, on the meaning of Adalard's departure. Levillain, *Loup de Ferrières, Correspondance,* 1:159 n. 6, took this to refer to Adalard's departure for the Aquitainian conflict. On the date of the letter, see Léon Levillain, "Étude sur les lettres de Loup de Ferrières," *Bibliothèque de l'École des chartes,* 63 (1902): 317–18.

left he would attend to the interests of Lupus's monastery, so that no harm would befall it at court.

Lupus's letter is crucial to setting straight the confusing chronology of Charles the Bald's visits to Saint-Martin. There has always been some uncertainty about the dates of four royal charters Charles the Bald issued at Saint-Martin, and thus about the timing of Adalard's replacement by Vivian and, indeed, about Charles's movements in 844–45. The old interpretation of Ferdinand Lot and Louis Halphen was that three of these crucial Turonian charters—variously dated to either January 844 or January 845—belonged to Charles's sojourn at Tours over the Christmas season of 843 and that, in fact, the king spent December 844 at the Synod of Ver and Christmas at Saint-Denis, from which he issued a charter on 9 December 844.[3] Were this interpretation of the dates of the charters true, then Vivian would have replaced Adalard as count of Tours and lay abbot of Saint-Martin in early January 844. But, as Lupus's letter suggests, Adalard had continued to hold both posts well into the summer of 844.[4] Even Georges Tessier, who had edited the four charters under the two different sets of dates, seems finally to have accepted the later dates as more reasonable.[5]

Thus, we are forced to conclude that Charles the Bald spent the first three Christmases after the Treaty of Verdun at Saint-Martin,[6] which would fit with his habit of regularizing where he and his court spent special religious seasons.[7] Saint-Martin itself seems to have had a special attraction for the young

---

Was Nithard, who speaks in the fourth book of his *Historiae* of the great wreck and ruin caused by Adalard, also aware in 843 of the divided loyalties and approaching departure of the count? See Nithard, *Historiae* 4.6, ed. and trans. P. Lauer, Nithard, *Histoire des fils de Louis le Pieux* (Paris, 1964), p. 142. Nelson argued that Nithard's anger in 843 was more personal: see Janet L. Nelson, *Politics and Ritual in Early Medieval Europe* (London, 1986), pp. 222–25.

3. See Ferdinand Lot and Louis Halphen, *Le règne de Charles le Chauve* (Paris, 1909), pp. 88 n. 1, 89 n. 2, and 130 n. 1. See also Lot, "Le sénéchal Alard," p. 188, rpt. in Lot, *Receuil des travaux historiques*, 2:594.

4. See also Karl Ferdinand Werner, "Untersuchungen zur Frühzeit des französischen Fürstentums (9.–10. Jahrhundert)," *Die Welt als Geschichte* 18 (1958): 274–75 and n. 89, who brings still other proofs to bear on the same question. Nelson, *Charles the Bald*, p. 142, also argued that Adalard stepped down in the summer of 844 and Vivian assumed the countship and lay abbacy of Saint-Martin by late 844.

5. In his edition of Charles the Bald's charters, Tessier gave charters 60–63 two sets of dates, placing charter 60 either on 30 December 843 or 844 and the other three on 5 January 844 or 845. See *Recueil des actes de Charles*, ed. Tessier, 1:170–84. He explained (1:170–71) that while these documents are dated to the fifth year of Charles's reign, and, therefore, would normally be placed between December 844 and January 845, the indiction given in the subscriptions fits with the year before. These charters were preserved by the monastery in copies, and there are other irregular features to be found in them. Later he clearly preferred the later dates for the four charters as more reasonable: see Georges Tessier, "Les diplômes carolingiens du chartrier de Saint-Martin de Tours," in *Mélanges d'histoire du Moyen Age dédiés à la mémoire de Louis Halphen* (Paris, 1951), p. 689. See also Nelson, *Frankish World*, p. 158 and n. 21.

6. For Christmas 843, see Charles the Bald charters 30–31, *Recueil des actes de Charles*, ed. Tessier, 1:75–82; for Christmas 844, see charters 60–63, 1:170–84; for Christmas 845, see charters 80–81, 1:223–29.

7. See Eugen Ewig, "Résidence et capitale pendant le haut Moyen Age," *Revue historique* 230 (1963): 64–69; Carlrichard Brühl, *Fodrum, Gistum, Sevitium regis*, Kölner historische Abhandlungen, 14.1

king and his family early in his reign. His mother Judith, for instance, was buried there after her death in Tours on 19 April 843, and the young king named his first child, who was born in 844, after her; it is this daughter who is apparently referred to at XI.38 in the First Bible verses. The king may also have had a particular devotion to Saint Martin, whom he called *peculiaris patronus noster,* "our special patron," in his charters.[8]

Vivian was Charles's chamberlain *(camerarius)* throughout 843 and much of 844, and served the king in that capacity at Saint-Martin on 27 December 843.[9] Two days later, when his brother, Rainaldus, became the lay abbot of Marmoutier, Vivian was probably in attendance.[10] Charles the Bald may have been preoccupied with Aquitainian affairs throughout most of 844, but he made a special point of visiting Saint-Martin at Christmas that year. The importance of that visit to the king is indicated by his busy schedule, since he was at Saint-Denis on 9 December and had arrived in Compiègne by 21 January 845.[11] The distance between these three points is not so great as to have prevented the king's travel to all three within six weeks, but it was a busy itinerary for the king and his court nonetheless.[12]

What doubtless drew the king to Saint-Martin in the midst of such a full schedule were two pressing problems. The first was that Nominoë, the Breton leader, had seized upon the opportunity of Charles's preoccupation with Aquitainian business in 844 to conduct a raid into the kingdom that had reached as far as Le Mans.[13] Tours was an important staging point for Charles the Bald after the Treaty of Verdun as he tried to put down troubles in Brittany and points to the south and west where his half brother Lothar continued, in association with Nominoë, to foment trouble.[14] Thus in late 844 Charles

---

(Cologne, 1968), pp. 39–47; Paul Edward Dutton, "Eriugena, the Royal Poet," in *Jean Scot Écrivain: Actes du IVe Colloque international, Montréal, 28 août-2 septembre 1983,* ed. G. H. Allard (Montreal, 1986), pp. 66–67.

8. Charles the Bald, charter 62, *Recueil des actes de Charles,* ed. Tessier, 1:179.6; charter 63, 1:183.8; charter 113 (16 April 849), 1:302.18; charter 114 (21 June 849), 1:304.29.

9. Charles the Bald, charter 30, *Recueil des actes de Charles,* ed. Tessier, 1:73. On *Vivianus camerarius,* see Charles the Bald, charter 19 (18 Feb. 843), 1:46.23; 24 (30 Aug. 843), 1:61.25; 28 (13 Nov. 843), 1:73.15; and 30 (27 Dec. 843), 1:77.18. See also Nelson, *Frankish World,* pp. 157–58.

10. Charles the Bald, charter 31, *Recueil des actes de Charles,* ed. Tessier, 1:80–82.

11. See Charles the Bald, charter 59 (9 December 844; Saint-Denis), *Recueil des actes de Charles,* ed. Tessier, 1:168–69; charter 65 (21 January 845; Compiègne), 1:191–93.

12. The distance between Saint-Denis and Tours, for instance, is approximately 250 km. and between Tours and Compiègne 325 km. Although one individual might ride 80 km. in a day, the average pace of daily travel on the heavy Carolingian horse might have been closer to 20–25 km. a day: see Caroll Gillmor, "War on the Rivers: Viking Numbers and Mobility on the Seine and Loire, 841–86," *Viator* 19 (1988): 101 and nn. 68–69.

13. *Annales de Saint-Bertin* 844, ed. F. Grat, J. Vieillard, and S. Clémencet (Paris, 1964), pp. 47–48.

14. See Julia M. H. Smith, *Province and Empire: Brittany and the Carolingians* (Cambridge, 1992), pp. 94–97; and Herbert Guillotel, "L'action de Charles le Chauve vis à vis de la Bretagne de 843 à 851," *Mémoires de la Société d'archéologie de Bretagne* 53 (1975–76): 6–19.

needed to plan a response to the Breton insurrection, and this was best done at Saint-Martin with the advice and assistance of his Turonian nobles. The second and, perhaps, more pressing problem was the need to deal with the vacuum left by Adalard's recent departure. Thus, Charles named Vivian the count of Tours by 5 January 845 at Saint-Martin, and Vivian immediately began to involve himself in Turonian affairs.[15]

The king's three charters from 5 January 845 suggest that during the royal visit to Tours over the Christmas season of 844 the king and the canons of Saint-Martin entered into a set of complex negotiations about their changing circumstances. In one of these charters Charles confirmed the monastery's possession of certain *villae* and agreed that the present and future archbishops of Tours should not presume to govern or interfere with the brothers or monastery of Saint-Martin and should not impose new demands upon them.[16] In another, he granted an estate to Saint-Martin but also agreed to limit lay impact upon the monastery. When the king visited Saint-Martin, none of his men were now allowed to accept lodging from the brothers, "nor is any layman allowed to possess lodging in the same monastery."[17] All of this was designed to insure that the canons could serve God better and more freely, King Charles said. Finally, in the last of the charters, Count Vivian asked the king to confirm an earlier grant of land to the monastery made by Amalricus, the master of the school of Saint-Martin, to insure the successful maintenance of the school and Amalricus's appointed successors.[18] These three charters would, therefore, seem to represent the beginnings of a bargaining process late in 844 between the king and the canons of Saint-Martin over the arrangement of their affairs and properties, and the appointment of a new abbot.

By the end of these negotiations in January 845 Vivian was the count of Tours, but might not yet have been made the lay abbot of the monastery. Indeed, he was not to be called the *rector monasterii* until 27 December 845, when the monastery's immunities were renewed.[19] In fact, as late as October 845, he was still being addressed by the king as "Vivianus, dilectus et amabilis nobis comes."[20] In early January 845, at the end of his visit to Saint-Martin,

---

15. Charles the Bald, charter 63, *Recueil des actes de Charles,* ed. Tessier, 1:182–84.

16. Charles the Bald, charter 61, *Recueil des actes de Charles,* ed. Tessier, 1:174–77, esp. 175.3–176.29.

17. Charles the Bald, charter 62, *Recueil des actes de Charles,* ed. Tessier, 1:179.24–26.

18. On Charles the Bald, charter 63, *Recueil des actes de Charles,* ed. Tessier, 1:182–84, and its implications for Carolingian education, see M. M. Hildebrandt, *The External School in Carolingian Society,* Education and Society in the Middle Ages and Renaissance, vol. 1 (Leiden, 1992), pp. 69–70, 98–99.

19. See Charles the Bald, charter 80, *Recueil des actes de Charles,* ed. Tessier et al., 1:224.34.

20. Charles the Bald, charter 77 (19 October 845), *Recueil des actes de Charles,* ed. Tessier, 1:218.19. The lack of mention in this charter of other titles the count might have held should not, however, be taken to mean that he did not hold them, for in fact there is not a single instance in the twelve royal charters that mention Vivian where he holds more than one official title. But there is also no royal reference to him as *rector monasterii* before 27 December 845: Charles the Bald, charter 80, 1:224.34.

Charles may simply have run out of time in his delicate negotiations with the canons over the appointment of a new abbot. He, thus, left for Compiègne with his business at Saint-Martin still unfinished.

He did, however, make plans to return to the famous monastery for the feast day of Saint Martin on 11 November 845 and ordered his court and retainers to appear there. Lupus of Ferrières was one of those summoned to Saint-Martin, but he informed his archbishop, Wenilo of Sens, that the king's plans had suddenly changed:

> When I was starting out [to join the king] and had sent men in advance to ask what the king wanted me to do, he commanded me to meet him on the feast of Saint Martin at the distinguished confessor's monastery. But since the kingdom's business had drawn him elsewhere, I dispatched messengers to him again and secured, through friends, the right to return [home]. The reason why our lord king did not go to Saint-Martin as he had planned, as I learned from my messengers, was that the Bretons were quarreling more than usual among themselves and had invited our king to Brittany so that the party which was upset with Nominoë might safely defect to him.[21]

Sometime around the start of November, then, Charles the Bald changed his plans and rapidly marched into Brittany with a small band of men. They fought an unsuccessful battle at Ballon near Redon on 22 November 845.[22] Charles retreated to Le Mans, where he apparently hoped to gather his forces for an assault upon his attackers, but he soon abandoned the plan. By Christmas 845, the king had proceeded to Saint-Martin, and on 27 December 845 he renewed the ancient immunities of the monastery.[23]

This specific set of events suggests that, in all likelihood, the First Bible of Charles the Bald was being made during 845 for presentation to the king on or around 11 November, when the king and his court were expected to assemble at the monastery. The emphasis in the verses at XI.15–18 on Martin, the bishops Brice (398–444) and Perpetuus (461–91), and the other saints special to Saint-Martin suggests that the poet's working assumption was that the king would receive the First Bible on or around the saint's feast day. Indeed Brice and Perpetuus had been the principal architects of Saint Martin's cult, and their work and prayers would have been specially remembered on 11 Novem-

---

21. Lupus of Ferrières, *epistola* 44, *Loup de Ferrières, Correspondance,* ed. Levillain, 1:184.

22. See *Annales de Saint-Bertin* 845, ed. Grat, Vielliard, and Clémencet, p. 51; and Lupus of Ferrières, *epistola* 44, *Loup de Ferrières, Correspondance,* ed. Levillain, 1:184. See also Guillotel, "L'action," pp. 16–17.

23. Charles the Bald, charter 80, *Recueil des actes de Charles,* ed. Tessier, 1:224–26.

ber.[24] Moreover, nothing in the verses specifically alludes to Christmas celebrations. Thus, when the First Bible was finally presented on or around 27 December 845, the content of its verses was already slightly out of sync with events or, at least, with Audradus's expectation of how and when those events would unfold.

Audradus and his fellow canons, therefore, probably knew well in advance, even if Lupus did not,[25] that the king intended to return to Saint-Martin on 11 November 845; the king may have given them such an indication of his intention in January, though all parties would have known that such plans were always contingent upon events in the kingdom. Still, Charles had probably indicated to the canons in January that upon his return he would settle the matter of their new abbot and renew their ancient immunities, for it is that renewal *(renovatio* and *renovasti)* for which thanks is specifically given at XI.23–30. Moreover, Audradus would seem to have known that Charles would merely add his signature (XI.29: *tua sancta manus nuper firmavit*) to the grant given earlier by his forefathers (XI.27–30), and, indeed, the charter that Charles finally signed on 27 December 845 is virtually identical to the earlier documents issued by Charlemagne and Louis the Pious.[26] Audradus also supplies us here with an indication of the expected order of events: the king would first renew Saint-Martin's immunities and then, shortly afterward (as implied by *nuper*) and, perhaps, as part of the same ceremony, receive the First Bible.

There may have been other occasions on which the First Bible could have been presented to Charles or even sent to him, but the specific mention in the verses of the renewal of the monastery's immunities, for which there is a securely dated document, and the depiction in the First Bible of a great ceremony of presentation suggest that the canons themselves had connected the two events. Indeed, no other occasion or specific reason for the canons to thank Charles is mentioned in the dedicatory verses. In this light, then, it would seem unnecessarily complicated to assign the making and presentation of the Bible to some other event or time. For surely the Presentation miniature was meant to portray an imagined moment when the king and his court would assemble at Saint-Martin, and there were not an endless number of such occa-

---

24. Traube may have taken "Perpetui" at XI.17 as an adjective, since in his index of names he identifies Brice as a bishop of Tours, but not Perpetuus: see *MGH PLAC* 3:767, 775. On Perpetuus as an architect of the cult of Saint Martin, see Raymond Van Dam, "Images of Saint Martin in Late Roman and Early Merovingian Gaul," *Viator* 19 (1988): 8; on Brice's role, see Christopher Donaldson, *Martin of Tours: Parish Priest, Mystic, and Exorcist* (London, 1980), pp. 146–47.

25. It is not clear from Lupus's report whether he was learning for the first time, as he set out to meet the king, that the court was going to collect at Saint-Martin on 11 November or was merely confirming, for his correspondent's benefit, the place and/or date of a meeting that had earlier been announced.

26. See the commentary at XI.27 in the appendix.

sions. Indeed, only one dovetails with the events mentioned in the verses and that was the grant of immunities on 27 December 845.[27]

The mention in the verses of the *villae* that Charles had earlier returned (XI.14: *reddiderat*) likely refers to the confirmation and grant of *villae* made on 5 January 845.[28] Thus, the two visits of Charles the Bald to Saint-Martin in 845, one in January and the other in December, were the events between which the First Bible was produced.[29]

Audradus laced his dedicatory verses with historical and political comments that also fit with the events of 844–45. He spoke, for instance, of the Bretons as restless (X.35). Until 843 Nominoë had been relatively supportive of Charles's interests, but after the Treaty of Verdun he had begun to ally himself with Lothar and to tug at the young king's shaky hold on Brittany.[30] His raid into Neustria in 844 must have increased the anxiety at Tours about the restlessness of these Bretons, over whom the church of Tours had special charge. The verses (X.35–36), however, contain no apparent awareness of the military defeat at Ballon on 22 November 845; nor does it seem likely that those lines could have been written in the summer of 846, when Charles and Nominoë had settled their differences and struck a peace treaty.[31] That peace would not last long, but Nominoë would not break into open revolt and overthrow the bishops of Brittany controlled by the metropolitan See of Tours until 849. In the summer of 845, Audradus and his brothers knew that the Breton problem was a troublesome one, and they realized that one of Charles's reasons for coming to Tours was to survey the situation in Brittany. But Audradus may also have considered the Breton problem in 845 to be an irritant and not a disaster on the scale of the Norse attack on Paris in March, which had so deeply shocked him.[32]

Of more immediate importance to Audradus and the canons of Saint-Martin was the damage done to the church's material interests. The theme of material want that runs through the verses of the First Bible matches worries that

---

27. We would like to thank Johannes Fried, who raised this issue with the authors. He was in the audience of the conference entitled "The Carolingian Bible and Its Impact" held at Princeton University on 4 April 1996, where the two authors delivered a paper entitled "Some Reasons for Rethinking the First Bible of Charles the Bald."

28. Charles the Bald, charter 61, *Recueil des actes de Charles,* ed. Tessier, 1:175.3–176.9.

29. Also consistent with such a date is the reference at XI.38 to a wife and child: Charles married Ermentrude on 12 December 842, and a daughter was born in early 844. A son was not born until 846. Although *prolis* might refer to the collective offspring and descendants of the king, it would also be an appropriate term for a single child.

30. See Smith, *Province and Empire,* pp. 94–97; and Guillotel, "L'action," pp. 6–10.

31. *Annales de Saint-Bertin* 846, ed. Grat, Vielliard, and Clémencet, p. 52.

32. For Audradus's shock over that assault and his disappointment at Charles the Bald's response, see 12 (*Liber revelationum*).4, ed. Traube, "O Roma nobilis," p. 379. See also Dutton, *Politics of Dreaming,* pp. 142–43.

were rising dramatically in the west Frankish church between 840 and 845; these anxieties had been brought on in part by the general disruption and specific displacement of properties caused by the civil war. In addition, west Francia experienced a *fames valida,* or severe food shortage, in 845, which harmed, if not killed, thousands of people.[33] This may account for the particular coloring of XI.21–22, in which the poet bewailed the foul hunger *(atra fames),* thirst, and cold that had fallen over the servants attached to Saint-Martin and the beggars who must have come to its door repeatedly during times of famine. The "famuli" serving the monastery were probably the thousands of dependent farmers who worked the lands of Saint-Martin[34] and who may have been suffering near-starvation in 845.

But Audradus's complaints about property were also general in tone and in agreement with recent synodal opinion. At the synod held at the villa of Thionville at Yütz in October 844, the three kings—Lothar, Louis the German, and Charles the Bald—had accepted the complaints of their high churchmen that church property had been compromised and dismembered during the recent troubles and that it was inappropriate to grant monasteries to laymen.[35] At Ver in December Charles the Bald had presided over a synod of west Frankish churchmen that echoed the same complaints and proclaimed that "Seculars should hold secular offices, ecclesiastics should receive ecclesiastical offices."[36] To avoid eternal torment and to obtain the joy of the Lord, the king was told to return God's things.[37] The language of the canons of Ver, which Lupus of Ferrières recorded,[38] reminds one at points of the verses of the First Bible.[39] The bishops called, for instance, on Charles to imitate that wisest

---

33. *Annales de Saint-Bertin* 845, ed. Grat, Vielliard, and Clémencet, p. 50: "Fames ualida Galliae inferiora consumit, adeo ut multa hominum milia eadem invalescente absumpta sint."

34. Although a polyptych like that of Saint-Germain-Des-Prés or statutes like those of Adalhard of Corbie do not survive for Saint-Martin, we may still infer that a monastery with two hundred or more canons would have had a large economic operation based upon extensive land holdings.

35. *Monumenta Germaniae Historica: Concilia* (hereafter *MGH Concilia*) 3, ed. Wilfried Hartmann (Hanover, 1984), pp. 29–35, esp. canon 3, p. 32.0. *Annales de Saint-Bertin* 844, ed. Grat, Vielliard, and Clémencet, p. 48: "et statum ecclesiarum, inminentibus necessitatibus foedissime rebus dilaceratum, ac personis minus congruis, id est laicis, uulgo contraditum, redintegraturos sese promittunt." See also Felten, *Äbte und Laienäbte,* pp. 298–99.

36. *MGH Concilia* 3, ed. Hartmann, p. 44.9–10. See Felten, *Äbte und Laienäbte,* p. 299.

37. *MGH Concilia* 3, ed. Hartmann, p. 44.7–9.

38. See *epistola* 44, *Loup de Ferrières, Correspondance,* ed. Levillain, 1:182. Almost the whole of this letter from 845, pp. 178–84, concerns Lupus's own loss of the cell of Saint-Josse to a layman.

39. Cf. "inclyte rex Karole" at *MGH Concilia* 3, ed. Hartmann, p. 38.27 with the same at I.190; the formula "clerus et populus" at *MGH Concilia* 3, ed. Hartmann, p. 42.6 and X.17; the use of the word "discordia" at *MGH Concilia* 3, ed. Hartmann, pp. 38.28 and 40.6 with I.139; and the description of the onset of evils at *MGH Concilia* 3, ed. Hartmann, p. 38.28 with I.173.

of all kings, Solomon, in his pursuit of justice,[40] a theme taken up by the First Bible (I.39–50, 179–82, 195). They called David "rex et propheta" and held him out as an example for Charles to imitate;[41] DAVID REX ET PROP<HETA> was, of course, to be the very label inscribed above the figure of dancing David in the famous frontispiece to the Psalms in the First Bible (figs. 8 and II).

Now this is not to suggest that Audradus had attended the Synod of Ver or that he was in direct contact with Lupus, though the latter seems a distinct possibility.[42] If Charles the Bald and his court had come to Saint-Martin in December 844, almost immediately after the Synod of Ver, Audradus might easily have learned the details of that council's specific complaints soon after they had been made. It may also have been at about this time that Audradus made or renewed his friendship with Hincmar, who was not yet archbishop of Rheims but quite likely traveling with the king's court.[43] In any event, late in 844 Audradus and the churchmen of west Francia shared a general set of concerns about the lay control of church property. These themes had been pointedly expressed at Ver and were to be articulated with even greater force at the synod that began to meet at Meaux in June 845 even as Audradus wrote and waited for the king to arrive in Tours.[44]

In the royal charter of 5 January 845 in which the canons of Tours attempted to limit lay interference, they had already revealed their own immediate concern with preserving Saint-Martin's autonomy and protecting its material resources.[45] Throughout the dedicatory verses of the First Bible,

---

40. Ver, canon 1, in *MGH Concilia* 3, ed. Hartmann, p. 39.19–25. Lupus, in a letter dated November–December 845, urged the king to remember that Solomon had especially sought out wisdom in order to rule the people of Israel, and that because of it he had ruled over them in perfect peace for a long time: see *epistola* 46, *Loup de Ferrières, Correspondance,* ed. Levillain, 1:196.

41. Ver, canon 1, in *MGH Concilia* 3, ed. Hartmann, pp. 39.27–40.2.

42. Lupus had been at Saint-Martin on 27 December 843: see Charles the Bald, charter 30, *Recueil des actes de Charles,* ed. Tessier, 1:76–77. Lupus's detailed knowledge of the contents of Saint-Martin's library also suggests that he had probably visited the monastery on a number of occasions before 846. He asked Ursmar, the archbishop of Tours, who died in that year, to supply him with a book held in the library by Amalricus and gave a physical description of the volume: see *epistola* 53, *Loup de Ferrières, Correspondance,* ed. Levillain, 1:214–16. Bernhard Bischoff also observed that Lupus had made notes in a number of a Turonian manuscripts: see Bischoff, *Manuscripts and Libraries in the Age of Charlemagne,* trans. and ed. M. Gorman (Cambridge, 1994), p. 125.

43. See Nelson, *Frankish World,* pp. 164–66. Audradus's contact with Hincmar in the early 840s at Saint-Martin might help us to date and understand the genesis of the *De fonte vitae,* Audradus's poetic dialogue with Hincmar.

44. *MGH Concilia* 3, ed. Hartmann, pp. 81–127. See especially canon 10, pp. 89–91 about laymen living in monasteries; canon 17, p. 94, about the restitution of church property; canon 24, p. 97, against the depredation of ecclesiastical properties; canon 61, p. 113, against those who spoil church properties; and canon 62, pp. 113–14, against those who steal or interfere with the collection of tithes and oppress clerics with poverty.

45. Charles the Bald, charter 62, *Recueil des actes de Charles,* ed. Tessier, 1:179.25–26.

Audradus was preoccupied with the same issue. He pointedly condemned the theft of church property at XI.33–34 and lamented the material want of Saint-Martin at XI.22. Even his emphasis on the Pauline primacy of charity (I.15–18, VI.23) and his evocation of the perfect bliss of paradise (I.119, XI.18) were reflections of the material concerns of Saint-Martin and of the special plea being presented to the king.

The theft of church property and lay intrusion into monasteries remained a special concern of Audradus, at least insofar as we can judge from his book of visions. In the third entry of the *Book of Revelations,* as reconstructed by Traube, Audradus reported that after the civil war the survivors had turned not to God, but toward the depredation of churches and the poor. These laymen, he said, had diverted churches from their proper mission, and the whole ecclesiastical order had been thrown into extreme agitation. God was so upset that he had informed Audradus that he would smite them with nine blows.[46] The first of those blows, as it turned out, was deemed to be the invasion of Paris by the Northmen in March 845.[47] In Audradus's longest and most interesting vision, Christ ordered the Carolingian kings to appear before him and spoke directly to Charles in a quasi tribunal set at the edge of heaven:

> If you, my boy, will be humble and obedient, if you will remain with me, if you will restore my churches to that state which I set out for them, if you will restore to each order a fitting head of religion, if you will set a proper law for each order to hold, and if you will free the whole population from rapine, depredation, and the violation of the churches that are entrusted to you, if you will deliver justice to each person, and if with a good and fine heart you will always follow my commands, then behold I shall give you the scepter and crown of the kingdom.[48]

Christ then appointed Saint Martin as Charles's special protector and guide. Thus Audradus's plea in 851–52 was for Charles to respect the autonomy, religious control, and property of the churches in his kingdom. In Audradus's next vision, the first one recorded after Vivian's death in 851, he continued to dream of Saint-Martin's restitution. He claimed that Charles himself had actually agreed "iterum atque iterum [again and again]" that he would restore the monastery [to canonical control], but had failed to fulfill his promise.[49]

---

46. Audradus 12 *(Liber revelationum).*3, ed. Traube, "O Roma nobilis," p. 379.

47. Audradus 12 *(Liber revelationum).*4, ed. Traube, "O Roma nobilis," pp. 379–80. This vision marks, in fact, the start of Audradus's system of *induciae.*

48. Audradus 12 *(Liber revelationum).*11, ed. Traube, "O Roma nobilis," p. 384.11–16.

49. Audradus 12 *(Liber revelationum).*12, ed. Traube, "O Roma nobilis," p. 386.6–7.

These are the very themes that course through the verses of the First Bible, though in a more subtly stated form. When Audradus composed those verses in 845, he was a more hopeful churchman than we find him later in the *Book of Revelations*. When he alluded in that book to an earlier meeting with King Charles, perhaps he was thinking of Christmas 845 and the presentation of the First Bible.[50] The advice he gave in 845, some six years before the fateful vision of 851–52, was couched in positive terms, but its principal themes were consistent: that a humble King Charles should deliver justice to Saint-Martin and to the Church. Yet, if anything, Audradus's high hopes in 845 in the First Bible, when he beseeched the Lord to let royal glory dominate and to let the power of kings prevail (XI.25–26), achieved their bitter counterpoint in the long vision of 851–52, when the saints informed Christ that it was "the fault of kings" that the kingdom was now in such a state of disrepair.[51]

Charles the Bald's difficult circumstances in the 840s had forced him to grant church properties to his supporters, so that, as he said, they might have a little material comfort while in his employ.[52] The See of Rheims, according to Hincmar, had particularly suffered from this alienation of properties.[53] Saint-Martin too felt itself compromised by Charles's secular needs. First it had been governed by Adalard, who had been appointed by Louis the Pious, and now was about to be compelled to receive another lay abbot in Vivian. The canons of Saint-Martin resolutely maintained a special sense of monastic or collective identity, which one finds reflected in Audradus's poems and visions.[54] Carolingian canons seem, in fact, to have thought of themselves as priests and monks living in urban monasteries under abbots. They were tonsured[55] and trained at monasteries such as Saint-Martin, slept in dormitories, and ate their meals in refectories.[56] In 849 the number of canons at Saint-Martin was capped at two hundred, twenty per table.[57] But canons, unlike monks,

---

50. Audradus 12 *(Liber revelationum)*. 12, ed. Traube, "O Roma nobilis," p. 386.1–2.

51. Audradus 12 *(Liber revelationum)*. 11, ed. Traube, "O Roma nobilis," p. 383.7: "culpa regum est."

52. See Flodoard, *Historia Remensis ecclesiae* 3.4, ed. J. Heller and G. Waitz, *MGH Scriptores* 13 (Hanover, 1881), p. 477.7–8. Also see Charles the Bald, charter 75, *Recueil des actes de Charles*, ed. Tessier, 1:212.

53. See *Politics of Dreaming*, pp. 170–81.

54. In his very first vision, the *verbum domini* descended upon Audradus, and said: "tu vir doloris, quia posuisti cor tuum, ut assidue pro salute fratrum tuorum periclantium te affligeres coram me": Audradus 12 *(Liber revelationum)*. 1, ed. Traube, "O Roma nobilis," p. 378.3–5, Audradus saw himself here and also on his way to Rome in 849 as working "pro salute fratrum." At the start of his poem in honor of Saint Martin, Audradus also addressed his fellow canons as "o socii": Audradus 7.3, ed. Traube *MGH PLAC* 3:86.

55. A fact that may be alluded to in I.38.

56. See canons 53 and 58 of the Synod of Meaux-Paris, *MGH Concilia* 3, ed. Hartmann, pp. 109 and 112. On the evolution of Saint-Martin, see Felten, *Äbte und Laienäbte*, pp. 229–46.

57. Charles the Bald, charter 113, *Recueil des actes de Charles*, ed. Tessier, 1:300–303. It was now stipulated that new canons would be allowed to enter the monastery only to replace deceased canons.

did not entirely or specifically follow the Rule of Saint Benedict and were able to hold personal property.

This element of compromise in canonical life may have made it easier for kings to commit these "irregular monasteries" to lay supervision. Charles the Bald himself would become the lay abbot of Saint-Denis in 867; and at Thionville in 844, he had recognized that the needs of the kingdom made it occasionally necessary to place monasteries under lay control.[58] Even under such circumstances, however, a monastery might have maintained some rights in the appointment of a lay abbot. In 831 Louis the Pious had, after all, recognized the right of Saint-Martin to select its own abbot, but soon compromised that right, since after Abbot Fridugis's death in 834 he appointed Adalard lay abbot.[59] Still Louis's concession gave the canons of Saint-Martin grounds for claiming a continuing and, perhaps, inalienable right to choose their own abbots.[60] That assertion of privilege forced Charles to negotiate delicately with them when he wished to name a new lay abbot, as he might have first contemplated doing during the Christmas season of 844.[61] The canons responded to Charles's initial move to replace Adalard, we may infer, by trying to limit future lay and episcopal impact upon the monastery. They also received a confirmation of lands and gained the assent of Charles and the new count of Tours to a grant of land to support the school.

But we should not assume that the canons of the chapter of Saint-Martin were particularly happy with the results of their dealings with Charles. Indeed, a concern with church property, regular appointments, and Charles's duty toward the Church bubbles persistently to the surface in the dedicatory verses of the First Bible. Much of what the poet wrote can be read as a plea for the king to respect the autonomy and property of Saint-Martin. Six years later Audradus would vent his fury over the disastrous appointment of Vivian. Then he envisaged Christ predicting the damnable count's death:

---

58. Canon 5, *MGH Concilia* 3, ed. Hartmann, p. 34.16–25.

59. On 4 November 831, Louis the Pious granted Saint-Martin a number of privileges, among them the right to choose its own abbot. See Émile Mabille, *La Pancarte Noire de Saint-Martin de Tours brulée en 1793, restituée d'après les textes imprimés et manuscrits* (Paris, 1866), p. 97 (no. 61, fol. 56); the document is edited in Bouquet, *Recueil des historiens des Gaules et de la France*, vol. 6 (Paris, 1749), p. 573. On Adalard's acquisition of the lay abbacy of Saint-Martin, see Lot, "Le sénéchal Alard," pp. 187–88, rpt. in Lot, *Recueil des travaux historiques*, 2:593–94.

60. Even in the early thirteenth century a Turonian chronicler still recalled that Louis the Pious had granted the canons of Saint-Martin the right to supervise the election of the abbot of Cormery and to elect their own abbot. See *Chronicon Sancti Martini Turonense*, ed. O. Holder-Egger, *MGH Scriptores* 26 (Hanover, 1882): "quod monachi Cormariacenses non possint eligere abbatem sine consensu canonicorum Sancti Martini Turonensis, immo sint ei subiecti; et quod canonici ex se ipsis eligant abbatem suum."

61. On the Carolingian king's power to appoint abbots, see Henri Lévy-Bruhl, *Les élections abbatiales en France* (Paris, 1913), pp. 31–33, 121–73.

And there [in Brittany] the treacherous and impious Vivian, who was not afraid to trample upon the nobility of my churches, glorifying himself as the abbot of the monastery of Saint-Martin and other places, will die, and then the beasts of the forest will devour his flesh.[62]

By then Audradus's complaint was no longer simply a principled rejection of lay abbacy, but a personal condemnation of Vivian as a proud pluralist and violator of churches, who deserved his animal-like death in 851.[63] Audradus's description of Vivian and his death are the most hateful words in all of the impassioned *Book of Revelations*. But it should not be forgotten that this vision also constituted an overt condemnation of Charles the Bald, who had appointed Vivian; indeed, the king apparently later heard and discussed this controversial vision in public.[64] Audradus also criticized the king's appointment of an outsider as the new bishop of Chartres in 853,[65] a position he doubtless thought should go to someone like himself.[66]

At XI.1–2 in the First Bible verses, however, the poet called Vivian a *heros* or noble warrior, a military and secular epithet that had occasionally been applied to Charles and his grandfather by other poets.[67] On one level this quick and effective characterization of Vivian was already a recognition of the military prowess for which he would later be celebrated in song,[68] but it also

---

62. Audradus 12 *(Liber revelationum)*.11, ed. Traube, "O Roma nobilis," p. 385.1–3.

63. For positive portraits of Vivian and his noble death, see Regino of Prüm, *Chronicon* 860, ed. F. Kurze, *Reginonis abbatis Prumiensis Chronicon cum continuatione Treverensi*, in *MGH Scriptores rerum Germanicarum in usum scholarum* (Hanover, 1890), pp. 78–79; *Chanson de Guillaume* 1–928, ed. J. Wathelet-Willem, in *Recherches sur la Chanson de Guillaume. Études accompagnées d'une édition*, 2 vols. (Paris, 1975), 1:282–321, 2:730–825; Ferdinand Lot, "Vivien et Larchamp," *Romania* 35 (1906): 258–77; André Moisan, "La fuite de Charles le Chauve devant les Bretons d'Érispoé (22–24 août 851) et la mort du comte Vivien de Tours," in *La chanson de geste et le mythe carolingien. Mélanges René Louis*, 2 vols. (Saint-Père-sous-Vézelay, 1982), 1:85–100.

64. See Audradus 12 *(Liber revelationum)*.12, ed. Traube, "O Roma nobilis," p. 386.1–7.

65. See Audradus 12 *(Liber revelationum)*.12, ed. Traube, "O Roma nobilis," pp. 386–87. Audradus's special pleading for Chartres in this case may suggest a connection with Chartres that would help to account for the appearance of his *Liber comitis* in the library of Saint-Père. That lectionary, however, is not identifiable in the eleventh-century list of Saint-Père's books: see Lucien Merlet, "Catalogue des livres de l'abbaye de Saint-Père de Chartres," *Bibliothèque de l'Ecole des Chartes* 15 (1853–54): 263–70. Item 98 on the list refers to a "Lectionarius antiquus" and item 99 to a "Lectionarius novus," either of which might have been a book like the *Liber comitis*.

66. First Bible X.19–24 indicates the high opinion of the episcopacy that Audradus held, an opinion that was reinforced at Saint-Martin by the model of Saint Martin himself, who had been both a monk and a bishop: see Audradus 7.29, ed. Traube *MGH PLAC* 3:87. In Audradus's case, he may also have come to identify with the Carolingian notion that bishops were the heirs of the prophets: see Pierre Riché, "La Bible et la vie politique dans le haut Moyen Age," in *Le Moyen Age et la Bible*, Bible de tous les temps, 4, ed. P. Riché and Guy Lobrichon (Paris, 1984), pp. 393–95.

67. See the commentary at XI.1 in the appendix.

68. See *Chanson de Guillaume* 790–928, ed. Wathelet-Willem, 2:730–825.

typed Vivian as what he was, a warrior.[69] The verses do not overtly criticize Vivian, but mention him and then quickly move on, never to name him again; indeed, Audradus may have employed the extravagant epithet *heros* as the most efficient way to flatter and then dispense with the count of Tours. In fact, the widespread assumption that Vivian commanded the creation of the First Bible[70] lacks support within the verses, in which Vivian is mentioned only once in 353 lines of poetry, and from all other sources. Poem XI.9–10 is quite specific in asserting that it was the canons who presented the book to the king, though XI.1–2 and the dedication miniature (figs. 17 and IV) did give Vivian a prominent place in the presentation ceremony. Still it seems more accurate to call the codex the First Bible of Charles the Bald[71] than the Vivian Bible, particularly since Charles was the certain recipient of the Bible and the evidence indicates that the monastery, and not Vivian, was its true donor.

In fact, it is quite likely that Vivian was not the lay abbot of Saint-Martin when Audradus was writing the verses and the First Bible was being prepared, though he may have actually come to hold the office about the time the Bible was finally presented. The ambiguous state of these unfolding events, in fact, helps to explain something of the First Bible's enigmatic character. When abbots took the relatively unusual step of seeking the

---

69. But not necessarily a dead one. Rita Lejeune, "Les portraits de Vivien de Tours et de l'artiste dans la Bible de Charles le Chauve: problèmes d'identification et de date," *Revue Bénédictine* 103 (1993): 174–85, argued that *heros* was a term applied exclusively to living kings and dead heroes. Hence, she reasoned that the very use of the phrase *heros Vivianus* in the First Bible must mean that the book had been prepared after Vivian's death in 851. In fact, *heros* might be applied to a still living, noble warrior, as Sedulius Scottus did twice in a poem in which he celebrated the return of the living Count Eberhard from a recent military triumph: see *carmen* 39.16 and 37, ed. Traube, *MGH PLAC* 3:203, "maximus heros" and "heros pietate plenus." See also Du Cange, *Glossarium mediae et infimae Latinitatis*, 4:203: "*Heroes*, Militum propria appellatio, episcopis tamen aliquando attributa." The epithet was also commonly applied to martyrs as Audradus himself did in his Julian poems: see 9.116, ed. Traube, *MGH PLAC* 3:94, "maximus heros." Even here, however, Audradus was probably influenced by Virgil, who had used the same phrase at *Aeneid* 6.192.

70. See Rand, *Survey of Manuscripts*, p. 156: "this most splendid of the great Bibles of Tours was done at the command of Abbot Vivian." John Michael Wallace-Hadrill, "A Carolingian Renaissance Prince: The Emperor Charles the Bald," *Proceedings of the British Academy* 64 (1978): 162, calls the First Bible "a thank-offering from Count Vivian." Rosamond McKitterick, "Charles the Bald and the Image of Kingship," *History Today* 38 (1988): 31: "Vivian appears to have chosen to acknowledge his gratitude by producing one of Tours' masterpieces as a gift for the king"; McKitterick, "Script and Book Production," in *Carolingian Culture: Emulation and Innovation*, ed. R. McKitterick (Cambridge, 1994), p. 221, states: "the gift was expressive of the patronage Count Vivian had enjoyed from the king and the count's own patronage of the abbey."

71. Of course, as a name the First Bible of Charles the Bald is also far from satisfactory. It is literally "the First" because it is Bibliothèque Nationale, lat. 1, and, thus, Bibliothèque Nationale, lat. 2 is known as the Second Bible of Charles the Bald. Since, however, the First Bible is the first great Bible known to have been specially made for and presented to Charles the Bald after he had become king of west Francia, the title may also be taken in this more meaningful sense.

renewal of their monastery's "perpetual" immunities, they often did so at the outset of their abbacies; it was their first and founding act, one that may have been meant, especially in the case of a lay abbot, to relieve anxieties within a monastery.[72] Vivian's own brother Rainaldus asked the king to renew the immunities of Marmoutier when he became its lay abbot in late 843.[73] This would also seem to have been the pattern followed in Vivian's case, so that a case can be made that he may not have become the lay abbot of Saint-Martin until 27 December 845, when the monastery's immunities were renewed.[74] Not until then did the king call Vivian the *rector monasterii,* the common title for a lay abbot.[75] There is, in fact, no evidence that Vivian was abbot throughout 845.

In January 845 the king, in his hurried visit to Saint-Martin, had named Vivian the count of Tours and had entered into negotiations with the canons about naming a new abbot. Vivian's candidacy probably surfaced at that time, and the first results of those dealings, including a land transaction in which Vivian participated, were expressed in the king's charters. The canons received protection from interference by the archbishop of Tours, a confirmation of lands, and a guarantee that strict limits would be placed upon royal and lay impact upon the monastery and its resources. But they likely also asked at the same time for the exceptional renewal of their "perpetual" immunities before they would agree to accept the imposition of another lay abbot, which would suggest that the king had already recommended Vivian as Adalard's successor. Whether because the king ran out of time in conducting those negotiations in early January 845 or because the negotiations themselves had broken down, Charles the Bald apparently postponed the decision to appoint a new abbot and to renew the monastery's immunities until his planned return to Saint-Martin on the saint's feast day in 845.

The verses of the First Bible support this interpretation, since the poet deliberately equivocates about the identity of the abbot of Saint-Martin.

---

72. See François Ganshof, "L'immunité dans la monarchie franque," in *Les liens de vassalité et les immunités,* Recueils de la Société Jean Bodin, vol. 1, 2d ed. (Brussels, 1958), p. 198 and n. 81: "Les confirmations [of immunity] accordées par des rois successifs ne contredisent point à ce caractère [of perpetual immunities]; on ne saurait quelques monastères, un nouvel abbé a sollicité du roi le renouvellement du privilège." "On rencontre des confirmations de ce type parmi les diplômes des divers chefs d'état carolingiens; ils sont trop peu nombreux pour être interprétés autrement que comme le résultat d'une précaution supplémentaire prise par les nouveaux abbés de certains monastères (notamment de Saint-Martin de Tours)." See also Felten, *Äbte und Laienäbte,* pp. 205–16.

73. Charles the Bald, charter 31, *Recueil des actes de Charles,* ed. Tessier, 1:80–82.

74. Charles the Bald, charter 80, *Recueil des actes de Charles,* ed. Tessier, 1:224.34.

75. On the terms for lay abbot in the ninth century, see Felten, *Äbte und Laienäbte,* pp. 1, 280, 287. *Comes et rector,* as Felten points out, was the typical formula.

The *heros Vivianus* mentioned at XI.1–2 seems not to be the *pater* of XI.3, though the poet may have wished by placing these two figures so close to each other to mislead his royal reader or, at least, to obscure the actual identity of the abbot. For one thing, *pater* was not commonly a specific or official term for abbot in the ninth century, but was rather a word that might be applied to many types of superiors.[76] If Saint-Martin was without an abbot for most of 845, the *pater* of XI.3 might well have been the acting abbot, perhaps the *praepositus* or prior of the monastery. The *praepositus* was the second most important official at Saint-Martin after the abbot and would normally have been the lay abbot's central agent within the monastery. When a lay abbot was absent, which must have been most of the time, the *praepositus* would have served as the effective abbot.[77] This canon would also have performed those religious functions at the monastery that a layman could not, such as celebrating mass in the presence of the king.[78] If, in fact, Vivian was not yet the lay abbot in 845 when the poet was at work preparing the First Bible, then the *pater* would probably have been the acting superior of the monastery. He was the person the canons had accepted as effective abbot in the interim; most likely that individual who had been the *praepositus* under Adalard in 844 or, perhaps, the canon they might have chosen as abbot had they been allowed to exercise the right granted to them by Louis the Pious.[79]

There is one puzzling piece of information that has been overlooked. In June 845 Ursmar, the archbishop of Tours, made a grant of lands to Saint-Martin that was witnessed by "Heirardus in Christo abba, Actardus episco-

---

76. See the strange case reported by Agnellus of Ravenna, *Liber Pontificalis ecclesiae Ravennatis* 165, ed. O. Holder-Egger, in *MGH Scriptorum rerum Langobardicarum et Italicarum, saec. VI–IX* (Hanover, 1878), p. 384. Charlemagne had objected when the archbishop of Ravenna had called him *pater*. See Dutton, *Politics of Dreaming*, pp. 124–25.

The Council of Paris's use of the word with respect to abbots in 829 was in order to urge the abbots of canons to set a fatherly example for their spiritual sons, but the council was not concerned here with the issue of lay abbacy, and the term "patres" was metaphorical rather than strictly titular: see 50.37, in *MGH Concilia* 2, ed. A. Werminghoff (Hanover, 1908), p. 636.

77. On the order of the officials at Saint-Martin, which was *abbas, praepositus,* and *decanus,* see Charles the Bald, charter 62, *Recueil des actes de Charles,* ed. Tessier, 1:179.22–23. On the various officials of the early medieval monastery, see Giles Constable, "The Authority of Superiors in Religious Communities," in *La notion d'autorité au Moyen Age: Islam, Byzance, Occident,* Colloques inernationaux de la Napoule (23–26 octobre 1979), ed. G. Makdisi, D. Sourdel, and J. Sourdel-Thomine (Paris, 1982), pp. 191–99, rpt. in Giles Constable, *Monks, Hermits, and Crusaders in Medieval Europe,* Variorum Collected Studies, 273 (London, 1988), item 3.

78. On the *praepositus* and *vicedominus* as the agents—one religious, the other as estate manager—of the lay abbot, see Felten, *Äbte und Laienäbte,* pp. 283–92.

79. See n. 59 above.

pus,[80] Grimaldus[81] presbyter atque decanus."[82] The compilers of the *Gallia Christiana* took "Heirardus" to be a corruption of "Adalardus,"[83] and since Adalard's name had on occasion been written as "Adarardus,"[84] the corruption to "Heirardus" is not an inconceivable one, however unlikely. Thus one possible interpretation of the charter might be that Adalard had continued as lay abbot through the summer of 845, even though he had certainly been replaced as the count of Tours six months earlier and had largely ceased to be a presence in west Francia. If this were true, it would account for the king's delay in appointing Vivian and his intention to return to Saint-Martin on 11 November to arrange Adalard's replacement.

But the specific chronology and paleographical improbability suggest that this is an unlikely scenario. The title *abba* was a word that strictly speaking meant "father" and would not normally have been applied to a lay abbot such as Adalard. It was, however, a term that could be applied to an abbot who was one of the flock.[85] But if this *abba Heirardus* was not Adalard, then who was he? Given the order of the witnesses listed in the charter, it is hard not to believe that this *abba,* placed before a bishop and Ursmar's own deacon, was the representative of Saint-Martin. If he was some unidentified abbot from elsewhere and not from Saint-Martin,[86] then the monastery would have had no signatory present to receive or witness Ursmar's generous gift of lands, which would have made this a most unusual contract. Might he, instead, have been a canon of Saint-Martin, perhaps the *praepositus,* who in the summer of

---

80. Bishop of Nantes (837–79).

81. Grimaldus was a priest and deacon of the cathedral of Tours, though some scholars have assumed that he was a deacon of Saint-Martin and, therefore, that he succeeded Sigualdus as deacon at Saint-Martin. This reasoning has led some to believe that the date of the creation of the First Bible could be based upon this succession: see Rand, *Survey of Manuscripts,* p. 156: "If Sigualdus gave place to Grimaldus as Dean in 845, then the Bible was done already in that year." Also see Rand and Howe, "Vatican Livy," p. 29. Dominique Alibert recently repeated this line of reasoning: "Les Carolingiens et leurs images. Iconographie et idéologie," Thèse de doctorat Nouveau Régime (Université de Paris-Sorbonne, 1994), p. 78 and n. 378.

The reasoning seems wrong on several counts. Grimaldus was not a deacon of Saint-Martin; Saint-Martin might have had several deacons at a time; and Sigualdus was not identified as deacon at XI.4 in the First Bible verses, so that the Bible might have been produced at any time while he was a member of the *grex.*

82. *Gallia Christiana,* 2d ed., vol. 14 (Paris, 1856), instr. 26, col. 33. See also Mabille, *Pancarte Noire,* p. 84 (no. 38, fol. 44). The document was dated by the formula, "Data in mense Junio, anno VI regnante Carolo rege," which could refer to either June 845 or 846.

83. *Gallia Christiana,* 2d ed., vol. 14, col. 165.

84. See Charles the Bald, charter 20, *Recueil des actes de Charles,* ed. Tessier, 1:48.5.

85. *Abba* was the etymological root of *abbas,* and, indeed, there was some confusion in the ninth century about its use, as scribes occasionally dropped the final *s* from *abbas.* See also the index to *MGH Concilia* 4: *Supplementum,* ed. L. Böhringer (Hanover, 1992), p. 280, in which *abba* stands for all *abbas* references.

86. The *abbas Heirardus* of Montreux who appears in several of Charles the Bald's charters was not active until very late in Charles's career: see Charles the Bald, charter 392, *Recueil des actes de Charles,* ed. Tessier, 2:375–76 and charter 440 (1 August 877), 2:486–88.

845 was effectively acting as abbot and hence was called *abba in Christo?* The subscription itself is particularly puzzling. Does the form *in Christo* suggest a title that was less than fully official, that Heirardus was somehow Christ's choice, rather than the king's? And was *abba* or "father" the closest Saint-Martin could come to calling Heirardus abbot without flouting the king's rights? The fact that both elements of Heirardus's title are oblique may hint at problems with the office or with the authenticity of the document.[87] But the archbishop of Tours between 856 and 871 was a certain Herardus, whose name was spelled in many ways, including Eirardus, Airardus, and Erardus; Lupus wrote to him as Herardus.[88] Since his predecessor, Amalricus, had gone from being canon and master of Saint-Martin to being archbishop of Tours (850–55) and Audradus himself had gone from being canon to suffragan bishop of Sens (847–49), it may not be unreasonable to wonder whether a certain Heirardus was a canon and the effective abbot of Saint-Martin in the summer of 845 and that he later went on to become the archbishop of Tours.

In any case, Saint-Martin seems to have been without an official abbot for most of 845. Both the poet and the painter of the Presentation miniature worked toward obscuring the identity of their abbot. The use of the term *pater* at XI.3 is, in fact, synonymous with the equivocal *abba* used to describe Heirardus in the charter of 845. Indeed, *pater* and *abba* may have been terms specifically chosen in order to identify the presiding officer of the monastery, without naming him *abbas* or *rector*. *Abba*, like *pater*, was, however, a word that skirted very close to the edge of presumptive announcement.

Irregular titles and the deliberate obfuscation of a poet, thus, underline the uncertain state of things at Saint-Martin in the summer of 845. Vivian was already the king's candidate to replace Adalard, but he had probably not yet become the official lay abbot of Saint-Martin when the poet and painters were at work preparing the First Bible. The mention of the renewal of the monastery's immunities at XI.23–30 and the depiction of Vivian in the Presentation miniature, however, imply that the *primi* knew that Vivian was shortly to become their lay abbot. The renewal of the immunities and the lay abbacy of Vivian, after all, went together. There would have been no manifest need for the renewal of the monastery's "perpetual" immunities if one of the

87. At the Synod of Germigny in September–October 843, one finds two abbots who subscribed in the following ways: "Hugo abbas dei Iesu Christi servus subscripsi" and "In dei nomine ego Lupus abbas." See *MGH Concilia* 3, ed. Hartmann, pp. 6.8 and 7.15. Bishops who were elected but not yet formally ratified generally signed as "episcopus vocatus."

88. On the variant spellings of his name in synodal proceedings, see *MGH Concilia* 3, ed. Hartmann, pp. 464.4, 468.9, 462.21, 472.23–25, 480.5–17, 481.10; Lupus of Ferrières, *epistola* 109, *Loup de Ferrières, Correspondance*, ed. Levillain, 2:148. Some of Herardus's writings survive: see the *Capitula Herardi, Commonitorium Herardi*, and the *Annuntiatio Herardi*, in J. P. Migne, *Patrologia Latina* (hereafter *PL*) 121:763–78.

canons had been elected abbot. The renewal was rather the end result of the negotiations of 845, for it not only reflected the basic anxiety of the canons, but was a putative guarantee, like Charles's earlier concessions in 845, against unwarranted lay interference in Saint-Martin's business. Vivian and the immunities, therefore, belonged together as part of a negotiated settlement. Thus, both the poet and the painter knew that they needed to give Vivian a prominent place in the First Bible, but they were careful not to present him as abbot or to exaggerate his role in the Bible itself or in the presentation ceremony. The final dedicatory verses do not even acknowledge Vivian's appointment as lay abbot, a silence that is striking. The canons may have hoped in the summer of 845 that they could still encourage the king to ponder carefully the fate of Saint-Martin and that they could try to limit the damage done by this and future appointments. In a certain light, then, the First Bible with its verses and paintings can be seen as the equivalent of the renewal of immunities, as a testamentary reminder of the king's undertaking to respect the monastery's rights. In doing so, the poet also reminded Charles the Bald, as sharply as he could, of the greater contract he had entered into with God.

Audradus informed the king at XI.13–14 that he should not think that the gift of the Bible represented anything other than an expression of their gratitude over his generous return of lands. This statement, however, suggests just the opposite: that the poet and painters had a deeper purpose in their preparation and presentation of the Bible. Audradus may have been worried that the king would react unfavorably to any overt attempt on the part of the canons to curry favor and influence the decisions he would make about Saint-Martin. But the gift of a precious book, particularly a Bible, was one of the few ways open for Saint-Martin to communicate with so great and distant a king. Gift books were frequently put to such ends in the ninth century, and Audradus himself did the same again in 849 when he presented Pope Leo IV in Rome with what must have been a handsomely decorated volume of his own writings.[89] In the worry-filled summer of 845, Audradus surely hoped that the king would finally begin to respect the monastery's autonomy and that the poetry and paintings of the First Bible would help the canons make their case.

Throughout the poems, Audradus set out a series of special concerns. At X.22, for instance, he laid emphasis upon Charles's proper appointment of church officials, a crucial concern of Audradus that was to surface later in his *Book of Revelations*.[90] The verses of the First Bible also praised Charles the

---

89. See Audradus, *Praefatio,* ed. Traube, *MGH PLAC* 3:740 and "O Roma nobilis," p. 375.

90. Audradus was very concerned about proper appointments. In 853–54, he complained to Charles the Bald and various bishops gathered at two different synods that it was wrong for Charles to name the outsider Burchard as bishop of Chartres: see Audradus 12 *(Liber revelationum).*12, ed. Traube, "O Roma nobilis," pp. 386–87 and Dutton, *Politics of Dreaming,* pp. 150–52. See nn. 65–66 above.

Bald's privileged position as the patron of the church (*fautor ecclesiae:* VI.4 and X.17) and a consoler of the clergy and people (X.17). And the poet also extolled the king as a respecter of tithes (X.23–24) and one who honored the priesthood (I.51–52). Indeed, he conferred honors upon the church in order to give each holy order what it needed (X.18) and to receive his own reward in heaven (I.53–54). The poet's praise in all these matters was formative, since he praised what he hoped to shape and encourage. But we should not imagine that these positive injunctions were without a sharper edge, for the poet still called upon the king to protect church property against the cruel crime of theft by evil men (XI.31–34). He also emphasized, as we have seen, the state of general poverty with which the canons were concerned, since they thought of themselves as intercessors for the poor (XI.21–24, I.41–46, X.25–26). One of the chief reasons, then, for the heavy emphasis upon justice and law throughout the poetry of the First Bible was to call upon Charles the Bald to protect the property and spiritual interests of Saint-Martin itself.

The poetry of the First Bible is a somewhat unstable amalgam of admonition and panegyric. Audradus employed an astounding twenty-two singular imperatives in the long first poem, six in the sixth poem, and one in each of the last two poems. These imperatives are not only abrupt, but often overly familiar, as when, in introducing the example of what a sharpened sword can do, Audradus said to the king, "Believe me!" (I.37–38). In fact, he frequently spoke to the king in the second-person singular and once addressed him as "tu" (I.183).[91] The poetic mood of the dedicatory verses is predominantly the hortative and jussive subjunctive, as the poet importuned the king in the second-person singular subjunctive. Charles was being educated by the poet and canons, who told him that he would find in the Bible what it was good "to learn" (I.3), that the law instructs and advises (I.140–41), and that it teaches (I.152) even those instructed in worldly ways (I.179). What needs to be remembered here is how young Charles the Bald was in the summer of 845. He had turned twenty-two years old on 23 June and was still being trained by his advisors. Lupus of Ferrières himself had written the king a hortatory letter in 843 in which, echoing the apostle Paul, he told him that it was now time to put

---

91. Although Classical Latin did not employ *vos* for *tu* as a formal address and classicizing Carolingian poets tried to follow classical norms, there is evidence that many Carolingian writers had begun to address their betters with the formal *vos.* Even the superior Latinist Lupus did so when addressing the elderly Einhard: see *epistola* 2, *Loup de Ferrières, Correspondance,* ed. Levillain, 1:10–12. For similar uses in poetry, see Sedulius Scottus, *carmen* 4.46, ed. Traube, *MGH PLAC* 3:169; 16.20, 184; 20.8, 186; 28.66 and 69–70, 194; 29.3, 195; etc. In view of the Carolingian tendency to employ formal address at least some of time when speaking to superiors, one has to wonder whether Audradus was simply observing classical norms in the First Bible or spoke so persistently to Charles in the second person singular because he was a young king not yet in secure control of his kingdom.

away childish things and put on mature wisdom.[92] In 844, in a similar letter, Lupus reminded Charles that a careful regard for justice would surely win him God's favor.[93] Of course, Lupus had his own worries over lost pieces of property, but his admonitory tone is not unlike Audradus's, and both reflected the continuing education of the young king. Indeed, at I.193 Audradus qualified his panegyrical praise of the king by noting that "even now" he surpassed all others, that is to say, that although he was still young he was already preeminent.

Despite that qualification, the poet praised the king in exaggerated terms more appropriate to Charlemagne than to Charles the Bald in 845. At I.190 he seems to employ the pun applied to Charlemagne, that the name CAROLVS came from CARA LVX, or dear light, and he played with the imagery of Charles the Bald as the brilliance of the land and light of the world (I.191), the latter being a phrase applied to Christ himself by the evangelists.[94] He also likened Charles to three biblical paragons: to David in power, to Solomon in intelligence, and to Joseph in appearance (I.195–96), a set of comparisons once applied to Charlemagne by Theodulf.[95] In that poem, Theodulf had also included a fourth figure, claiming that in his name Charlemagne recalled his grandfather, that is, Charles Martel; and this may lead us to suspect that Audradus's fourth comparison at I.196 to "spe induperator ovans" was to Charles's own grandfather, the emperor Charlemagne. At the Synod of Ver, as recorded by Lupus, Charles was reminded that Emperor Charlemagne, the light of Francia, had brought great renown to his name and his family.[96] It would have been natural for a Carolingian poet to flatter young Charles the Bald with a reminder of his likeness to Charlemagne and to his imperial future.[97] Freculf of Lisieux had begun this game of allusions in the 830s when Charles was but a boy.[98] Moreover, the imperial theme of the First Bible verses

---

92. Lupus of Ferrières, *epistola* 31, *Loup de Ferrières, Correspondance,* ed. Levillain, 1:140–46 and *epistola* 37, 1:160–64. See 1 Cor. 13:11.

93. Lupus of Ferrières, *epistola* 37, *Loup de Ferrières, Correspondance,* ed. Levillain, 1:162.3–5: "Observantia justitiae non solum apud Deum meritum vobis comparat, verum etiam terrenam potestatem confirmat."

94. See Gabriel Silagi, "Karolus—cara lux," *Deutsches Archiv* 37 (1981), 786–91; and Dutton, *Politics of Dreaming,* p. 21.

95. Theodulf, *carmen* 25.29–30, ed. Dümmler, *MGH PLAC* 1:484. See also the later poem once attributed to Theodulf: *carmen* 76.13–14, ed. Dümmler, *MGH PLAC* 1:577.

96. Ver 1, in *MGH Concilia* 3, ed. Hartmann, p. 39.29–30: "domesticum lumen imperator Karolus, qui nomen, quod familiae vestrae peperit, clarissimis actibus adornavit." Solomon, David, and Ezechias were cited as other examples for Charles in the previous lines.

97. William Diebold, "'Nos quoque morem illius imitari cupientes': Charles the Bald's Evocation and Imitation of Charlemagne," *Archiv für Kulturgeschichte* 75 (1993): 271–300.

98. See Freculf, *epistola,* in "Epistolae variorum" 14, ed. Dümmler, *MGH Epistolae* 5 (Berlin, 1898), p. 319.15–16 and "Epistolae variorum" 13, ed. Dümmler, *MGH Epistolae* 5:317.12–14.

was hardly accidental, since at XI.15 the poet addressed Charles as *Caesar.*[99] This title was also applied to Charlemagne and the word *imperium* invoked in the verses inscribed in the copy of Boethius's *De arithmetica* (Bamberg, Staats-bibliothek, Class. 5, fols. 1v–2r), which was also made for Charles the Bald at Saint-Martin about 845.[100] This imperial language, which was most boldly stated in the First Bible, was a way of connecting the young king with the imperial inheritance of his father and grandfather.[101]

The imperial theme was also one that the architect tried to insert into the very design of the First Bible. At the first full opening of the codex (fols. 1v–2r, figs. 2–3, frontispiece, and fig. I) the king encountered the lines of the first set of verses laid out as though in a diptych design with golden rustic-capital letters on purple panels.[102] Between the purple panels on folio 1v one sees two medallion portraits, the top one labeled DAVID REX IMPERATOR +[103] and the bottom one KAROLVS REX FRANCO<RVM> (fig. 37). These bear a rough resemblance to Roman imperial coins having bust portraits in profile.[104]

---

99. The poet's usage here has confused some scholars, who have spoken of Emperor Charles the Bald in the First Bible: see, for instance, C. R. Dodwell, *Painting in Europe, 800 to 1200*, Pelican History of Art, rev. ed. (New Haven, 1993), p. 71. An inscription in Caroline minuscule in the top margin of fol. 422v of the First Bible refers to the monks of Saint-Martin presenting the book to *Imperator Karolus*. Since Charles the Bald did become emperor in late 875, perhaps a later reader or librarian at Metz, where the book may have been deposited in 869, remembered him in this way, or there may have been a simple confusion with Charle-magne.

100. Ed. K. Strecker, *MGH PLAC* 4 (Berlin, 1881; rpt. 1964), pp. 1076.2–3, 1077.16.

101. Janet Nelson's comment that "perhaps as early as 849, Charles voiced imperial pretensions or, at least, let those around him do so in his name," could at Tours, therefore, be pushed back several years to 844–45. See Janet L. Nelson, "Translating Images of Authority: The Christian Roman Emperors in the Car-olingian World," in *Images of Authority: Papers Presented to Joyce Reynolds on the Occasion of Her Seven-tieth Birthday,* ed. M. M. MacKenzie and C. Roueché (Cambridge, 1989), p. 196 and rpt. in Nelson, *Frank-ish World*, pp. 89–98.

102. See Calkins, *Illuminated Books,* p. 96.

103. There remains some disagreement about whether the complete inscription is original, though we were able to examine the inscription both on microfilm and in person and could find only one hand at work. See the conclusion below. Rainer Kahsnitz, "Ein Bildnis der Theophanau? Zur Tradition der Münz- und Medaillon-Bildnisse in der karolingischen und ottonischen Buchmalerei," in *Kaiserin Theophanau: Begeg-nung des Ostens und Westens um die Wende des ersten Jahrhunderts,* vol. 2, ed. Anton von Euw and Peter Schreiner (Cologne, 1991), p. 120, observed that IMPERATOR was added to the inscription at some later date by a different hand. Diebold, "Nos quoque morem," p. 287 n. 57, thought the full inscription was orig-inal.

104. They are not very similar to Carolingian coins. Charles the Bald's coins, for instance, lacked bust portraits, and Charlemagne's coins with bust portaits all date from his imperial period. Those bust portraits also faced in the opposite direction, and no Carolingian coin inscription is exactly like either of the two inscriptions on fol. 1v of the First Bible. The closest was KARLVS REX FR, which appeared on coins of both Charlemagne and Charles the Bald. See Philip Grierson, "Money and Coinage under Charlemagne," in *Karl der Grosse. Lebenswerk und Nachleben,* ed. W. Braunfels, vol. 1: *Persönlichkeit und Geschichte,* ed. Helmut Beumann (Düsseldorf, 1965), p. 505; Karl F. Morrison, *Carolingian Coinage* (New York, 1967), pp. 177–258; Grierson, "The 'Gratia Dei Rex' Coinage of Charles the Bald," in *Charles the Bald: Court and Kingdom,* ed. M. T. Gibson and J. L Nelson, 2d ed. (Aldershot, 1990), p. 53; and Kahsnitz, "Ein Bildnis der Theophanau?" 118–24.

On folio 2r, between the purple panels and paralleling the medallion portraits on folio 1v, are two more medallion portraits, one the bust of a full-faced
figure and the other a half-portrait of a haloed figure (fig. 3). Though these
figures lack inscriptions, they were probably meant to represent biblical
figures. Outline drawings of other figures such as Moses, Jerome, and Judith
appear in various initials throughout the Bible; some are labeled, most are not.
Their placement, context, and general features, however, often allow identification. It is, thus, tempting to wonder whether the top figure on folio 2r might
be Solomon and the bottom one handsome young Joseph, hence the reason for
showing more of his physical form.[105] There is, after all, only one group of
four men mentioned in the first dedicatory poem, to which the medallion portraits are specifically tied. The architect of the First Bible may have wished at
the first opening of the great Bible to illustrate Charles's relationship to these
four great paragons of virtue. If so, then the Charles medallion may have been
meant to represent Charlemagne and not his grandson or, at least, to fuse the
identity of the two Charleses.

The most persistent fusion of identities was certainly of Charles and
David,[106] whose medallion portrait surmounts Charles's. Throughout the
First Bible verses David is both a model of virtue and another name for King
Charles. It had also been the pet name of Charlemagne at his court. In 844
Lupus of Ferrières reminded Charles the Bald that David was the one figure
whom he should imitate,[107] and at the Synod of Ver in December the bishops,
in Lupus's words, reminded Charles that David was both king and prophet,
"rex et propheta," and they held him out as a source of truth for King
Charles.[108] REX ET PROP<HETA>, as already noted, was the very label
inscribed above the portrait of David in the Psalms frontispiece of the First
Bible, thus once again fusing David and Charles the Bald, Charlemagne and
his grandson.

But if flattery and extravagant praise was one element of the poet's message,
it was the honey laid down to catch a fly, for Audradus's imperative admonition overrides all the praise. It would be misleading to think of the verses as a

---

105. Joseph had also become for the Carolingians and especially Charles's court a symbol of a younger
son forced to survive against hostile brothers. See the commentary at I.196 in the appendix.

106. See Kessler, "Lay Abbot as Patron," pp. 662–65.

107. Lupus of Ferrières, *epistola* 37, *Loup de Ferrières, Correspondance,* ed. Levillain, 1:160–64.

108. Canon 1, in *MGH Concilia* 3, ed. Hartmann, pp. 39.27–40.4. David was also referred to as "rex et
propheta" in the context of his dancing before the ark in *Libri carolini* 2.26, ed. Bastgen, in *MGH Concilia*
2.*Supplementum* (Hanover, 1924), p. 86.32–35: "ante quam egregius propheta et rex infulatus magna cum
exsultatione ludere non erubescat et eam ad locum destinatum in musicis concentibus hymnorumque suavi-
sonis modulaminibus introducat: quae, dum et suis et opificis tot signorum eminuerit praerogativis, non
inmerito arcae testamenti Domini poterit coaequari."

typical species of *Fürstenspiegel* or Mirror of Princes,[109] since the poet laid out no examples of evil rulers for Charles to ponder, and that had been a characteristic feature of the genre. Audradus's emphasis on the importance of wisdom was, however, a familiar feature of the mirrors.[110] Indeed, when he warned that even those trained in arms could still fall to the enemy of humankind, the devil (I.163–64), and when he hinted at the insufficiency of worldly training (I.179), he borrowed from *Fürstenspiegel* themes.[111] But his deeper purpose was to persuade the young king that the Bible itself was the single source of truth, one that would supply him with virtually everything he needed to know. Thus, the Bible was, to Turonian eyes, the mirror of mirrors, and the canons of Saint-Martin, as depicted in the Presentation miniature, were the supreme suppliers of the Bible, the visible heirs of Jerome's holy *translatio.*

The poet particularly wanted the king to realize that the Bible was the best of all teachers. It cultivated intelligence, as the example of Solomon showed (I.33, 40, 181–87, 195), would teach him about the natural world, logic, and morality, that is, the liberal arts (I.131), provided the model of the four virtues (I.165), and supplied all the riches he needed (I.133–34). Audradus portrayed the Bible as the place where the young king could find everything he needed to know. What it especially taught was the law, for justice (see I.49–50, 135–46) is one of the main themes binding together the dedicatory verses and paintings. And justice achieved its final and clearest expression in the last two sets of verses and in the Presentation miniature, where the poet and painter imagined the king and canons finally setting their worlds right.

---

109. At the Fifth Saint Louis Conference on Manuscript Studies, held 12–14 October 1978, Eleanor Scheifele made such an argument based on an interpretation and analysis of the paintings. A precis of her talk is to be found in *Manuscripta* 23 (1979), pp. 21–22. See also Anton's analysis of the First Bible verses in this regard, *Fürstenspiegel und Herrscherethos*, pp. 254–58.

110. See Anton, *Fürstenspiegel und Herrscherethos*, pp. 255–56 especially nn. 555 and 559.

111. Sedulius Scottus, *De rectoribus christianis* 14, ed. S. Hellmann, *Sedulius Scottus*, Quellen und Untersuchungen zur lateinischen Philologie des Mittelalters, 1 (Munich, 1906), pp. 62–66, later employed the same theme of the foolishness of kings who have a false confidence in military might and training.

CHAPTER 3

Preparing the Codex

Sometime, then, perhaps as late as the summer of 845, a decision was made at Saint-Martin to prepare a deluxe Bible for Charles the Bald. The immediate cause of the Bible's creation was probably an announcement by the king that he would visit the monastery on Saint Martin's feast day in November 845 to renew the monastery's immunities and appoint a new abbot.

The First Bible could have been made entirely in 845, given E. K. Rand's observation that six scribes worked on the manuscript.[1] But the codex seems, in fact, already to have been in production as part of the steady output of the scriptorium of Saint-Martin,[2] which during the 830s and 840s was producing approximately two pandects per year.[3] This is indicated, first of all, by the four core illuminations (figs. 6, 7, 10, 13) and accompanying *tituli* (III, IV, VII, IX), all of which are shared with the Moutier-Grandval Bible. The idea that the First Bible was a relatively hasty adaptation of a manuscript already in production[4] is furthermore indicated by a series of alterations still evident in the volume.

Of these, the most important is the rewriting of the end of the Epistle to the Hebrews (13:13–25) onto folio 415r (fig. 12). Scripture there spills over onto the back of a miniature, a feature that is unique in the First Bible.[5] Originally,

---

1. Rand, *Survey of Manuscripts,* p. 155.

2. See Rosamond McKitterick, "Carolingian Book Production: Some Problems," *Library,* 6th series, 12 (1990): 29–30 and rpt. in McKitterick, *Books, Scribes and Learning in the Frankish Kingdoms, 6th–9th Centuries,* Variorum Collected Studies, 452 (Aldershot, 1994), item 12; David Ganz, "Mass Production of Early Medieval Manuscripts: The Carolingian Bibles from Tours," in *The Early Medieval Bible: Its Production, Decoration, and Use,* ed. R. Gameson (Cambridge, 1994), pp. 53–62; Rosamond McKitterick, "Carolingian Bible Production: the Tours Anomaly," in *The Early Medieval Bible,* pp. 63–77.

3. See B. Bischoff, *Latin Palaeography: Antiquity and the Middle Ages,* trans. D. Ó Cróinín and D. Ganz (Cambridge, 1990), p. 208 and Ganz, "Mass Production," p. 53. Of these, several contained pictorial decorations, in addition to the Moutier-Grandval Bible and Bamberg Bible from nearby Marmoutier (Staatsbibliothek, Misc. class. Bibl. 1). See Kessler, *Illustrated Bibles,* pp. 6–8.

4. Rand, *Survey of Manuscripts,* p. 63: "There is no obvious sign in the script—in fact, quite the contrary—that it was begun at an earlier date."

5. On the unusualness of fol. 415r, see also Mildred Budny, "Assembly Marks in the Vivian Bible and

these lines of text had been transcribed on the conjoint leaf (now fol. 416r, fig. 14) that opened immediately across from folio 414v.[6] The original text, which had been written in Caroline minuscule, can still be discerned, though it is now whited out in broad strokes, beneath the repainted and paneled surface of the left column that contains the title to Jerome's preface to Revelation.[7] Above and below the fourth panel daubs of paint cover the characters of the beginning (EXPLICIT) and end (AD HEBRAEOS) of the original *explicit* of Hebrews. Traces of rustic-capital letters, with which all the letters of Paul conclude, actually show through the fourth panel. Immediately below the square-capital letters one reads the word <E>PISTOLA, the *S* beneath the large *M* being particularly evident. The *E* is now covered by the left side of the frame, as is the *E* of EXPLICIT and the *A* of AD.

Thus, even the frame of folio 416r was added after the original inscription of Hebrews had been painted over, since it also covers the second line of the original inscription. Other prologues and prefaces of Jerome are presented on framed pages (fol. 130r, the prologue to Isaiah, and fol. 324r, the preface to the Gospels), but this frame was introduced late in the transformation of the page. The new frame also bleeds through to folio 416v, particularly along the inside margin, thus suggesting that that surface had been inscribed before the introduction of the frame on the recto.

The original *Incipit praefatio* to Jerome's preface had been inscribed in the upper portion of the right column of folio 416r (see fig. A). When the panels were introduced into the left column, that *incipit* was no longer needed in its usual place, and a fuller one with few abbreviations was inscribed in the new left-column panels. The scribe at this point probably removed the original *incipit,* which, if it was inscribed in gold letters, as was often the case, might have been stripped away. He then introduced panels and adjusted the lettering of the opening words of the preface in the right column. He also increased the size of the capital *I* of IOHANNES in order to bring it into nearer alignment with its new referent. The page's original arrangement, with the conclusion of a text and an expansive rustic-capital *explicit* below it in the left column, and the *incipit* and preface to a new biblical book starting with an initial letter in the next column, occurs elsewhere in the manuscript: at the end of Deuteronomy and Jerome's preface to Joshua (fol. 73r), at the beginning of the Book of Ruth (fol. 88v), and at the opening of Acts (fol. 366v). Although the new left-column panels imitate others in the manuscript, they have an improvised

---

Scribal, Editorial, and Organizational Marks in Medieval Books," in Making the Medieval Book: Techniques of Production, ed. L. L. Brownrigg *(Los Altos Hills, Calif., 1995), pp. 202, 231–32.*

6. For a detailed schematization of the relevant quires here, see Budny, "Assembly Marks," p. 202, fig. 4.

7. Budny, "Assembly Marks," pp. 231–33 and figs. 30–31.

A. Conjectural reconstruction of the original layout of Paris, BN lat. 1, fol. 416r

appearance; and nowhere else in the Bible is a full column given over to a title, a capacious elaborateness that seems somewhat unsuited to a preface *incipit.*

The reason for the change can be easily surmised: a decision was made after the text had been basically completed to insert the Apocalypse miniature at the start of the Book of Revelation, that is, at the center of that quire, which is gathering 58. No other frontispiece was so situated in the codex, for gatherings had normally been designed to allow frontispieces to stand alone before new quires.[8] Most likely, then, Revelation was not originally supposed to have a frontispiece. When it was decided to insert the picture there, the assemblers realized that it would separate the last portion of the epistle, which had already been inscribed, from the rest of the text. Hence a decision was made to score twenty-seven lines lightly in the upper left quadrant of the blank side of the Apocalypse folio, now folio 415r (fig. 12). The scribe was aware that a precious miniature occupied the obverse; not only did he score only as many lines as he thought he needed, but in recopying the text he slightly reduced the size of the letters and the spaces between letters and words. He thus marginally decreased the physical size of the inscribed text on folio 415r to twenty-three lines plus the *explicit,* which now occupies only two scored lines, and found that he did not need two of the scored lines. His estimate of the amount of space required had probably been based upon the approximately twenty-seven lines of text inscribed in the left column of what is now folio 416r (fig. 14). He then painted over that original text, inserted the panels, wrote out the new *incipit,* and rearranged the opening of the preface text. The nature of these changes suggests that the preface (fol. 416rb), the *capitula* to Revelation (fol. 416va), and start of Revelation (fol. 416vb) already occupied the folio and that the rest of the conjoint (fol. 414) already contained the text of the Letter to the Hebrews. In order both to preserve these inscribed texts and, perhaps, because time was precious, the alterations described were made to folio 416r.

While it is conceivable that the preparers of the codex had simply forgotten the miniature and had to rectify their mistake, both the specific codicology and special iconography of the Apocalypse miniature suggest otherwise (figs. 13 and III). The image of the Bible being opened at the end of time and of the revelation of the *facies bibliothecae* or the very countenance of the whole Bible properly belonged at the volume's conclusion, and had been so placed in the Moutier-Grandval Bible (fig. 26).[9] In the First Bible this painting was also originally designed to stand at the end of the codex, and the text of Hebrews was written accordingly. At some point late in the preparation of the volume,

8. See Budny, "Assembly Marks," p. 202.

9. Herbert L. Kessler, "'Facies bibliothecae revelata': Carolingian Art as Spiritual Seeing," in *Testo e immagine nell'alto medioevo,* Settimane di studio del Centro Italiano di Studi sull'alto medioevo, 41 (Spoleto, 1994), pp. 559–61.

the program was changed, and the miniature was transformed into a frontispiece to Revelation. The same scribe who had copied the Letter to the Hebrews on folio 414v seems to have recopied the end of the epistle onto the back of the present 415r, thus suggesting that the change itself was contemporaneous with the final phase of the production of the First Bible. The hypothesis of the shift of the Apocalypse miniature is further indicated by the anomalous presence of two single leaves (fols. 420–21) rather than a bifolium at the end of the text of Revelation.[10]

The picture was probably not fully painted when the program was altered, and at least three small scenes were introduced (figs. 19–21). The new inscription of the end of Hebrews on folio 415r conforms to the frame of the miniature on the verso and the scribe was conscious that scoring lines might have left marks that would mar the colored surface already occupying the verso of the folio. It seems likely, therefore, that the borders and general composition of the miniature already existed, at least in outline, but that the surface may still not have been completely painted when this change was conceived and alterations to the painting were introduced. Both the rewriting and repainting, to which we shall return, attest to the codex's changing program, perhaps in the early autumn of 845.

Moreover, in this rare case we are able to trace the way in which the specific codicological changes were introduced. In an important discovery, Mildred Budny detected matching assembly marks on folios 414v and 415r and also on folios 420v and 421r.[11] Although she regarded these as constituent features of the First Bible and suspected that more assembly marks might be found,[12] we are tempted to think that these assembly marks were exceptional signs introduced late in the production of the First Bible in order to handle the specific relocation of the Apocalypse miniature. Once the decision had been made by the volume's architect to introduce a folio of verse and the Presentation miniature at the end of the volume, he needed to relocate the Apocalypse miniature to folio 415r and to have the end of the text of the Letter to the Hebrews repaired. The matching assembly marks on folios 414v and 415r were employed to bring together two folios that had originally been separated. Similarly the assembly marks on 420v–421r were designed to unite folios at the end of Revelation that had previously been associated with the Apocalypse miniature and that were now in danger of dislocation.

---

10. See Budny, "Assembly Marks," pp. 202–3.

11. Budny, "Assembly Marks," pp. 202–3 and figs. 4, 7, and 8.

12. Her first example, the marks found on fols. 27v–28r and associated with the Exodus Frontispiece, are perhaps less convincing than the others. The one on fol. 28r is an *r* set high in the left margin near an initial letter and might have served purposes other than assembly. See Budny, "Assembly Marks," pp. 203–4 and fig. 6.

Thus, the assembly marks provide further evidence of the extraordinary changes made to the First Bible as it was being prepared for presentation to the king in the autumn of 845. What caused the change was the designer's decision to include verses and a portrait of the king at the end of the volume; these were now to serve in place of the Apocalypse miniature as the manuscript's tailpieces.

The only other miniature with text on the back, the Majestas Domini (fol. 329r, fig. 9), provides another indication of the changes introduced late in the production of the First Bible;[13] here, the text of poem VI was written freehand on unscored vellum. In this case the painting was apparently already completed when the decision was made to add dedicatory verses between the Old and New Testaments. The architect of the volume probably decided not to risk damaging the surface of the miniature by ruling the page. This is the only set of dedicatory verses not inscribed on purple vellum, a fact of which the architect seems to have been aware, since poem VI was inscribed in alternating lines of red and gold rustic-capital letters as though to approximate the effect of the other verse pages.

The poem itself also has an ad hoc character. Indeed, it is likely that poem VI was the last set of verses composed, since it reverberates with phrases and themes found in the longer poems.[14] Of course, the function of poem VI was not only to serve as the poetic hinge between the Old and New Testaments, but also to reinforce the poet's main topics. This made the introduction of poem VI particularly important to Audradus's cycle of poems, but its exceptional codicological features also suggest that it was conceived of late in the preparation of the First Bible. Indeed, there are two interesting scribal mistakes in poem VI, both probably products of haste. At VI.23 the scribe had written the nonsensical HICCA VITA RITAS in line 8 of the second column of folio 329r (fig. 9). Someone recognized the error, but he may have thought it unwise to erase it and risk damaging the folio with its illuminated surface lying on the other side. Moreover, since folio 329r was unpainted, he could not simply paint over the error, which was the usual technique of correction applied to the painted pages that contained the other dedicatory verses. Hence the corrector introduced diacritical marks above the *CA* to indicate the necessary exchange

---

13. Budny, "Assembly Marks," p. 202, notes that aside from the Apocalypse miniature only the Gospels frontispiece does not stand as a single sheet at the start of a quire, but rather was inserted between the first and second folios of a gathering. This was probably done so that it would fall immediately before the commencement of the first Gospel on fol. 330r.

14. The following phrases are the most notable examples: "eclesiae fautor/fotor" at VI.4 and X.17; "clare primordia" at VI.7 and I.157; "verumque fidesque" at VI.23 and XI.5; "nova rite" at VI.6 and I.113; and "actio munda" at VI.21 and "actio pura" at X.16. Particular note should also be made of the similar treatments of the evangelists at VI.7–18 and I.91–104.

I. Poem I.101–50, with portraits; Paris, BN lat. 1, fol. 2r

II. Psalms frontispiece; Paris, BN lat. 1, fol. 215v

III. Apocalypse frontispiece; Paris, BN lat. 1, fol. 415v

IV. Presentation miniature; Paris, BN lat. 1, fol. 423r

of letters. This mistake was one of the eye and not the ear, as the scribe may have allowed his eye to wander ahead a few letters when copying from an exemplar. At VI.11 the same scribe wrote PARTIS where PARTES seems called for. This error is an interesting one, because it may suggest that the scribe's exemplar was written in rustic-capital letters, in which it is sometimes difficult to distinguish between *E* and *I*. What is also telling in this case is that no one caught this particular mistake, perhaps because the Bible was soon presented to the king and soon carried away.

The other changes to the First Bible being readied for presentation to the king are all codicologically discrete. Poem I was written on a separate bifolium, and the Jerome, David, and Paul frontispieces are all singletons with blank rectos. All these folios, along with the end matter, could easily have been inserted into a manuscript already under production. Only the relocation of the Apocalypse frontispiece, made necessary by the special addition of poems X and XI and the Presentation portrait, required major modifications in the nearly completed work. This is not to suggest that the four new illuminations were absolute innovations in the Turonian pandect project, since the Bible of San Paolo fuori le mura made for Charles the Bald around 870 repeats some of the same themes.[15] But the modifications do suggest that the original plan for the First Bible was much more like that of the Moutier-Grandval Bible and that the program was adapted when a decision was made to present the manuscript to the king on his announced visit to the monastery in 845. That the dedicatory verses and paintings were put together relatively quickly is suggested by the fact that the inserted pages are slightly larger than normal, the ruling is not always consistent, and even the decoration of the inserted pages may not always be perfectly consistent with the rest of the volume.[16]

Furthermore, there are some indications that Audradus may have composed some of the verses rather quickly.[17] The verses in the First Bible seem somewhat inferior to his other compositions and are either more or, perhaps, less successfully derivative.[18] The use of intensified constructions such as *sic sic* (I.21) and *hic hic* (I.133), although not untypical of Audradus's work, may also

---

15. Joachim E. Gaehde, "The Turonian Sources of the Bible of San Paolo fuori le Mura in Rome," *Frühmittelalterliche Studien*, 5 (1971): 359–400 and "Le fonti Turonesi," in *Commentario della Bibbia di San Paolo fuori le mura* (Rome, 1993), pp. 281–98.

16. See Berger, *Histoire de la Vulgate*, p. 218; Edward K. Rand, "How Many Leaves at a Time?" *Palaeographica Latina* 5 (1927): 70; Budny, "Assembly Marks," pp. 231–32.

17. The first dedicatory verse is the one with the most compositional and scribal problems.

18. The variations in Audradus's poetic style in different poems may reflect the different sources and models he drew upon. Traube was able to demonstrate this dependence in the case of three of the sets of poems on Julian and his friends in which Audradus drew directly upon an extant hagiographical tradition: see Audradus 9–11, ed. Traube, *MGH PLAC* 3:91–121, in which Traube printed the relevant chapters from the *Acta beati Iuliani et sociorum martyrum* at the bottom of the pages.

suggest that he was pressed for time when composing the long first poem. Although familiar with the intricacies and phraseology of classical poetry, when composing the First Bible verses he turned specifically to the examples of the verses prepared for other Carolingian Bibles. The poet did not, in other words, hit upon the idea of beginning with a two-hundred-line poem accidentally, but drew upon the models provided by the Theodulfian and Alcuinian Bibles. Audradus's heavy reliance upon the size, design, and content of these biblical verses may suggest that he was pressed for time when preparing the First Bible's longest and most difficult set of verses. Theodulf's Bible, for instance, began with a poem of 250 lines and Audradus borrowed and reworked a number of its lines.[19] But the influence of Alcuin on Audradus was even greater. In fact, the 204-line poem Alcuin placed at the start of one Bible was effectively 200 lines long, since the last four lines are a separable colophon.[20] Hence, Audradus imitated the specific length and structure of that poem in his own first verse. After Virgil Alcuin had the greatest influence upon Audradus's poetic style. In his long poem Alcuin had, for instance, run off lists of nouns,[21] as Audradus would. He also introduced Job immediately after Ruth, a peculiarity copied by Audradus even though it has no obvious relationship to the arrangement of biblical materials in the First Bible.[22] Audradus also closely followed Alcuinian images[23] and employed many of his particular phrases.[24] He may have drawn on these older biblical verse cycles because he was in some haste to prepare the first poem, but in so doing he also reinforced an Alcuinian poetical tradition at Tours.[25] He was certainly aware of the Turonian tradition of Bible making when he sat down to compose the verses for the First Bible and consulted the monastery's extant Bibles and biblical sources. Indeed, the singular emphasis on the importance of the Bible in the

---

19. Theodulf, *carmen* 41, ed. Dümmler, *MGH PLAC* 1:532–38. Cf. Theodulf, *carmen* 41.87, ed. Dümmler, *MGH PLAC* 1:534 and I.91; Theodulf, *carmen* 41.143, p. 536 and I.147: "per compita mundi"; Theodulf, *carmen* 41.149, p. 536 and I.137 and X.13; Theodulf, *carmen* 41.151, p. 536 and I.135; Theodulf, *carmen* 41.203–4, p. 537 and X.31, and the other more subtle influences listed in the notes to the verses in the appendix.

20. Alcuin, *carmen* 69, ed. Dümmler, *MGH PLAC* 1:288–92. On the tradition of these verses at Tours, see Bonifatius Fischer, *Lateinische Bibelhandschriften im frühen Mittelalter* (Freiburg, 1985), pp. 222–50.

21. Alcuin, *carmen* 69.103, ed. Dümmler, *MGH PLAC* 1:290; *carmen* 69.173–74, p. 291; *carmen* 69.178, p. 292; *carmen* 69.182, p. 292; *carmen* 69.190, p. 292.

22. Cf. Alcuin, *carmen* 69.106–108, ed. Dümmler, *MGH PLAC* 1:290, I.71–72. While Ruth falls on fols. 88vb–89vb of the First Bible, Job is to be found on fols. 206va–214vb.

23. Cf. Alcuin, *carmen* 69.113–16, ed. Dümmler, *MGH PLAC* 1:290, I.77–80.

24. Cf. Alcuin, *carmen* 69.6, ed. Dümmler, *MGH PLAC* 1:288, "pietatis opus" and X.30; Alcuin, *carmen* 69.9, p. 288 and XI.11, "laudetur ametur"; Alcuin, *carmen* 69.31, p. 288 and I.187, "sapientia vera"; Alcuin, *carmen* 69.103, p. 290, "Quorum gesta, genus, tempus, locus, bella, triumphos," and I.69, "Horum facta, genus, tempus, loca, bella, triumphi,"; Alcuin, *carmen* 69.198, p. 292, "ab arce pius," and VI.12, "ab arce piae," and X.42, "ab arce pia."

25. See Fischer, *Lateinische Bibelhandschriften*, pp. 222–46.

verses and the demonstration of that importance in the Jerome frontispiece underlined the fundamental mission of Saint-Martin.

The sixth poem, as demonstrated, seems almost to have been an after-thought in a quickly evolving composition and, thus, was another sign of the speed with which the volume was being rushed to completion. There are, how-ever, signs of careful and deliberate design to the composition and layout of the other poems. Thus, the long first poem falls precisely into eight columns of twenty-five lines spread over four pages, or two folios. This exact division of verses cannot have been simply fortuitous; either Audradus had decided in advance that he would compose enough lines of verse to fill the purple pages of an already existing bifolium (fols. 1–2) evenly or he ordered the preparation of the bifolium based on the length of the anticipated or already completed poem. In either case, this would seem another indication of Audradus as the poet-architect of the remade codex making his empurpled work the first, prominent feature of the First Bible.

One also has to wonder whether the poet when composing read parts of his poetry orally to secretaries or scribes, who then wrote out exemplars of the verses for use by the First Bible's scribes. The difference in orthography between *fautor* at VI.4 and *fotor* at X.17 might be accounted for by such oral transmission. The same might be said of *componit* at I.7 and *conposuit* at II.6 and of *paradise* at XI.18 and *paradyse* at I.119, though they are more minor in effect. The evidence suggests that exemplars of the dedicatory verses, probably already containing small orthographical variants and other anomalies, existed before final inscription. In the case of the older *tituli,* it is certain that these poems existed in written form at Saint-Martin. Even the dedicatory verses were probably copied from exemplars, perhaps written in rustic-capital letters; both HICCA VITA RITAS (VI.23) and PARTIS for PARTES at VI.11, as already noted, imply the existence of those exemplars. The corrections that were introduced to the codex may also suggest that the scribes had access to copies of the verses or, perhaps, that the poet himself took an active role in correcting the inscribed poems. Thus, at I.58 the scribe seems originally to have written HERI, which was subsequently corrected to ERI by painting over the letter *H.* Other scribal mistakes were caught by a corrector before the codex left Tours. At VIII.3, ANNANIAM was corrected to ANANIAM by painting over the extra letter, thus once again demonstrating the corrector's reluctance to erase letters on an illuminated folio. The same phenomenon is seen at II.5, where a corrector inserted a medial point in gold at TRANS-LATA·S VI to help the reader separate words that had been improperly joined. It is interesting that no such errors occur in the *tituli* of the four core illumina-tions, for which there were certainly established and reliable copies. The mistakes and corrections of the new poetry may once again, then, suggest the haste with which the codex was being readied for presentation.

The addition of the dedicatory verses and the four new miniatures, the modification of the position and content of the Apocalypse miniature, the introduction of poem VI on an illuminated folio, and the various anomalies, oversights, and corrections to the poetry all point to the late transformation of a pandect that had once more closely resembled the Moutier-Grandval Bible (figs. 23–26). This volume, before the changes, would have begun with the elaborately framed page that now stands at folio 4r and introduces Jerome's letter to Paulinus. It would have had four principal illuminations: to Genesis (fig. 6), Exodus (fig. 7), the Gospels (Majestas Domini, fig. 10), and Apocalypse (figs. 13 and III), which then stood at the end of the codex. As originally conceived, the volume might have had no other poetry than the *tituli* found on the four illuminations.[26]

In this scenario, then, one can suppose that a volume very like the Moutier-Grandval Bible either stood ready or was in the midst of preparation in 845 when it was learned that the king intended to return to Saint-Martin that year on 11 November in order to celebrate the feast of Saint Martin, renew the immunities of the monastery, and arrange for a new abbot. A decision was made at Saint-Martin, probably by the *primi* and *pater,* to transform the codex into one for presentation to the king. We know something of the sequence of commands that led to the production of other royal books in the scriptorium of Saint-Martin from the verses found in the gospel book made for the emperor Lothar around 849 (Paris, B.N. lat. 266, fig. 34).[27] Sigilaus's verses suggest that, once the decision had been made to create that special volume, the abbot or *praesul* put Sigilaus himself in charge of its preparation. Sigilaus was, therefore, the poet-architect of the Lothar Gospels. He directed the *grex Martini* or, at least, the brothers who worked in the scriptorium to prepare the precious book, perhaps even providing them with specific orders about its illumination while he readied the verses. It is not unwarranted, then, given Sigilaus's description of the command structure at work in the preparation of a later royal book at Saint-Martin, to think that in 845 the *pater* of the monastery had in similar fashion placed the poet and *primus* Audradus Modicus in charge of producing a precious Bible for Charles the Bald. It was decided that the dedicatory volume would not only have new poems dedicated to the king, but new illuminations and a new

26. In Princeton on 4 April 1996 after the authors presented their paper, "Some Reasons for Rethinking the First Bible of Charles the Bald," to the conference devoted to the theme of "The Carolingian Bible and Its Impact," Lawrence Nees wondered for whom such a precious book might have been prepared. Unfortunately the First Bible in its finished form does not seem to preserve any information that would allow us at this point to speculate on its earlier purpose or destination.

27. *Sigilai versus ad Hlotharium imperatorem* 10–22, ed. E. Dümmler, *MGH PLAC* 2:671.

and very special design, quite unlike anything seen before in Carolingian Europe.

But the specialness and demonstrable spontaneity of the specific design of the codex raises questions about the First Bible's influence upon the creation of other illuminated manuscripts. If in a moment of inspired and hurried innovation the Apocalypse painting was displaced by the poems and Presentation miniature and transformed from a tailpiece into a frontispiece, then it is unlikely that it is a mere coincidence that the Bible of San Paolo fuori le mura repeats the same changed order of miniatures. Although the king's portrait in the latter manuscript now stands at the front of that codex (fol. 1r), it originally stood on folio 337v as the volume's tailpiece,[28] and the Apocalypse miniature there is properly a frontispiece (fol. 331v). It may be reasonable to suppose, therefore, that the artists of the First Bible kept a descriptive record of some sort of the basic structure and verses of the First Bible.

As we have already noted, the scribes of the codex seem to have worked from copies of the poems, which may well have still been available at Saint-Martin in the late 840s. In fact, poem X.39–41 was later reworked in the Lothar Gospels (fig. 34). Sigilaus rearranged the order of the three lines of verse, transformed a pentameter into a hexameter, and introduced a few vocabulary changes.[29] Although not absolutely unique as a design feature, it is nevertheless striking that those verses occupy the recto of a folio that contains a miniature of the Majestas Domini on the verso (Paris, B.N. lat. 266, fol. 2). The conjunction of dedicatory verses and the Majestas Domini was, as we have seen, quite likely a last-minute innovation of the architect of the First Bible, so its repetition in a later manuscript made at Saint-Martin would seem dependent on that earlier innovation. Since both of these examples of the Majestas Domini were painted by the celebrated illuminator called Master C by Koehler,[30] one may suspect that in working on later manuscripts he simply remembered and repeated some of the First Bible's codicological characteristics. He may also have been the chief illuminator of a lost pandect that incorporated some of the First Bible's new features.[31] But what we can never fully

---

28. See William J. Diebold, "The Ruler Portrait of Charles the Bald in the S. Paolo Bible," *Art Bulletin* 86 (1994): 7 and n. 2.

29. See the commentary at X.39–41 in the appendix for a comparison of the lines and Lowden, "The Royal/Imperial Book," p. 221. On the politics of Saint-Martin's connection with Lothar in 849, see Joachim Wollasch, "Kaiser und Könige als Brüder der Mönche. Zum Herrscherbild in liturgischen Handschriften des 9. bis 11. Jahrhunderts," *Deutsches Archiv für Erforschung des Mittelalters* 40 (1984): 19.

30. On the division and differentiation of Masters A, B, and C, see Koehler, *Die karolingischen Miniaturen*, 1:2, pp. 27–64. Master A is thought to have painted the Genesis and Apocalypse miniatures; Master B the Exodus and Epistles frontispieces; and Master C the Jerome, Majestas Domini, Psalms, and Presentation miniatures.

31. See Gaehde, "Turonian Sources," 359–400. On the lost "bibliotheca cum imaginibus et maioribus characteribus" that Lothar gave to the Benedictine abbey at Prüm, and its possible influence on the San Paolo Bible, see Kessler, *Illustrated Bibles*, pp. 6–8.

recapture, of course, in attempting to reconstruct the descent of manuscripts at a scriptorium as busy as that of Saint-Martin, are the number of manuscripts that have been lost or so damaged as to be beyond reconstruction and the individual influence of those codices.[32] Since copies of the verses of the First Bible and of the Moutier-Grandval Bible and its *tituli* were once preserved at Saint-Martin, it seems reasonable to suppose that the scriptorium was in the practice of keeping written records of its work. Thus, the First Bible, either because of the living memory of the canons or some description kept in the scriptorium, came to have a significant impact on the subsequent design and structure of Turonian biblical manuscripts.

But this influence was not iconographically exact, since certain novel elements and much of the specific message of the First Bible was not copied and did not, for instance, resurface in the San Paolo Bible, which was dependent upon Turonian exemplars. Features such as the three vignettes on the Apocalypse miniature, the special treatment of David on the Psalms frontispiece, and, of course, the unique Presentation miniature, all of which we shall shortly discuss, were not to be repeated in Turonian Bibles ever again. That too, we think, is further proof of the specialness and, indeed, of the highly politicized program of the First Bible, for many of the things that will most concern us in the following chapters were precisely the elements that were dropped from the continuing Turonian tradition. Thus, the Bible makers of Tours confirmed the particularity and political character of much of the First Bible's content by choosing not to repeat it.

---

32. See Ganz, "Mass Production," pp. 53–62.

CHAPTER 4

The Biblical Frontispieces

An analysis of the paintings and other decorations of the First Bible discloses a history consistent with the one detected in our analysis of the poetry, context, and codicology. Two of the four miniatures that repeat comparable subjects found in the Moutier-Grandval Bible—the Genesis and Exodus frontispieces—differ from the earlier depictions in the details, selection, and treatment of individual episodes (figs. 6–7, 23–24),[1] but exhibit no special response to the specific circumstances behind the gift. Even the Majestas Domini miniature, with the addition of the portraits of the evangelists in the corners of the page, may match themes important to the poet, but was probably prepared before the redesign (fig. 10). These three paintings along with the original Apocalypse miniature formed the core of what was to have been a luxurious, albeit familiar Turonian pandect.[2]

The fourth full-page painting, the Apocalypse miniature (figs. 13 and III), follows the same pattern in its basic composition,[3] but the painter introduced three small vignettes that were absent in the earlier Turonian pandect. To the left in the middle of the page (fig. 19), he painted a scene of the elder consoling John from Revelation 5:2–5; in the top half of the page above the closed book (fig. 20), he added the appearance of the first horseman from Revelation 6:1–2; and, finally, to the right in the middle of the page (fig. 21), he illustrated the account of John eating the book from Revelation 10:2–11:1. These scenes were without precedent at Tours and are not present in the Moutier-Grandval Apocalypse tailpiece. They seem to have been introduced as a means of transforming the complex original composition, designed for the end of the codex, into a more suitable frontispiece for the Book of Revelation. Thus, this shared

---

1. Cf. Kessler, *Illustrated Bibles,* pp. 13–83; Kessler, "Traces of an Early Illustrated Pentateuch," *Journal of Jewish Art* 8 (1981): 20–27; and Peter Klein, "Les images de la Genèse de la bible carolingienne de Bamberg et la tradition des frontispices bibliques de Tours," *Texte et Image* (Chantilly, 1982), pp. 77–107.

2. Cf. Nordenfalk, "Beiträge zur Geschichte," pp. 281–304.

3. Cf. Yves Christe,"Trois images carolingiennes en forme de commentaires sur l'Apocalypse," *Cahiers archéologiques,* 25 (1976): 77–92 and Kessler, "Facies bibliothecae revelata," pp. 559–66.

painting, now relocated in the process of adapting the Bible to the specific circumstances of Charles the Bald's visit to Saint-Martin, became a hybrid made up of old and new elements.

The three new frontispieces with their *tituli* convey a distinctly different history. Judging from the San Paolo Bible, miniatures of Jerome Preparing the Vulgate, David Composing the Psalms, and the Conversion of Paul may have become part of the standing Turonian repertory;[4] but a comparison with their counterparts reveals the special character of these treatments in the First Bible.

The Jerome sequence in the San Paolo Bible, for instance, preserves a distinctly narrative aspect, even though it is based on no known text, while that in the First Bible (fig. 5) sacrifices episodic clarity to centralized compositions in the second and third registers.[5] The depiction of Jerome explaining the Bible to Paula and Eustochium and translating the Vulgate conflates two moments that, in the later Bible, are pictured separately. The monk directly behind the saint is part of the first episode, and, as in the San Paolo Bible, he records Jerome's commentary on Scripture. The two men behind him, however, are from the second; with backs turned to the main action, they are at work inscribing the translation itself. The accompanying couplet mentions only the two women and does not refer to the men; whereas the final line of the *titulus* (II.6) refers not only to the translation, but also to Jerome's own commentaries. These features suggest not only that the poet knew the picture's original context, but also that the *titulus* (poem II) and the conflated images were created together. Moreover, the caption characterizes the Bible as sacred law, as does the picture; Jerome is shown seated on a *sella curulis,* the animal-headed faldstool that from ancient times had signaled a magistrate's juridical role. Like Christ in the venerable *traditio legis,* the saint dispenses the divine law to men on his left and right.[6]

In many respects the frontispiece to the Pauline Epistles is a counterpart to the Jerome page and contains a similar telltale indication of interaction between the miniaturist and poet. In this case, the revealing detail is in the first couplet (VIII.1–2), which contains the seeming redundancy, "post trahitur caecus, ut ire queat." This verse makes sense only when read against the depiction of the soldier standing in an entranceway and drawing Saul forward by

---

4. Cf. Christoph Eggenberger, *Psalterium Aureum Sancti Galli* (Sigmaringen, 1987), pp. 39–60 and Gaehde, "Turonian Sources," pp. 376–400.

5. For a full discussion, see Kessler, *Illustrated Bibles,* pp. 84–95; Rosamond McKitterick, "Women in the Ottonian Church: An Iconographic Perspective," in *Women in the Church,* ed. D. Wood, Studies in Church History, 27 (Oxford, 1990), pp. 82–86 and rpt. in McKitterick, *Frankish Kings and Culture,* item 11; and Staubach, *Grundlegung der "religion royale."*

6. Kessler, "Lay Abbot as Patron," p. 669.

the wrist; thus, the blind soldier can only proceed into Damascus because he is being guided through the doorway. The miniature's double action of guiding and advancing is particularly significant in view of the fact that the pictorial tradition on which it may have been based shows Saul's companion simply walking alongside him in the same direction.[7]

Although the *titulus* of the Psalter frontispiece is too terse to allow similar arguments, its emphasis on David's splendor is consonant with the picture's celestial setting (figs. 8 and II). As well, it is hard not to see the influence of the self-styled prophet Audradus in the inscription above David's head, DAVID REX ET PROP<HETA>, and in the inclusion and labeling of the four virtues in the corners of the painting.[8] This quadrivium of virtues is highlighted in the verses, in which the royal reader was alerted that the *quadrivium virtutis nobile* leads humans to the stars (I.165–66), and there in the illumination one finds David surrounded by these heavenly virtues. Thus, the frontispiece itself types the virtues as specifically Davidian and divine. The poet later at X.29 presented these virtues in adjectival form as descriptions of Charles's own character.[9]

The implication that the author of the captions played a role in planning the new frontispieces is reinforced by the deeply Virgilian tone of the paintings. Just as Audradus reflected Virgil's language and spirit in his poems, so too did the composers of the Jerome, David, and Paul pages, who freely quoted pictorial elements from the fourth- or fifth-century Vatican Virgil (Biblioteca Apostolica, Cod. lat. 3225).[10] Scholia suggest that this very codex, one of most impressive illustrated manuscripts to survive from late antiquity, was at Tours during the ninth century; and among the ninth-century Turonian annotations in the codex is one on the word *olli*.[11] Wilhelm Koehler recognized that the

---

7. Kessler, *Illustrated Bibles,* pp. 111–24, and "An Apostle in Armor and the Mission of Carolingian Art," *Arte medievale,* 2d series, 4 (1990): 17–39.

8. See Sibylle Mähl, *Quadriga virtutum: Die Kardinaltugenden in der Geistesgeschichte der Karolingerzeit,* Beihefte zum Archiv für Kulturgeschichte, 9 (Cologne, 1969), pp. 171–73.

9. The one substantial change was of *temperantia* into *moderatus.*

10. *Vergilius Vaticanus Commentarium* (Graz, 1984). David Wright, "When the Vatican Vergil Was in Tours," *Studien zur mittelalterlichen Kunst 800–1250. Festschrift für Florentine Mütherich zum 70. Geburtstag* (Munich, 1985), pp. 53–66 and *The Vatican Vergil: A Masterpiece of Late Antique Art* (Berkeley, 1993); Kessler, "Apostle in Armor," pp. 17–39.

11. Cf. Wright, "Vatican Vergil in Tours," p. 56, fig. C. Bern, Burgerbibliothek 165 contains the so-called Turonian Virgil. At *Aeneid* 1.254 and 5.10, Bern 165 (pp. 58 and 104) glosses "olli" with "tunc." At *Aeneid* 6.321 (Bern 165, p. 124), "olli" is glossed by "pro tunc vel illi." On Bern 165, see B. Munk Olsen, *L'étude des auteurs classiques latins aux XIe et XIIe siècles,* vol. 2: *Catalogue des manuscrits classiques latins copiés du IXe au XIIe siècle: Livius-Vitruvius, Florilèges-Essais de plume* (Paris, 1985), pp. 703–4; B. Matthias von Scarpatetti, *Catalogue des manuscrits datés en Suisse en écriture latine du début du Moyen Age jusqu'en 1550,* vol. 2: *Les manuscrits des bibliothèques de Berne-Porrentru* (Zurich, 1983), p. 192 and plates 669–71; Hermann Hagen, *Scholia Bernensia ad Vergilii Bucolica atque Georgica* (Leipzig, 1867; rpt. Hildesheim, 1967), pp. 317–26.

illustrations provided materials for the Turonian illuminators.[12] Thus, the ship that transports Jerome from Rome to Palestine in the first miniature (fig. 5) has very close counterparts in the Vatican Virgil; its tunnel-like cockpit, patterned sail, square rudder port, and plumed stern ornament specifically recall those of the ship bearing Aeneas in picture 17 of the Vatican Virgil (fig. 27). *Roma* inside the walled city in the same scene has parallels in pictures 13 and 18 (fig. 28). The personifications of the virtues on the Psalms frontispiece as cowled, half-length women floating on cloud banks and reaching forward into the central field are quite like Juno in picture 2. David's guards, who reappear in the presentation painting, are similar to the figures of Messapus and Nisus in pictures 48 and 49 (figs. 32–33): their postures, pleated skirts, and outer cloaks are all strikingly similar.[13] Moreover, one needs to bear in mind that the Vatican Virgil when it was in Tours had pictures that are now lost. Most important of all, as David Wright observed, Paul's companions in the lowest register of the Epistles frontispiece are based on Achates and Aeneas before the Cumean Sibyl in picture 31 (fig. 29); indeed, Wright detected that these figures in the Vatican manuscript were actually traced over with a stylus, perhaps as part of the process of copying them for the First Bible.[14] Furthermore, the arches in the Epistles frontispiece (fig. 11) and Saul's armor were also adapted from this late-antique model.[15] Even the circular composition of the presentation scene, to which we shall return, may have been suggested by picture 49 of the Vatican Virgil (fig. 33).

References to the late-antique Virgil were not, of course, unique to Charles the Bald's Bible. The illuminators of the Moutier-Grandval Bible had also quoted from it and imitated its appearance.[16] But the extent of dependence on this richly illustrated copy of Virgil's works and the innovative response to it is far greater in the First Bible, and the understanding underlying those borrowings is deeper and more meaningful.

While the *tituli* are closely connected to the miniatures they accompany, in at least one case a First Bible painter may have diverged not only from the Tur-

---

12. Koehler, *Die karolingischen Miniaturen,* 1:2, pp. 214–15.

13. It has been argued that the depiction of armaments—shields, helmets, and lances—shown in Carolingian manuscripts such as the First Bible was influenced by actual Carolingian objects: see Simon Coupland, "Carolingian Arms and Armor in the Ninth Century, *Viator* 21 (1990): 29–50, esp. pp. 31–35, 46–48. The lances depicted in the First Bible, for instance, have wings; one of these wings can be seen immediately above the banner on the lance held by Phelethi in the Psalms frontispiece (figs. 8 and II). Winged lances first appeared in Carolingian Europe and are entirely absent in the depictions in the Vatican Virgil.

14. Wright, "Vatican Vergil in Tours," p. 53, fig. A. The compositions in the First Bible were, themselves, drawn in with a stylus rather than a pen; these stylus marks are particularly evident on fol. 215r.

15. Kessler, "Apostle in Armor," pp. 17–39.

16. Koehler, *Die karolingischen Miniaturen,* 1:2, p. 166; Alfred A. Schmid, "Die Buchkunst," in Duft et al., *Die Bibel von Moutier-Grandval,* p. 162; and Kessler, "Facies bibliothecae revelata," pp. 557–58.

onian exemplar, but also from the content of the received *titulus*. Poem IV.1–2 speaks of the *corusca regis dextra superi,* which refers to the shimmering or radiating right hand of God. Indeed, the Moutier-Grandval illumination (fol. 25v, fig. 24) appropriately depicts the *dextra dei* surrounded by rays of light. In the First Bible (fol. 27v, fig. 7), however, the painter copied the same basic design but chose not to illustrate rays of light surrounding the downthrust hand of God, though another painter did so depict the hand of God above the king in the Presentation miniature (figs. 17 and IV). Either these rays, which were meant to express the sense of *corusca* (or vice versa), were absent in the Exodus models drawn upon and the Moutier-Grandval illuminator, after reading the poem, had supplied them, or, more likely, they were present in that description and the First Bible illuminator, for some reason, ignored this specific poetic information when painting the Exodus frontispiece. In this case, then, there was a small parting of the ways between *titulus* and illustration.

The First Bible illuminators also chose in every case to arrange the *tituli* in a manner different from the one found in the Moutier-Grandval Bible. In the Genesis frontispiece, Moutier-Grandval had divided the poetry into four lines that were inscribed on the four bands separating registers; the First Bible painter divided the poem into three: III.1–6 was inscribed in the top margin in units related to the scenes below, and III.6–10 and III.11–12 were written in single lines on the two bands that separated the three registers. In the Exodus frontispiece, Moutier-Grandval presents the whole poem in one line in a band that separates the two registers of the illumination, while in the same location in the First Bible the poem is inscribed in two lines. The Gospels frontispiece contains the largest variation, for the Moutier-Grandval painter set the *titulus* within the mandorla in six short, divided lines that surround the upper body of Christ, while in the First Bible the *titulus* is inscribed in one line in the top margin immediately above the top border of the illumination. Finally, while in the Moutier-Grandval Bible the Apocalypse *titulus* falls in two lines in a variegated band between the two registers of the illumination, the First Bible painters placed IX.1–2 in the top margin above the first register and IX.3–5 in a single line in the band that separated the two registers of the illumination. The degree of variation in the placement of the *tituli* may suggest that at Tours the poems stood on their own, separated from any iconographical models, thus forcing the illuminators to make individual decisions about their placement. The First Bible painters and scribes seem generally to have wanted to bring the *tituli* into closer proximity to the scenes described. Thus, on the Exodus frontispiece, the poem was broken into two lines, the upper line referring to the scene above and the lower line to the scene below. Similarly the First Bible divided the Genesis *titulus* into units specifically placed to refer to the scenes depicted below. The arrangement of *tituli* on the four core illuminations of the First Bible suggests that the painters had an active awareness of the *tituli* and their integral importance to describing the illuminations.

The dedicatory verses each have a different relationship with the illuminations. Poem I does not, for instance, have a painting to which it directly refers, while portions of X and XI directly describe the Presentation illumination, as we shall see. Poem VI, however, has the strangest relationship of all, since the Majestas Domini illumination that shares the same folio possesses its own older *titulus*. But this illumination, unlike the one in the Moutier-Grandval Bible, gives a prominent place to the seated evangelists, who are all engaged in writing the Gospels while looking with awe on Christ. This emphasis upon the evangelists is reflected in the tone and purpose of poem VI, for the poet took great pains at VI.7–14 to demonstrate how they actively spread the story of Christ to the world: Matthew (located in the upper right of the illumination; fig. 10) recites from the beginning, Mark (in the lower-left quadrant) roars, Luke (in the bottom right) carries the light to the four corners of the world, and John (in the ethereal quadrant in the upper left) sings the words of the Word. The evangelical symbols had been explained earlier at I.95–104, but here the poet emphasized the active nature of the evangelical work that flowed from One through four. The prophets, who are mentioned in the *titulus* proper (VII.2), remain unnoted in poem VI.

In general, Audradus's first dedicatory verse does not describe the specific biblical pictures that adorn the First Bible; neither the older sequence of paintings shared with the Moutier-Grandval Bible nor the three new paintings is directly governed by the poem. For example, two of the frontispieces are dedicated to Genesis and Exodus, but poem I virtually skips over the Pentateuch, alluding only to the five joined volumes of Moses (I.63–64). And, though I.159 speaks of the First Person of the Trinity as the creator of the world (I.159–60), the Genesis frontispiece (fig. 6), dependent on older Turonian models shaped by the ancient tradition of the Cotton Genesis,[17] depicts Christ as the agent of creation. The miniatures also seem to make no explicit statement about church property and poverty, themes that so preoccupied the poet. Even the paradisiacal setting of the final scene of the Genesis frontispiece (fig. 6), which stands in such sharp contrast to the apparent poverty and hardship endured by the couple in the same scene in the Moutier-Grandval Bible (fig. 23), referred to and reinforced christological and mariological typology.

The decoration of the initial letters throughout the First Bible occasionally

---

17. See Kurt Weitzmann and Herbert L. Kessler, *The Cotton Genesis* (Princeton, 1986).

and, probably, incidentally contains allusions to some of the poet's themes. The Book of Isaiah (fol. 130v), for instance, begins with a vignette of an angel touching the prophet's lips with a glowing coal, which plays upon the eating metaphor encountered in the poems.

But just as Audradus seems to have been influenced by the language of the shared *tituli* in at least one instance, so too the dedicatory verses seem to play upon and explain the Bible's extant decorations in several others. This was true, as we have seen, in the case of the Majestas Domini illumination, since poem VI focused special attention on the active evangelical work of the evangelists in a way that the older *titulus* neglected. *Titulus* VII, which had been sufficient for the Moutier-Grandval illumination (fig. 25), may, therefore, have seemed too terse for Audradus. Since the First Bible's Majestas illumination was probably already painted when Audradus took control of the preparation of the redesign of the First Bible and since the evangelists now occupied a prominent place in the miniature, Audradus may have felt called upon to explain their crucial importance in spreading word of Christ to the world. Thus, poem VI would seem to have been, in part, a response of the poet to the illumination and not the reverse. As well, in his brief precis of Paul's epistles (I.110), Audradus characterized the apostle as one "From whom formerly a wolf's voice and now a sheep's voice flashes forth." At the head of the Epistle to the Romans (fol. 387r, fig. 18), an upright lamb confronts a cowering wolf. This motif, employed already to adorn an initial in the Moutier-Grandval Bible (fol. 411v), was almost certainly a feature of the manuscript's original decoration before the changes were introduced to create the presentation codex;[18] and although the wolf-lamb metaphor had a long history in descriptions of Paul's conversion, this suggests that its origin in the First Bible may have been pictorial. Hence, the reference to a sheep and wolf in the poem may be another example of the poet responding to an existing illustrated page and of the priority, in a few cases, of the image over the word.

An example of the opposite is supplied on folios 1v–2r (figs. 2–3), where the four medallion pictures set between the columns seem to illustrate, as already discussed, the four paragons of virtue named in the accompanying verse (I.195–96). Since Wilmart and Rand assumed that Audradus himself had been both a manuscript decorator and calligrapher at an earlier stage of his career, it would be interesting to know if he himself worked on the design and decorations of folios 1v–2r.[19] A close comparison of these pages with the designs in

18. Kessler, "Apostle in Armor," pp. 17–39.
19. Wilmart, "Le lectionnaire de Saint-Père," pp. 276–78; and Rand, *Survey of Manuscripts,* pp. 133–34.

the *Liber comitis* might once have provided an answer, but the destruction of that precious manuscript now makes that impossible to determine.[20]

In other instances, a case can be made that Audradus as the apparent architect of the First Bible directed or recommended that specific illustrations and scenes be included in the First Bible. His view of the relative importance of David is already evident in the first poem, in which five out of the twenty-four lines dedicated to characterizing the books of the Old Testament (I.63–86) are devoted to David (I.76–80). There, for instance, he described David as the great and rhythmical singer of the Psalms, and the *titulus* of the Psalms frontispiece (V.1–2), which he probably also composed, specifically invokes the musicianship of David and his heavenly band of singers. In the final poem of the First Bible at XI.35–38, Audradus returned again to the image of the singers and their instruments, though now it was the canons who were singing psalms for their David, King Charles. The David frontispiece with David portrayed playing a lyre and surrounded by his four musicians fits so perfectly with the poetical imagining of Audradus as to suggest that he probably influenced the choice of subject. Moreover, there is another important Audradan theme at work in that miniature, to which we shall turn in the next chapter.

If the pictures and dedication verses share a limited number of specific cross-references, they are nonetheless remarkably consonant in general themes. Two of Audradus's main topics recur in the paintings with an insistence that forcefully unites the First Bible's verbal and pictorial images. One of them is the claim that the Bible, even though it comprises many books, constitutes a single revelation whose unity can be discerned by reading the Old Testament with the knowledge of the New and the New with an understanding of the Old. The second is that the Bible is the law.

The first of these themes was introduced in the opening couplet of the first poem, in which King Charles was invited to read the two Testaments of the Bible *(biblioteca)* over again and again (I.1–2). The poet asserted (I.113–15) the theme of the unity of the two Testaments; for him the Old Testament was the shadow or outline, and the New Testament its cause or fulfillment. And, "Thus the journey is double, [but] the achievement of both is in one." The Tur-

---

20. Aside from fol. 2r (which is our fig. 22), Wilmart printed plates of fols. 2v, 3r, 4r, and 22v in his article, "Le lectionnaire de Saint-Père," pp. 269–78. More photographs of the manuscript once existed, since Wilmart says, on p. 272 n. 1 of his article, that not only had Yves Delaporte, the archivist of the diocese of Chartres, originally pointed out Audradus's name to him, but "m'a mis en mains plusieurs photographies du manuscrit, dont cinq se trouvent réproduites ici." Whether these photographs still exist is not clear. The Bibliothèque municipale de Chartres today apparently has only photographs of fols. 2v, 3v, and 4r: see *Catalogue général des manuscrits des bibliothèques publiques de France,* vol. 53: *Manuscrits des bibliothèques sinistrées de 1940 à 1944,* p. 15.

onian pictorial project was to provide a program of illustrations for manuscripts comprising all of Scripture in one volume, and thus the theme of scriptural concord also underlies the illuminations in the Moutier-Grandval Bible,
and the related San Paolo Bible as well. In the Genesis frontispiece (fig. 6), for
instance, the Creator is identified as Christ and is so named in the caption
(III.3). In the Exodus miniature (fig. 7), Moses is portrayed as Paul, with characteristic bald pate and rounded beard,[21] and the *titulus* speaks of him teaching the people of Christ (IV.4). Moreover, the Hebrew prophet holds tablets
inscribed, not with the Ten Commandments, but with the passage Jesus
quoted from Deut. 6:5 to sum up Jewish law, "Love the Lord your God with
all your heart, soul, and mind" (Matt. 22:37). By inserting portraits of the
evangelists in the act of composing the Gospels, the First Bible painter also
intensified the demonstration of the essential harmony underlying the unity of
the Gospels and Old Testament, so that it would serve the even broader purpose of asserting the essential coherence of the entire Bible.

The claim of verses and pictures, and of the Bible manuscript itself—that
the Old and New Testaments are two paths to the same goal—culminates in
the Apocalypse miniature (figs. 13 and III).[22] Divided like the Exodus frontispiece into two fields, the miniature in the top register pictures an enormous
codex resting on a draped throne, its seals being opened by the Lamb of God.
According to a long exegetical tradition incorporated in Jerome's preface, Revelation was a "book sealed inside and out" comprehending both Testaments,
whose fundamental harmony would be disclosed, literally "unveiled," when it
was opened at the end of time.[23] The same theme is reformulated below, where
an enthroned man is encircled by four symbols lifting an enormous sheet to
expose his visage. Bearing the facial features of Moses-Paul, albeit gray-
haired, and also John, the author of Revelation, the man personifies all the
authors of the Bible, who had enunciated God's message. This is emphasized
by the "tuba" of prophecy raised to his face, which bears lips precisely at the
place where it overlaps the man's mouth, symbolizing God's inspiration of biblical pronouncements.[24] The enthroned man is thus the embodiment of the

21. Cf. Schmid, "Die Buchkunst," p. 174; Archer St. Clair, "A New Moses: Typological Iconography in
the Moutier-Grandval Bible Illustrations of Exodus," *Gesta* 26 (1987): 19–28; and Kessler, "Facies bibliothecae revelata," pp. 554–56, 566–73.

22. Christe, "Trois images carolingiennes"; Kessler, *Illustrated Bibles,* pp. 69–83, and "Facies bibliothecae revelata," pp. 559–84.

23. Victorinus of Pettau, *Commentarii in Apocalypsin,* ed. J. Haussleiter, in *Victorini Episcopi Petavio-
nensis opera,* vol. 1, Corpus Scriptorum Ecclesiasticorum Latinorum, 49 (Leipzig, 1916), p. 60; Jerome, "Ad
Paulinum Presbyterum" (included as a preface to the Bible in BN lat. 1), ed. Donatien De Bruyne, *Préfaces
de la Bible Latine* (Namur, 1920), pp. 13–14; and Alcuin, *Commentariorum in Apocalypsin,* 3.5 (*PL*
100:1120A–B). Cf. Kessler, "Facies bibliothecae revelata," pp. 560–61.

24. Kessler, "Facies bibliothecae revelata," pp. 573–76. And see Ps. 46:6: "Ascendit Deus in iubilo, Et
Dominus in voce tubae."

written document being opened above; Beatus of Liébana said that the face of the Bible had been veiled from Moses until Christ and was revealed at the end of the Bible to John. For Beatus the entire Bible was one book, veiled at the beginning, but made manifest at the end. He thought that the complete Bible, with its two Testaments, both Old and New, the law, and the Gospels, was to be understood as just one person.[25]

The First Bible enhances the typological reading of these compositions inherited from the earlier exemplar. Thus, Eve is presented as Mary in the final episode on the Genesis page, clothed in a maphorion and holding the child upright in her lap. A cross in the pediment marks the Exodus tabernacle as a type of the Christian Church, and the rivers beneath the evangelists in the Majestas Domini refer back to Eden.[26] In the Apocalypse miniature, the narrative additions further the notion of scriptural harmony. According to the Apocalypse commentary of Ambrosius Autpertus, which had served as a primary source for the image in the Moutier-Grandval Bible (fig. 26), the elder consoling John in the upper-left corner of the lower miniature is "an Old Testament prophet who foretold the coming of the Son of God."[27] The horseman rising from the book in the upper scene is the fulfillment of that prophecy; the horse and rider symbolize Christ, who, in Mary's womb, fused flesh and spirit.[28] In turn, the figure is an allegory of the spiritual reading of the Old Testament that Christ allows; the man is the spirit rising up from the literal meaning of Old Testament law. The bow in his hand, furthermore, stands for the two Testaments, and the two arrows the divine utterances propelled from the Bible.[29] The interpolated figure not only enhances the narrative aspect of the Apocalypse frontispiece, it also introduces the claim found in Audradus's

---

25. Beatus, *Adversus Elipandum,* 1.99, in *Beati Liebanensis et Eterii Oxomensis Adversus Elipandum libri duo,* ed. B. Löfstedt, Corpus Christianorum: Continuatio Mediaevalis, 59 (Turnhout, 1984), p. 76: "Velata fuit Moysi usque ad Christum bibliotecae facies, et in fine eius bibliotecae reuelata est. Et inde sic incipitur reuelatio Ihesu Christi, 'quam dedit illi Deus palam facere servis suis, quae oportet fieri cito' (Rev. 1:1). Haec Iohanni reuelatum est. Quae tota biblioteca unus liber est, in capite uelatus, in fine manifestus. Qui liber duo testamenta dicuntur, Vetus et Novum. Et unum est tamquam unus 'gladius ex utraque parte acutus' (Rev. 1:16). Et hinc inde, id est in lege et evangelio, acuitur, ut fideles armet, interficiat infideles, sicut idem Apocalipsin de ore Domini gladium ex utraque parte acutum egredere testatur, id est verbum eius. Quaelibet biblioteca totus sic est intellegendus tamquam unus homo." Cf. Kessler, "Facies bibliothecae revelata," pp. 569, 577–80.

26. Cf. Søren Kaspersen, "Majestas Domini-Regnum et Sacerdotium: Zu Entstehung und Leben des Motivs bis zum Investiturstreit," *Hafnia: Copenhagen Papers in the History of Art* 8 (1981): 95.

27. *In Apocalypsin,* I, in *Ambrosii Autperti opera: Expositionis in Apocalypsin libri I–V,* ed. Robert Weber, in Corpus Christianorum: Continuatio Mediaevalis, 27 (Turnhout, 1975), p. 60. Cf. Alcuin, *Commentariorum in Apocalypsin libri quinque,* 3.5, in *PL* 100:1121B. Alcuin cites Autpertus, whose commentary may have been known at Tours (*PL* 100:1088); see E. Ann Matter, "The Apocalypse in Early Medieval Exegesis," in *The Apocalypse in the Middle Ages,* ed. R. Emmerson and B. McGinn (Ithaca, N.Y., 1992), p. 48.

28. *In Apocalypsin,* IV, ed. Weber, p. 276.64–68.

29. *In Apocalypsin,* IV, ed. Weber, pp. 276–77.

verses at I.115 that the *iter duplex* of Scripture makes possible a heavenly ascent. Finally, John eating the book signifies the complete consumption of the full Bible containing the Old Testament and the New. To Autpertus, the scene represented the process of the authoritative interpretation through which congruence emerges, for just as food enters the stomach through the mouth, sacred Scripture as God's law when meditated day and night passes to those on earth through the Church's holy preachers.[30]

The theme of biblical concord is expanded still further in the three full-page frontispieces added to the core cycle. The first miniature, for instance, features Jerome studying Hebrew and producing *bibliothecae* containing both Testaments in one language. Moreover, as the caption and picture stress, these composite volumes include Jerome's own prefaces to the books of the Bible; among these, most notably, was his letter to Paulinus of Nola, with its summary treatment of the Bible and its many parts, which begins immediately across from the frontispiece on folio 4r.[31] The Bible's fundamental unity is one of the principal themes of the verses and paintings. David, for instance, is characterized as Christ and stands at the center of a mandorla surrounded by his guards and four musicians; he recounts "the many mysteries of Christ" (I.78). And the conversion of Paul focuses on a Jewish soldier setting forth to persecute Christians, who was blinded and then restored by one of the deacons in order to teach the pagans "the vital lessons of life from the heavenly Old and New Testaments" (VIII.5–6).

To discover the fundamental consonance beneath the Bible's diverse figures requires diligent reading and rereading (I.2), that is, constant study and contemplation. Like the new image of John eating the book that was introduced into the Apocalypse painting, Audradus played persistently with the metaphor of the Bible as spiritual food. The Bible was to be the king's sustenance and drink (I.8, VI.22), his holy nectar (I.118, IV.3–4), and a heavenly and paradisiacal banquet for the hungry and parched (I.117–22). Thus, humans as returning exiles turn to the Bible as to a rich religious feast (I.171–72) and, indeed, to salvation (VI.22) through their reading, rereading, and understanding of the reread Bible (I.172).

For Audradus, the aim of this process of interpretation was the comprehension of God's law, and that is the second great theme that ties the poems and pictures together.[32] It should be remembered that the very form of the

---

30. *In Apocalypsin,* V, ed. Weber, p. 400. For Autpertus, the image of John eating the book conjured up the lifting of the veil from Moses's face and hence refers to the motif central to the illustration: *In Apocalypsin,* V, ed. Weber, pp. 390–91.

31. De Bruyne, *Préfaces,* pp. 1–7.

32. Among the numerous references, the verses expound how the *culpa* of Adam and Eve made the giving of holy law necessary, redeemed only by the *gratia Christi* (I.19–21), how Joshua conquered by means of the law (I.65–66), and how the Maccabees fought on its behalf (I.85).

unified Bible, containing both the Old and New Testaments in a single volume, was understood during the ninth century to be the counterpart to ancient legal compendia. In the dedication poem included in the Moutier-Grandval Bible, Alcuin had called such volumes "pandects," a term derived from legal tracts and first applied to Scripture by Cassiodorus in the sixth century.[33] Though the opening line of the First Bible calls the volume a *biblioteca,* Audradus clearly conceived of the Bible as the sacred law. At I.135, the poet boldly informed the king that the Bible is the law and that nothing was more important than this law. A few lines later he asserted that the Bible was, in effect, a written statement of justice (I.144). It had the capacity to instruct and guide the unlearned (I.141) but was particularly suited to a king. Joshua had not only risen up in arms to lead his people, but had laid the law upon his land and people (I.65–66), just as Charles was asked to lay the divine rules of law upon his own kingdom (X.41–42). Charles was called upon to love justice and to follow its righteous way (I.49–50).

The paintings make the same essential claim. Jerome appears in the final register of the first miniature (fig. 5), in a *traditio legis* setting, as the promulgator of the *ius divinum.*[34] The *titulus* reinforces the theme of the painting, since it not only describes him as the translator of the honorable Hebrew law (II.2), but as the bestower of the "divine laws of salvation" (II.4). In the following miniature (fig. 6), Adam and Eve are instructed by God, then punished for disobeying him.[35] In the next (fig. 7), Moses is pictured receiving the written commandments, which the *titulus* calls the law (IV.1), and instructing the Chosen People in their teachings. Because he submits to God's will, David is then shown elevated as "king and prophet" (figs. 8 and II). Christ, the source of this law, rules the universe through his book, and David teaches Christ's many mysteries (I.78). Paul, in the bottom register of the frontispiece to the Epistles (fig. 11), teaches the new law of the two Testaments to the pagans. And John in the Apocalypse frontispiece (fig. 21) holds a "cane, a kind of measuring rod," while he consumes the Bible. As Autpertus explained, this *calamus similis virgae* signified both the preaching of divine words, since a book is written with a pen or *calamus,* and also the true doctrine of Christ established through his Church, since the measuring stick is a straight edge. At I.144, in the midst of his discourse on the law and its importance to Charles, Audradus

33. Alcuin, *carmen* 65.1.1, ed. Dümmler, *MGH PLAC* 1:283; Cassiodorus, *Institutiones,* 1.12, ed. R. A. B Mynors (Oxford, 1937), pp. 36–38 and *PL* 70:1124B12–16; Fischer, *Lateinische Bibelhandschriften,* pp. 246–50; and James W. Halporn, "Pandectes, Pandecta, and the Cassiodorian Commentary on the Psalms," *Revue Bénédictine* 90 (1980): 290–300.

34. Cf. Anton von Euw, "Studien zu den Elfenbeinarbeiten der Hofschulen Karls des Grossen," *Aachener Kunstblätter* 34 (1967): 36–54; and William Diebold, "Verbal, Visual, and Cultural Literacy in Medieval Art: Word and Image in the Psalter of Charles the Bald," *Word and Image* 8 (1992): 89–99.

35. Cf. Søren Kaspersen, "Cotton-Genesis, die Toursbibeln und die Bronzetüren—Vorlage und Aktualität," in *Bernwardinische Kunst* (Göttingen, 1988), pp. 79–103.

had called this "the mighty pen of justice"; *stilus* here being synonymous with *calamus,* the straight rod of justice that John carries.

The very act of giving the young king a Bible in the Presentation painting (figs. 17 and IV) dramatized Scripture's status as divine law, since it had been stipulated in Deut. 17:18–20 that a king should possess such a book of law:

When he has ascended to the throne of the kingdom, he shall make a copy of this law in a book at the dictation of the Levitical priests. He shall keep it by him and read from it all his life, so that he may learn to fear the Lord his God and keep all the words of this law and observe these statutes. In this way he shall not become prouder than his fellow countrymen, nor shall he turn from these commandments to right or to left; then he and his sons will reign for long over his kingdom in Israel.

For the Carolingians, this passage was a guiding reference to proper kingship, for the just monarch should govern according to this sacred law.[36] Jonas of Orléans inserted just this excerpt from Deuteronomy in his chapter on good kingship in the *De institutione regia,* written around 830.[37] The same had been incorporated in the acts of the Council of Paris in 829.[38] Even Jonas's officially sanctioned definition of kingship depended on Deuteronomy: "A king is called a king by acting rightly. If he rules piously, justly, and with mercy, he is properly called a king; if he lacks these, he loses the name of king."[39] Thus for a new king to hold in his hands a Bible, the literal law, was the fulfillment of God's own command in Deuteronomy. For him to act piously, justly, and with mercy was what Audradus and the canons of Saint-Martin wanted most of all. What better instrument than the gift of a majestic Bible could there be, then, to mark the anticipated renewal of the monastery's immunities? What better way to remind Charles of Audradus's resounding call for him to be a defensive wall and nurturing father for a beleaguered church?

The stage was set for Charles's return to Saint-Martin and for the real unfolding of that high and ceremonious moment Audradus and the canons had been imagining throughout 845.

---

36. Riché, "Bible et vie politique," p. 399, lists this as a fundamental and frequent Carolingian political citation of the Bible.

37. Jonas of Orléans, *De instituione regia* 3, ed. J. Reviron, in Jean Reviron, *Les idées politico-religieuses d'un évêque du IXe siècle: Jonas d'Orléans et son "De institutione regia,"* L'église et l'état au Moyen Age, 1 (Paris, 1930), p. 139.

38. *Concilium Parisiense* (829), ed. Weminghoff, *MGH Concilia* 2:649–51. Jonas of Orléans became a member of Charles's faction after 840 (see Charles the Bald, charter 25, *Recueil des actes de Charles,* ed. Tessier, 1:63–65), though he was certainly dead by 845.

39. Jonas of Orléans, *De institutione regia* 3, ed. Reviron, p. 138. See also *Concilium Parisiense* (829), ed. Werminghoff, *MGH Concilia* 2:607.44–45, 612–14, 649–51.

CHAPTER 5

The Presentation Miniature

The theme of Scripture as divine law, which ties together the poetry and paintings of the First Bible, also informs its final miniature (figs. 17 and IV).[1] The picture's ostensible subject is the presentation to the young king of the majestic pandect prepared by the canons of Saint-Martin. But the scene also carried the biblical mandate of Deuteronomy into the Carolingian present,[2] and the accompanying verses reminded Charles of his royal obligation to lay the divine rules of law upon his kingdom (X.42). The radiating *manus dei* above the king's head, surmounted by stars and separated by a curtain symbolizing heaven,[3] signified Charles's status as God's intermediary on earth.[4] Effecting a transition between the celestial and terrestrial realms, personifications holding palm fronds in the arch's spandrels proffer crowns to the ruler.

These overtly panegyrical elements yield to the overall impression that the miniature pictures an actual event. Paul Zumthor once called the dedication

---

1. Scheifele, *Manuscripta* 23 (1979): 21–22, noted the legal implications of the portrait and observed that Charles "was considered the embodiment and disseminator of the Law, based on Scripture."

2. Martina Pippal, "Distanzierung und Aktualisierung in der Vivianbibel: Zur Struktur der touronischen Miniaturen in den 40er Jahren des 9. Jahrhunderts," *Aachener Kunstblätter* 60 (1994): 73, noted the importance of this passage of Deuteronomy. On Scripture as a legal source for Carolingian rulers, see Peter McKeon, "The Empire of Louis the Pious: Faith, Politics, and Personality," *Revue Bénédictine*, 90 (1980): 50–62; and Riché, "Bible et vie politique," pp. 385–400.

3. "Velum, coelum": Hrabanus Maurus, *Allegoria in sacram scripturam*, PL 112:1073. Cf. Johann Eberlein, *Apparitio regis-revelatio veritatis* (Basel, 1982), pp. 110–12.

4. In the Geneva Hrabanus commentary, as the *tituli* make explicit, God's protection and supervision of rulers were symbolized by the *manus dei* in Judith's portrait: see Elisabeth Sears, "Louis the Pious as *Miles Christi:* The Dedicatory Image in Hrabanus Maurus's *De laudibus sanctae crucis,*" in *Charlemagne's Heir: New Perspectives on the Reign of Louis the Pious (814–40)*, ed. P. Godman and R. Collins (Oxford, 1990), p. 620. In the case of the *manus dei* seen in the John frontispiece to the Codex Aureus of Saint-Emmeram (Munich, Bayerische Staatsbibliothek, Clm 14000, fol. 97ᵛ), see Paul Edward Dutton and Edouard Jeauneau, "The Verses of the 'Codex Aureus' of Saint-Emmeram," *Studi medievali*, 3ª series, 24 (1983): 96, rpt. in Jeauneau, *Études érigéniennes* (Paris, 1987), p. 614. See also Jean-Claude Schmitt, *La raison des gestes* (Paris, 1990), pp. 93–133. On the intersection of divine and royal natures in the king, see Dutton, *Politics of Dreaming*, p. 53.

portrait "le plus ancien tableau conu inspiré par un evénément actuel,"[5] and similar claims have often been made. In fact, the staging of the presentation as a unitary event within a receding space and the abundance of specific details partially obscures the fact that the painting is a careful construction of an ideal polity. Composed before the occasion it represents,[6] the Presentation miniature was, like the poems that describe it, an anticipatory realization.

The Bible was reminiscent of the gift of the sacred books corrected and combined into one magnificent collection that Alcuin, as abbot of Saint-Martin, had once delivered to Charlemagne.[7] Moreover, as Koehler noted, the circular composition and several details recall the scene of Nisus and Euryalus before Ascanius in picture 49 of the Vatican Virgil (fig. 33).[8] The personifications derive from the same source, while the pose of Charles himself may have been based on the dignified figure of Latinus in pictures 41 and 42 (figs. 30–31), who holds a long staff in his left hand and turns toward the right, his right arm outstretched to receive men bearing gifts. Thus, like the three other compositions introduced into the First Bible, the Presentation picture shares a Virgilian tenor with the accompanying verses.

The very idea of including a depiction of a living monarch in a volume of Scripture, however, probably derived from a different tradition, that of the compendia of secular law. Numerous antecedents can be cited, including the early-ninth-century Breviary of Alaric in Paris (Bibliothèque Nationale, MS lat. 4404), which features Theodosius II attended by his heirs and other jurists (fols. 1v–2r);[9] and Charles the Bald may have been pictured in the collection of charters assembled by Ansegis, though the degree to which the Ottonian copies of this tract adhere to the ninth-century original is uncertain.[10] Soon after the First Bible was completed, Charles was again portrayed in another biblical text, a psalter in Paris (Bibliothèque Nationale, MS lat. 1152, fol. 3v) where he is described in the *titulus* as "similar to Josiah and equal to Theodosius,"[11] the two great legislators and legal reformers.[12]

---

5. Paul Zumthor, *Charles le Chauve* (Paris, 1957), p. 89.

6. The arguments made above about the Bretons, references to Saint Martin and his cult, Vivian not yet being lay abbot, the specificity of the reference to the renewal of the immunities, and the return of the properties all point to the painting being composed before the presentation and not after Charles's departure.

7. Cf. Fischer, *Lateinische Bibelhandschriften,* p. 211; Ganz, "Mass Production," pp. 56–57.

8. *Die karolingische Miniaturen,* 1:1, p. 270.

9. Kessler, "Lay Abbot as Patron," p. 654; Florentine Mütherich, "Frühmittelalterliche Rechtshandschriften," *Aachener Kunstblätter,* 60 (1994): 89–99.

10. See Gotha, Forschungsbibliothek, Membr. I 84, fol. 2v; and Koehler, *Die karolingischen Miniaturen,* 1:2, pp. 229–31.

11. "Bibliothecarum et Psalteriorum Versus" 1.2.2, ed. Traube, *MGH PLAC* 3:243. See Rosamond McKitterick, *The Frankish Church and the Carolingian Reforms, 789–895* (London, 1977), pp. 2–3, but the misprinting of HONORI instead of the manuscript's HONORE complicates the reading there. On the figures of Josiah and Theodosius in Carolingian art, see Lawrence Nees, "Carolingian Art and Politics," in Sullivan, *Gentle Voices of Teachers,* pp. 207–9.

12. See Diebold, "Literacy in Medieval Art," pp. 89–99.

Charles's portrait might, in fact, allude to Theodosius II, whose code had secured the immunity of the Church in Roman law.[13] Even the circular composition of the Presentation miniature finds a parallel within this tradition, recurring twice in the Vatican Agrimensores (Cod. Palat. lat. 1564, fols. 2r and 3r), a compendium probably made for Charles's father and containing excerpts from the Theodosian Code, Justinianic Digest, other legal tracts, and Roman treatises on land surveying.[14] Late in the summer of 844 Lupus of Ferrières, who was involved in his own legal dispute with the king, also recommended that Charles imitate Trajan and Theodosius.[15]

Although it is unique among the miniatures of the First Bible in having no words on the surface of the page, the Presentation painting is intimately tied to the accompanying verses. Poems X and XI were inscribed on a single folio that, with the Presentation miniature, effectively displaced the Apocalypse miniature as the final sequence in the codex. They serve as an introduction and extended *titulus* for the Presentation miniature on folio 423r. Speaking of the painting directly, the verses refer to the exceptional skill with which Charles was portrayed (X.4) and describe the depicted scene for the benefit of the king (XI.1–10). Poems X and XI share, in fact, a parallel structure, for in each the poem begins by talking about the painting (X.1–10, XI.1–10). Next both turn to discuss the king's virtues and contemporary events and concerns, which included poverty, restless Bretons, and the theft of church property (X.11–36, XI.11–34). Finally both poems finish by singing the king's praises and praying for his well-being (X.37–44, XI.35–42).

Despite the specificity of the poems and the painting, uncertainty has always surrounded the identity of the men named in the text.[16] Viewed now in the light of our new understanding of the poems, context, and codicology, however, this uncertainty should probably be seen as a strategy of deliberate equivocation on the part of the poet and the painter. Charles, as the central

---

13. Cf. Cod. Theod. XI 21, 22; XVI 13, 14, 15, 29, 30, 40. From entirely different criteria, Koehler speculated that the dedication miniature may have been based on a model from the orbit of Theodosius II, but concluded that, "das sind unbeweisbare Hypothesen" (*Die karolingische Miniaturen,* 1:2, p. 230). On the importance of Theodosius for Charles's notion of kingship later in his reign, see Nelson, "Translating Images of Authority," pp. 194–203; Diebold, "Literacy in Medieval Art," pp. 89–99; Lawrence Nees, *A Tainted Mantle: Hercules and the Classical Tradition at the Carolingian Court* (Philadelphia, 1991), pp. 164–65, 265–66.

14. Florentine Mütherich, "Der karolingisches Agrimensoren-Codex in Rom," *Aachener Kunstblätter,* 44 (1974): 59–71.

15. *Epistola* 37, ed. Levillain, *Loup de Ferrières, Correspondance,* 1:164.

16. The history of efforts to identify the individuals is very old. For some of the attempts at identification, see Du Cange, *Glossarium mediae et infimae Latinitatis,* 1:392–94; Philippe Lauer, "Iconographie carolingienne: Vivien et Charlemagne," *Mélanges en hommage à la Mémoire de Fr. Martroye* (Paris, 1940), pp. 194–95; Wolfgang Braunfels, *Die Welt der Karolinger und ihre Kunst* (Munich, 1968), p. 390 n. 292; Kessler, "Lay Abbot as Patron," pp. 648–52; Dutton, *Politics of Dreaming,* pp. 147–48. See Lejeune, "Les portraits," pp. 171–73 for a review of the various identifications.

and dominant figure in the composition, is easy to spot, but the men immediately flanking the enthroned king are not referred to in the verses. The two retainers to his left and right wait on the king and may represent idealized courtiers or palace officials.[17] The guards in classical dress standing outside them are also to be found standing, with some slight changes, beside King David on the Psalms frontispiece (figs. 8 and II).[18] Labeled CERETHI and PHELETHI on that miniature, they were meant to represent not individuals, but two different Old Testament families that had guarded King David.[19] In the Presentation miniature, then, these guards collectively represent not only Charles's army and his military might, but the divine protection afforded a Christian king; they are the only arms-bearers in the Presentation miniature. Adapted from figures in the Vatican Virgil, they also contribute to the imperial theme explored by the poet at the beginning of the codex (fols. 1v–2r). These figures would, in fact, reappear in reworked form and with a new dynamism as the guards flanking the throne of Emperor Lothar in his Gospels (fol. 1v, fig. 34) made at Saint-Martin around 849. In that miniature, also painted by Master C, Lothar's idealized guards wear the same helmets and hold the same stylized shield, sword, and lance as those found in the Presentation miniature. The king's retainers and guards in the First Bible were probably not meant to portray real participants in the presentation ceremony and so remained unmentioned by the poet. Still, by introducing them into the painting, the illuminator was able to create a horizontal layer, intermediate between the divine and the holy, occupied by the king and his secular realm. The Davidian guards, crown-bearing personifications, and downthrust hand of God, however, effectively bracket the king with divine forces and raise him into the sphere of the celestial.

Ever since Koehler presented arguments to support the identification of Vivian, scholarly consensus has accepted that the man in a vermillion mantle at the miniature's center right is meant to represent this noble, who is mentioned at XI.1–2. But Koehler also believed that Vivian, as the count of Tours, was already the lay abbot of Saint-Martin at the time the portrait was painted and so assumed that he was the *pater* referred to in the ambiguous phrase "ante ubi post patrem primi" (XI.3). In a somewhat convoluted explanation, he accounted for the apparent contradiction between the poem locat-

17. Koehler, *Die karolingischen Miniaturen,* 1:2, p. 226 identified them as the *ostiarius* and *sacellarius.* See also Alibert, "Carolingiens et leurs images," pp. 211–15 and Lejeune, "Les portraits," p. 174 and plate 3, who identified Vivian as the figure to the king's immediate right.

18. The guard on our right in the Presentation miniature differs from Phelethi on fol. 215v in lacking a lance, in the changed position of his right hand, and the different attitude of his head. The figures of the left guard and Cerethi are different only in the treatment of their armaments.

19. See 2 Sam. 8:18, 15:18, 20:7, and 2 Kings 11:19.

ing the *primi* "after the father" and the painting situating them in the foreground as the result of differences in literary and artistic convention. Thus, for Koehler, the canons stand after or behind the lay abbot from the perspective of Charles's throne; but from the perspective of the viewer of the page, the canons stand before or in front of Father Vivian. Philippe Lauer challenged Koehler's reading soon after it was published.[20] Conjecturing that Vivian might have taken minor orders and been tonsured, he proposed that Vivian should be identified with the canon at the bottom middle with his back turned to the spectator. But the historical evidence strongly suggests that Vivian was never ordained and, instead, remained a layman. As such he would not have been tonsured or allowed to participate in the execution of the liturgy. Everything indicates, in fact, that Koehler's basic identification was correct, that Vivian is the prominent figure in lay dress pictured on our right, but that Lauer was right to identify the *pater* as the central figure with his back turned toward us.[21]

Karl Morrison accepted the basic premise of these two readings and identified the isolated figure at the bottom center as the *choregus,* or choir master.[22] Others have wondered whether that central individual might be the main celebrant of the presentation ceremony.[23] Our reading of both the historical evidence and the verses leads us to believe that the central figure is, indeed, the *pater* mentioned at XI.3. This tonsured *pater* was, therefore, neither Vivian nor Adalard. Vivian cannot be this *pater,* since as the layman pictured on the right he does not have brothers both before and after him, as the verses suggest the *pater* should. Moreover, Adalard was no longer the lay abbot of Saint-Martin by December 845, and, like Vivian, was never tonsured. The *pater* of the poem and the painting was more likely the *praepositus* of the monastery or an acting abbot such as the enigmatic *abba Heirardus*. In both the verses and the painting this individual's identity is cleverly and effectively obscured, presumably because in the summer of 845 Saint-Martin was still without an official abbot, and this figure was something of a cipher.[24] But the canon with his back to the viewer is far from inconsequential in the presentation ceremony. He is the only figure in the entire miniature whose body comes into contact with no other; his

20. Lauer, "Iconographie Carolingienne," pp. 191–205.

21. See also Donald Bullough, "*Imagines regum* and Their Significance in the Early Medieval West," in *Studies in Memory of David Talbot Rice,* ed. G. Robertson and G. Henderson (Edinburgh, 1975), pp. 223–76 and rpt. in Bullough, *Carolingian Renewal: Sources and Heritage* (Manchester, 1991), pp. 39–96; and Søren Kaspersen, "Majestas Domini-Regnum et Sacerdotium," pp. 83–146. Cf. Lejeune, "Les portraits," pp. 174–80.

22. Karl F. Morrison, "'Know Thyself': Music in the Carolingian Renaissance," in *Committenti e produzione,* Settimane di studio, 39, pp. 443–44.

23. Dutton, *Politics of Dreaming,* p. 147.

24. See chapter 2.

arms are raised in prayer or song; and he stands opposite the king as one of the four cardinal points of the quartered circle of the composition.[25] The canons seem to walk toward him from our left and to gaze toward him from the right.

This conclusion fits perfectly with the recent reading of XI.3 that posits that the four *primi* are depicted twice, both before and after the *pater*.[26] *Ubi* in this odd grammatical construction has relative force, that is, "where" stands for "in which," meaning the painting. To our left, the four principal canons and the two book-bearers as they process into the presence of the king and *pater* are properly *ante patrem;* that is, from the vantage point of the enthroned king, the three named canons—Tesmundus, Sigualdus, and Aregarius—are arrayed before the *pater* (XI.3–4). It is as though the king with a sweep of his eyes was looking from the Bible forward to the *pater.* Both the portrait figure and the poem are, therefore, attuned to the king's particular perspective of the scene; he was, after all, the only intended audience of his First Bible, as he was reminded at the conclusion of the description of the painting (XI.9–10). Vivian and the two book-bearers stand on a horizontal plane intermediate between the canons and the king, and Charles had already at XI.1–2 acknowledged Vivian's presence before turning toward the proffered Bible.

The poet, thus, gives us critical information about the order of the four *primi,* for he tells us not only the order in which the king sees the canons, but also how the first and fourth brothers physically relate to the others. To the immediate left of the *pater* is Aregarius, who is called the first or supreme canon *(summus);* he is the distinguished, gray-bearded brother dressed in a dark blue chasuble.[27] Next comes just Sigualdus, who is dressed in pale blue; then beloved Tesmundus, dressed in vermillion. The poet himself is the fourth, as he follows and clings *(iunctus haeret)* to the other three and breaks into individual song, as poets are wont to do (XI.7–8). Clothed in salmon pink, Audradus presents himself, in typical fashion, as both the least important and the most prominent, for though he is the *quartus,* he stands closest to the all-important Bible that the king is about to receive, and the king's gaze in the imagined ceremony would have fallen on him first among the *primi.* Behind him come the two unnamed canons who, with draped hands, bear the represented First Bible.[28]

---

25. See Morrison, "Know Thyself," pp. 446–47 and Dutton, *Politics of Dreaming,* p. 147.

26. Dutton, *Politics of Dreaming,* pp. 147–48.

27. Additional support for the identification of Aregarius as the oldest and, hence, gray-haired canon in the illumination, may be supplied by Rand and Howe, "Vatican Livy," pp. 30–31, who estimate because of his place on the Saint-Gall list that he would have been in his seventies in the mid-840s.

28. Dutton, *Politics of Dreaming,* p. 147 and fig. 18, though the general reading of the scene has been that three canons are depicted carrying the Bible. In fact, the two canons closest to the guard have their draped hands under the Bible, while the third has his hands fully visible, the right one with a maniple, and uplifted, as do the three canons in front of him.

The same intricate hierarchy is repeated on the right, where the group of four canons has reassembled *post patrem*. The *pater* may now look toward them, but this is because the *primi* have processed past him and he is a pivotal figure who has now turned toward them to lead them in song. Indeed, the ceremony as imagined by the poet and painter would have had both an entrance and exit, or a beginning as the codex was brought in and an end after it had been given to the king and psalms were sung to him. Aregarius is once again the *summus* canon on our right, and his figure, standing higher than the other canons, now almost breaks the rough symmetry of the ceremonial circle. Here, however, the four *primi* form a solid square of monastic virtue, as they stand in pairs, side by side, and personify the quadrivium of monastic virtues assigned to them at XI.5. Now Tesmundus stands to Aregarius's immediate left, and Sigualdus opposite him stands in front of Aregarius. The poet Audradus, again the least and yet most important, stands closest to the *pater*.[29] This group of four canons now looks back toward the *pater* and the Bible.

A late-ninth-century ivory panel in Cambridge depicting the Introit of the Roman Mass (Fitzwilliam Museum, McClean Bequest M.12/1904, fig. 35),[30] offers an analogue to the compositional structure of the First Bible painting, but one that only points up the miniature's composite aspect and unusual complexity. As in the presentation portrait, singing monks form a semicircle before an enormously enlarged central figure, in this case a bishop. Moreover, one of them, with his back turned toward the spectator, is shown at the bottom center with his arms raised in acclamation. On the plaque, however, the attention of the singers is undivided, and the scene, unified in time and space, lacks the Presentation miniature's compositional intricacy.

There are, in fact, few precedents for the First Bible's double depiction of personages. In the First Bible itself, Master C, the creator of the Presentation miniature, had also painted the Jerome frontispiece, in which Jerome is depicted twice in the first register, both leaving Rome and paying his Hebrew teacher (fig. 5); but there the effect is different for Jerome appears in two distinct narrative units. In the second register of the same miniature, however, Jerome occupies a pivotal role more like that of the *pater* in the Presentation

---

29. Though the facial features of the *primi* left and right are fully consistent and their gowns are basically the same, there are some slight differences. The left-hand gown of Audradus, for instance, does not today reveal any trace of the floral pattern so evident on the right. But all the gowns on the left-hand side of the page show, in fact, signs of progressive fading as they come closer to the left margin.

30. See Adolph Goldschmidt, *Die Elfenbeinskulpturen aus der Zeit der karolingischen und sächsischen Kaiser*, vol. 1 (Berlin, 1914), p. 61; Carl Nordenfalk, "Karolingisch oder Ottonisch? Zur Datierung und Lokalisierung der Elfenbeine Goldschmidt I, 120–31," *Kolloquium über spätantike und frühmittelalterliche Skulptur, Heidelberg, 1972,* vol. 3 (Mainz, 1974), pp. 45–58; Helmut Trnek, "Das Oeuvre des Meisters der Vienner Gregorplatte," in *Zu Gast in der Kunstkammer* (Vienna, 1991), pp. 13–14, 25–27; and Susan Rankin, "Carolingian Music," in McKitterick, *Carolingian Culture,* pp. 274–75.

miniature, since he explains Scripture to the two women in front of him, while the work of inscribing his translation goes on behind him. These activities were understood, as already noted, as two different sets of action and were so divided into separate scenes by the San Paolo illuminator. Probably the closest parallel to the doubled action of the Presentation miniature is the San Paolo Bible's Judith frontispiece (fol. 234v, fig. 36).[31] It pictures Judith and her hand-maiden leaving Bethulia at the upper left of the three-tiered composition and then, at the upper right, returning with Holofernes's head; and the *titulus* underscores the opposition of two moments through the use of *pergo* at the left and *revertor* at the right.[32] The result is that the beginning and end of the narrative take place in the same setting; indeed, the returning women salute the same townspeople who watched them depart.

In the Presentation miniature of the First Bible, however, something truly unusual and adventurous was attempted, for the doubled *primi* express different moments in the same unfolding ceremony, while the other figures—the king, Vivian, the *pater,* and the book bearers—serve as fixed points around the ceremonial circle. There are now two chief pivotal figures around whom the action of the ceremony turns, for both the *pater* and King Charles are touched by the temporal flow of action around them: the king in turning from Vivian to the Bible and later listening to songs in his praise, and the *pater* in presiding over different stages of the ceremony. The doubling of the *primi* was, thus, a bold and precocious attempt to capture on parchment the passing of ceremonial and symbolic time,[33] for what Master C and Audradus sought to express, as we shall see, was the profound spiritual and temporal transformation of a king.

Despite the complexity of the scene, there is a striking correspondence between the actual depiction and the verse description. In painting, for instance, a squared assembly of canons along the rim of a circle, Master C personified the four *primi* as the quaternity of monastic virtues mentioned at precisely that point in the facing poem (XI.5). Moreover, the double depiction of the *primi* and the poet's "ante ubi post" directly reflected a shared vision of a complex and almost inexpressible image. The high degree of correspondence between the Presentation miniature and the last dedicatory verses demonstrates just how closely the poet and this painter worked together. Audradus and Master C may have worked almost side by side in order to achieve the Pre-

---

31. Cf. Joachim Gaehde, "The Pictorial Sources of the Illustrations to the Books of Kings, Proverbs, Judith, and Maccabees in the Carolingian Bible of San Paolo Fuori Le Mura in Rome," *Frühmittelalterliche Studien,* 9 (1975): 381–82 and "Le miniature," in *Bibbia di San Paolo,* pp. 379–83.

32. See Gaehde, "Pictorial Sources," pp. 359–89 and "Le fonti Turonesi," pp. 318–20.

33. On medieval artistic reflections of time and history, see Giles Constable, "A Living Past: The Historical Environment of the Middle Ages," *Harvard Library Bulletin,* new series 1 (1990): 49–70.

sentation miniature and its verses, for they could not have achieved their complicated vision in the busy autumn of 845 without mutual understanding of
what it was they wished to show the king.

It was, thus, an exceedingly sophisticated, almost idiosyncratic vision that
Charles the Bald encountered when he turned to the last opening of the First
Bible at Christmastide 845. He confronted a miniature that both represented
the present ceremony and celebrated his recent renewal of the privileges
granted by his great-grandfather, grandfather, and father. The king's subsequent actions, the verses and picture suggest, should be the careful and
respectful consideration of the true needs of the monastery and church. The
unnamed *pater* standing directly across from the painted king was a visual
challenge for the real king to do his moral and royal best, and his prominent
depiction may have given Charles the Bald momentary pause.

Like the portrait, the verses convey a certain tension between the actual
moment of presentation and the ideal situation that would be established
should Charles enact his promises. They credit the king with already having
submitted to the church (X.22), for returning properties to the monastery
(XI.15), and for renewing privileges (XI.27 and 29); but they also exhort him
not to falter in his commitment to honor and preserve the charters granted to
the community of Saint-Martin (XI.27–30). Charles was meant to learn, love,
and live the law contained in the book given to him by the canons so that he
might then act in the interests of the Church and his own salvation (VI.21–26).
But beyond merely receiving the Bible, he was to progress to action based on
its precepts.

A change in person marks a significant shift just six lines from the end of the
last poem in the Bible. Instead of the first person singular and the hortatory
second- and third-person verbs that had predominated throughout the poems,
the poet now switched to the collective *nos,*[34] thereby moving from promise to
realization as the canons, the *grex Martini,* together turned to pray for the king
and his family (XI.37–38). This prayerful "we" was not, however, limited to the
primi or confined to the present ceremony and its audience, for the poet
promised that the successive generations of brethren at Saint-Martin would
continually pray for the king and his family (XI.39–40),[35] thereby conferring
upon Charles the gift of perpetual prayer for his well-being. Thus, the word
nos expressed the collective mission and commitments of the canons that,

---

34. See also I.177, where "nos" was employed.

35. On continual prayers for Carolingian rulers, see Michael McCormick, "The Liturgy of War in the
Early Middle Ages: Crisis, Litanies, and the Carolingian Monarchy," *Viator* 15 (1984): 3–6. For general
background, see Ernst H. Kantorowicz, *Laudes regiae: A Study in Liturgical Acclamations and Medieval
Ruler Worship* (Berkeley, 1958), pp. 13–111.

being extended in time and space, represented the sempiternal presence of Saint Martin himself in heaven, ever ready to intercede for Charles.[36] The prayers of the *nos,* moreover, brought to realization the poet's request at X.37–44 for the whole world to join with him in praying for the king.

Both Morrison and Lowden observed that the canons pictured on the facing page actually seem to be singing these lines of poetic prayer.[37] As part of the ceremony of presentation, actual lines from the verses of the First Bible may have been sung to the king by the assembled canons of Saint-Martin. At X.39–44 the poet, who had been most often speaking to Charles in the second-person singular, shifted to the third-person singular subjunctive as though giving formal direction to the assembled audience on how to pray for a king. At the point in the ceremony when these prayers were taken up, poems would have merged with pictures; and both images—written and painted—would have coalesced with the unfolding event and the assembled people. Having read the Bible as the first stanza on folio 1r directed him to and in anticipation of his acting according to the precepts gleaned from it (X.43), Charles was saluted by the canons for "proceed[ing] along a holy way in your speech and deeds" (X.14).

Yet the poems and paintings of the First Bible convey, despite all the imperative posturing of the poet, a mood of deep anxiety, as the canons worried about the impending appointment of a new abbot and his intentions toward the abbey.[38] Throughout 845, the canons had been attempting to erect their own defensive walls against lay intrusion. Measures designed to thwart such intrusion had been granted in charters, and, in fact, the renewal of the monastery's "perpetual" immunities was sought by the canons as the most important of these guarantees. Vivian, as the count of Tours, may have supported the property interests of Saint-Martin in early 845, but Audradus and the canons could not be sure his benevolence would continue. As the poet wrote and Master C painted in the late summer and early fall of 845, they probably wondered whether Vivian would remain a true and beneficial patron. Audradus, at least, would have preferred him to remain a local, noble supporter of the monastery at the royal court, rather than its lay abbot. Not long after the Bible was presented and Vivian was appointed the *rector monasterii,* tensions began to increase, and Audradus's disillusionment quickly grew. When the Northmen sacked Saint-Martin in 853, Audradus thought of the

---

36. See especially, Audradus 12 *(Liber revelationum).*2, ed. Traube, "O Roma nobilis," p. 379, in which Saint Martin stands in heaven and intervenes with the Virgin and Christ on behalf of the Frankish kings and their people.

37. Morrison, "Know Thyself," p. 437 and Lowden, "Royal/Imperial Book," pp. 216–22.

38. Kessler, "Lay Abbot as Patron," p. 668.

event as divine punishment for Charles's arrogance in making false appointments. He believed, in part, that God was still angry over Vivian's inappropriate appointment, even though the count had died in the forests of Brittany two years before. The extraordinary loathing for the "treacherous and impious Vivian" became one of the sustaining furies of Audradus's later life.[39] But that anger was not yet evident in the First Bible verses, in part because Vivian was not yet officially lay abbot and could still be treated with cool distance. Audradus probably hoped that the king could be persuaded by the Bible to respect Saint-Martin's best interests.

But what Audradus and the canons wanted was not simple, or, at least, it could not be simply or directly expressed. Instead Audradus and the painters had to approach the king on a number of levels and indirectly. The argument that a young Christian king was obliged to subject himself to God's precepts was particularly advanced in the Presentation picture through the association of Charles's portrait with the earlier depiction of David. Just as the poems repeatedly addressed this Carolingian king as David, so too the final miniature identified Charles with DAVID REX ET PROP<HETA> by means of facial features, crown, shared bodyguards, and personified virtues. Indeed, the personifications provided a double link; for while, in the painting, Charles is attended by only two female figures, the accompanying verse attributes all four of David's divine virtues to him (X.29).[40] Furthermore, the framing arch with twisted vine columns properly belonged to David's iconography, as is seen in Charles's later Bible in San Paolo fuori le mura in Rome (fol. 170v).[41] Moreover, Charles was now protected by David's guards, and the *primi* now served as the king's Davidian singers, so that at XI.35–38, with mention of their lyre and sweet song, Audradus imagined himself and the other chief canons singing psalms to their own King David. They too, these importunate canons, had become part of reconstructed biblical history. Thus, the fusion of David and Charles announced by the medallion portraits on folio 1v and reinforced by the connecting verses[42] achieved its fulfillment and most satisfying expression in the Presentation miniature.

In the early 840s, the traditional equation between the contemporary ruler and biblical king had acquired precise political connotations.[43] The fact that

---

39. See Dutton, *Politics of Dreaming,* pp. 144–46.

40. Cf. Kaspersen, "Majestas Domini-Regnum et Sacerdotium," pp. 102–3; and Diebold, "Ruler Portrait," pp. 6–18.

41. Eggenberger, *Psalterium Aureum Sancti Galli,* pp. 44–45.

42. See especially VI.1–6, which, as the central poem of the First Bible, connects the Old Testament and the New. It is also the first poem after the Psalms frontispiece (fol. 215v) and seals the continuing and unmistakeable identification of Charles with David.

43. Anton, *Fürstenspiegel und Herrscherethos,* pp. 421–30.

David had been selected to rule Israel ahead of Jesse's other sons took on obvious implications for the sons of Louis the Pious, still contending with each other for control of their father's kingdom; it is that aspect of David's life that is underscored by the *titulus* bridging the emperor's portrait to David's in the Lothar Psalter (London, British Library, Add. MS 37768), in which the poet said that God had selected this king as the one from many brothers fit to hold the scepters of power.[44]

In the First Bible, however, a different aspect of David's elevation to power is seen at work, his humility.[45] Alone among ninth-century psalter portraits and, indeed, virtually unique in the entire history of medieval art, David is portrayed dancing naked.[46] The reference here is to 2 Sam. 6:12–22, which describes how David, who was "wearing a linen ephod, danced without restraint before the Lord" (2 Sam. 6:14). He danced to citharas, harps, tambourines, sistrums, and cymbals (2 Sam. 6:5). When he led the ark into Jerusalem, Saul's daughter chastised him for his unseemly deportment:

> What a glorious day for the king of Israel, when he exposed his person in the sight of the servants' slave-girls like any empty-headed fool. (2 Sam. 6:20)

The key to the episode's political meaning and, hence, to the significance of the Bible's imagery here is David's reply to Michal's rebuke:

> But it was done in the presence of the Lord, who chose me instead of your father and his family and appointed me prince over Israel, the people of the Lord. Before the Lord I will dance for joy, yes, and I will earn yet more disgrace and lower myself still more in your eyes. But those girls of whom you speak, they will honor me for it. (2 Sam. 6:21–22)

In Scripture, nudity signals David's willingness to submit to God's will even at the cost of a king's dignity. He would humble himself, but they would honor him for his humility before the Lord.

No wonder, then, that during the Carolingian period, David's reply to

---

44. *MGH PLAC,* 6.1: *Nachträge zu den Poetae aevi Carolini,* ed. K. Strecker (Berlin, 1951; rpt. 1978), p. 163: "Rex fuit eximius, de multis fratribus unum quem deus elegit, regnandi ut sceptra teneret." See also Wilhelm Koehler and Florentine Mütherich, *Die karolingische Miniaturen,* vol. 4: *Die Hofschule Kaiser Lothars: Einzelhandschriften aus Lotharingen* (Berlin, 1971), pp. 14–16, 28–30; and Kessler, "Lay Abbot as Patron," p. 663.

45. Kessler, "Lay Abbot as Patron," pp. 663–66.

46. An exception is the eleventh-century psalter in Munich (Bayerische Staatsbibliothek, Clm 13067, fol. 18r); cf. Kessler, *Illustrated Bibles,* fig. 143.

Michal was taken as a prime example of proper royal humility,[47] as in Smaragdus's *Via Regia* written for Louis the Pious: "You see, therefore, O king, that [Saul] . . . was cast down from the royal throne by pride, and [David] was elevated to the glory of kingship by humility."[48] Citing Smaragdus and other texts in his important article on the Prayerbook of Charles the Bald, Robert Deshman noted that the generations following Charlemagne consistently transformed the *imitatio David regis* trope to stress the "ideal of David as the humble royal penitent, as the king who was exalted because of his selfless submission to God's will."[49] The specific implications are clear: just as David was chosen over the sitting ruler, Charles—whose face and crown he bears—would be victorious over his enemies, especially Lothar, who had continued to harass him, and through his humility he would be "appointed prince over the people of the Lord."[50]

In the context of the First Bible, this special emphasis takes on a further meaning. As Deut. 17 states, one reason the Levites were to give the divine law to a new king was to teach him humility. In Audradus's vision of 851–52, he envisaged Christ reminding Charles of the need for royal humility and obedience. In that very vision, Christ overthrows Lothar because of his pride. If young Charles was "humble and obedient," however, Christ promised to bestow upon him the scepter and crown of his kingdom.[51] Thus, for Audradus, humility was constitutive of kingship, pride its sure unmaking.[52] In the First Bible verses he reminded Charles that the law brought salvation to all and lifted up even the unlearned and made them wise (I.141–44). He attempted as

47. Theodosius I, the Great, was another example of a humble ruler praised because of his penance by the Carolingians. See Mayke de Jong, "Power and Humility in Carolingian Society: The Public Penance of Louis the Pious," *Early Medieval Europe* 1 (1992): 29–52; and Dutton, *Politics of Dreaming,* p. 74.

48. *PL* 102:956.

49. "The Exalted Servant: The Ruler Theology of the Prayerbook of Charles the Bald," *Viator* 11 (1980): 385–417. The topos derives ultimately from Luke 14:11. See also the situation described by Ioli Kalavrezou, Nicolette Trahoulia, and Shalom Sabar, "Critique of the Emperor in the Vatican Psalter gr. 752," *Dumbarton Oaks Papers* 47 (1993): 195–219.

50. The First Bible's subsequent history might be telling in this regard. Charles apparently presented the manuscript to the Cathedral of Metz when he was crowned king of Lotharingia in 869, that is, at the moment this goal was finally accomplished. And to replace it, he commissioned the San Paolo Bible, which may actually copy, in part, Lothar's Turonian pandect in Prüm, a monastery then briefly in Charles's hands and the former site of the king's imprisonment and humiliation by Lothar. Thus, just at the moment when the First Bible's message was no longer appropriate, the manuscript was discarded and a replacement made. Cf. Florentine Mütherich, "Eine Kopie nach der Vivian-Bibel," *Miscellanea pro Arte: Hermann Schnitzler zur Vollendung des 60. Lebensjahre am 13. Januar 1965* (Düsseldorf 1965), pp. 54–59 and *Metz Enluminée*. On the fate of the Bible, see also, Konrad Hoffmann, "Zur Entstehung des Königsportals in Saint-Denis," *Zeitschrift für Kunstgeschichte,* 48 (1985): 37 and n. 59.

51. See chapter 2 above and Dutton, *Politics of Dreaming,* pp. 143–46.

52. For Audradus, even the theft of church property was a sin of pride: see Audradus 12 *(Liber revelationum).*3, ed. Traube, "O Roma nobilis," p. 379.20. See also the last of the visions in which God the Father remained angry at those, who "mente superba in suis sceleribus obstinatissime obduruerunt": Audradus 12 *(Liber revelationum).*14, ed. Traube, "O Roma nobilis," p. 389.13.

well to teach the young king the importance of confession (I.13–14, 145) and submission to bishops (X.22), for the humility of those acts would bring him everlasting rewards. At I.183, on the only occasion when Audradus referred to Charles directly as *tu,* he called him *humilis* and *prudens.* He had just finished making the point that Solomon had been placed higher than all other kings because of the wisdom God gave him (I.179–82). If Charles was humble and prudent, and pursued wisdom, he too, the poet seemed to say, would prevail over his worldly enemies and achieve some measure of the greatness of the four great paragons of royal virtue (I.195–96).

The theme of the reward for humble submission to God is nowhere better captured than in the David frontispiece. David's elevation is brilliantly expressed by setting the naked king against an enormous blue mandorla surrounded by heavenly virtues and filled with celestial song. Indeed, Master C structured his entire composition in order to demonstrate the heavenly prize granted to David for his dance of humility. The tautly modeled naked man floating against a blue sky recalls no one as much as Amphion, Zeus's music-making son, portrayed in the contemporary *Aratea* manuscript in Leiden (Bibliotheek der Rijksuniversiteit, MS. Voss. lat. Q 79, fol. 16v).[53]

Implicit in the doubling of David and Charles is also a resemblance to Christ, albeit an oblique one.[54] Raised into a mandorla and accompanied by four co-psalmists, David is likened visually to the next effigy page, the Majestas Domini, which is also a quadripartite heavenly vision structured within a cosmological scheme.[55] Jerome's preface, the Carolingian *titulus* (poem V), and the "Origo Psalmorum" prologue facing the Psalms portrait all assert that the king of Israel is a *persona Christi,* whose hymns proclaim the mysteries of his carnal descendant Jesus.[56]

The poetry of the First Bible, in turn, applies divine and christological epithets directly to Charles, for to refer to him as the *splendor populi, lux mundi,* and *gloria regni* (I. 191) was to invoke the splendor of God (Ps. 89:17), Christ as the light of the world (John 8:12), and the glory of God's kingdom (Ps. 144:11). Charles was also hailed as "gloria, laus, honor" (X.3); these were the

---

53. Cf. Koehler and Mütherich, *Die Hofschule Kaiser Lothars,* pp. 79–83, 108–16; *Aratea: Ein Leitstern des abendlandischen Weltbildes* (Luzern, 1987); Anton von Euw, *Aratea: Sternenhimmel in Antike und Mittelalter* (Cologne, 1987); Hermann J. Hermann, *Die illuminierten Handschriften und Inkunablen der Nationalbibliothek in Wien,* 1 (Leipzig, 1923), pp. 145–52; Florentine Mütherich, "Die Buchmalerei am Hofe Karls des Grossen," in *Karl der Grosse: Lebenswerk und Nachleben,* vol. 3, ed. W. Braunfels (Düsseldorf, 1965), pp. 50–51; Ranee Katzenstein and Emilie Savage-Smith, *The Leiden Aratea: Ancient Constellations in a Medieval Manuscript* (Malibu, Calif., 1988), p. 23.

54. Cf. Morrison, "Know Thyself," pp. 433–37.

55. Kessler, *Illustrated Bibles,* pp. 51–52.

56. The *Origo psalmorum* faces the Psalms frontispiece in the First Bible of Charles the Bald. For the *Origo,* see De Bruyne, *Préfaces,* p. 43. Cf. First Bible V.1–2.

terms in which God the Father had expressed his recognition and honor of Christ (2 Pet. 1:17). Theodulf, Alcuin, and Audradus in his *Liber de fonte vitae* had all sung variations of these praises of Christ.[57] And the painting, too, places the Carolingian monarch in a sacred sphere by showing him dressed in golden raiment and elevated into a cloudy region above the darkened earth.[58] The tie between Charles and Christ is expressed most emphatically in the dedicatory verses addressed to the Carolingian monarch that were transcribed on the obverse of the Majestas Domini miniature itself (VI, fig. 10). These explicitly situate Charles the Bald at the hinge of the Old and New Testament; albeit only through words and not yet by means of a picture, they refer back to Jewish scripture and introduce the Gospels, exhorting Charles to govern wisely so that Christ would place him among the saints. Marking the two books of Scripture used in the liturgy, the Psalter and the Gospels, and leading to a third that ends the composite volume, the First Bible's monumental portrait pages thus form a subset of pictures that encompass three epochs of salvation, as Alibert proposed, the period of Jewish law, the age of grace, and the present.[59]

Through subtle ties with the Apocalypse miniature, the presentation portrait goes one step further to suggest the future as well. In the first poem, Audradus had already called on Charles to be not only a father and mother, and brother and sister for his people, but also a lamb (I.47) or savior, which may have been the poet's way of foreshadowing the innocent Lamb of God (IX.1) Charles would later see in the Apocalypse frontispiece. The connection between that miniature and the Presentation illumination is secured through all three of the vignettes, which were only introduced when the decision was made to adapt the codex to the special circumstances surrounding Charles's visit to Tours in 845. All of these new scenes might be interpreted as conveying a special message to King Charles, and each obtains its own correlative in the Presentation miniature. Thus, the question asked by the angel at Rev. 5:2 is, "Who is worthy to open the scroll and break its seals?" The first vignette (fig. 19) shows John being consoled by an elder, who informs him that one from the line of David will open the scroll (Rev. 5:5). In the Presentation miniature, it is, of course, King Charles, this new David graced with christological epithets, who stands ready to answer the angel's question, for he is about to open the First Bible, both physically and spiritually. In the second vignette (fig. 20), the painter moves us forward to the point at Rev. 6:1–2 where the very first seal has

---

57. Theodulf, *carmen* 69.1, ed. Dümmler, *MGH PLAC* 1:558; Alcuin, *carmen* 45.26, ed. Dümmler, *MGH PLAC* 1:257; and Audradus 5.147, ed. Traube, *MGH PLAC* 3:77.

58. See Dominique Alibert, "La majesté sacrée du roi: Images du souverain carolingien," *Histoire de l'art* 5–6 (1989): 23–36.

59. Alibert, "Majesté sacrée du roi," pp. 30–31.

been broken and the book opens to reveal a royal rider on a white horse, who was "given a crown and rode forth victorious to further his victories." In the Presentation miniature Charles is the living personification of this breaker of the first seal and is offered crowns by the virtuous figures set high above him at the edge of heaven. This vignette may have been intended to remind the king of the victories that would come to him if he humbly submitted to the Bible and its holy representatives.

Finally, the vignette of John eating the codex (fig. 21), in this steady progression of scenes, treats Rev. 10:2–11:1 and constitutes the final biblical moment pictured in the manuscript. Indeed, this vignette condenses all the themes of the Bible's pictorial program—the essential unity of the Old and New Testaments, the Bible as *ius divinum,* and the embodiment of sacred law in God's chosen agents. The scene of the angel standing on sea and land and handing the small book of Scripture to John, who carries in his right hand the *calamus similis virgae,* leads directly to the representation of the canons of Saint-Martin delivering their Bible to King Charles, who cradles a scepter, his own powerful straight stick of justice (I.144), in his hand. Autpertus's commentary on Revelation's "cane like a measuring rod" had facilitated this association; in quoting Ps. 44:7–8, "your royal scepter [is] a scepter of righteousness; you have loved right and hated wrong," Autpertus had concluded that John's *calamus* symbolized the success achieved by a ruler who adhered unbendingly to justice.[60] That straight stick, the *stilus* or "mighty pen of justice" invoked by Audradus at I.144, not only signified the pen used to write Scripture (I.108) and the Church's true doctrine, but also stood for the scepter of a monarch who ruled rightly according to the sacred law.[61] King Charles was also, through reference to the last Apocalypse vignette, being urged in the Presentation miniature to hold tight his mighty stick of justice, as John had, and also, like John, to consume the Bible he was about to receive from the canons.

But these new scenes swirl around and lead the eye back to the sacred book resting on a throne and the *agnus* in the upper register and to the *facies bibliothecae* in the lower, with its moment of transcendent revelation and completion. Physically replacing the Apocalypse page, the Presentation miniature employs the very conventions of typology used in the Apocalypse miniature to assert the concord of Scripture and to establish Charles's proper role in this new biblical history. It, too, depicts Scripture yielding to a man enthroned

---

60. *In Apocalypsin,* V, ed. Weber, p. 406.

61. This explains why the Presentation picture is the final folio in the manuscript, replacing the more suitable Apocalypse miniature, which in the earlier Moutier-Grandval Bible serves as the colophon picture; see Kessler, "Facies bibliothecae revelata," p. 559 and n. 2.

beneath a celestial curtain, who is a *persona* of his biblical predecessors. Here, however, the purpose was not to show the new law and the future church prophesied by John, but to establish the continuity of biblical law in ninth-century Gaul by providing a glimpse of a reformed terrestrial church restored and guarded by a Carolingian king.[62] The enthroned king in the refashioned codex now physically occupied the place of both the *agnus* and the *facies bibliothecae,* for Audradus had called on Charles at the start of the codex to become an *agnus* to his people (I.47) and to consume and become the Bible. By the end, in the Presentation miniature of the First Bible, the king has become this final fulfillment of the Bible's mandate, as constructed by Audradus, to achieve oneness and to personify justice.

It was this complete transformation of king and kingdom that Audradus hoped the Bible would bring about, for in the First Bible verses he said that the law would transform the world and lead to the restoration of the Church (I.153–54). One feels here the stirrings of the prophet Audradus whose prophetic calling quickened in 845. In early March of that year he had been praying to God "for the well-being of his churches," when God's presence swept over him.[63] Audradus's preoccupation in 845 with the onset of prophecy surfaces in the First Bible, where David takes the title of prophet and the verses alert the young king to the terrifying revelations of things "that will surely come to pass" (I.156) and the wisdom of the law that remains. The Apocalypse frontispiece introduced and qualified the way in which the canons wanted the king to understand the Presentation miniature. There Audradus and the painters pushed the king not only toward a specific reading of the Presentation miniature, but also toward the perfect future the final painting imagined for him. Throughout the poems Audradus had urged Charles the Bald to think of the Bible as food, and in the final two paintings we first see John eating the book and then the king about to consume the contents of the First Bible. Moreover, the mighty pen or firm rod of justice (I.144), which Audradus had so wanted the king to take up, was finally shown, first in John's hand and then in the king's. In the final painting of the First Bible, Charles has become David, and the *primi* have become both his psalm singers and the bearers of biblical truth now feeding their king the First Bible with all its inspired poems and paintings.

---

62. Pippal, "Distanzierung und Aktualisierung," p. 62, emphasizes the importance of the theme of church power within the First Bible's sacred narrative.

63. See Audradus 12 *(Liber revelationum)*.4, ed. Traube, "O Roma nobilis," p. 379.

Conclusion: Poems and Paintings, Bible and King

The poems of the First Bible interact with the miniatures to imagine a living monarch who has read and reread the Bible and, hence, stands on the verge of becoming Scripture's true agent and embodiment. Once Charles had consumed the Bible's everlasting nectar (I.118), he himself would become the food of his people (X.26). Just as the "holy nectar" (IV.4) inscribed on Moses' tablet in the Exodus frontispiece (fig. 7)—the commandment to "love God with all your heart, soul, and mind"—transforms Jewish law into a personated precept and just as "the vital lessons of life from the heavenly Old and New Testaments" (VIII.5–6) are delivered to the pagans by Paul viva voce in the Epistles frontispiece (fig. 11), so too the Bible presented by the canons of Saint-Martin in the presentation portrait (figs. 17 and IV) was designed to become part of Charles's very being. Over and over again, the poems apply eating metaphors to Charles's apprehension of Scripture to make this point, referring to the Bible as his sustenance, drink, and blessed salvation (I.8, VI.22). Verse I.29–48 contains, as it were, a poetic discourse on a replacement diet for the king. For as the Bible became his spiritual food, Charles was urged to restrain his own physical appetite and to chasten his body with fasting (I.31). As rich as he was (I.41) and as strong as his desires were (I.42), Charles was invited to redistribute goods, to give to the poor and become, as we have seen, their food (I.43–48). To the same end, the Presentation portrait refigures the vignette of John eating the book that concludes the sequence of biblical miniatures (fig. 21). Literally replacing the Apocalypse miniature, which had originally been designed to close the manuscript, the portrait restates the claim that "the Bible is to be understood as just one man."[1] Charles, now fully fed by poet and painter with the stuff of the Bible, should have become this man, this food for his people, this paradise.

One of the distinctive characteristics of the First Bible is its unified quality,

---

1. Cf. chapter 4, n. 25 above.

as the poetry and paintings speak to each other in extremely subtle ways and move together toward the final fulfillment of the Presentation miniature. Even if the codex had begun its history in the summer of 845 as a somewhat plainer and less directed book, by the time that it was reworked and presented to Charles the Bald in December it conveyed a consistent and profound message. Beginning with a Turonian pandect more or less like the Moutier-Grandval Bible, Audradus and the painters had worked systematically to redirect the imagery to the specific moment of the gift's presentation to Charles the Bald and to his obligations in 845 as understood by the canons of Saint-Martin.

The poet expanded upon the two basic premises underlying the standard program, that Scripture is the work of one Author whose identity emerges by excavating the essential harmony beneath the diverse texts the Bible comprises, and that the unified Bible constitutes divine law. Thus, the poems assert that God speaks here (I.177);[2] and the Psalter frontispiece figures David as Christ. But the architect of the First Bible of Charles the Bald expanded this imagery to resituate the inherited program in the present. Applying the same techniques to the new subjects, Audradus imagined and Master C painted Jerome issuing Bibles composed in a single tongue and a single tome, which seems a striking reference to the canons of Saint-Martin distributing unified pandects throughout west Francia.[3] He also portrayed David as naked and humbled as a way of sending a message to Louis the Pious's youngest son that to secure his kingdom, he must submit to God's law—a message rooted in Deuteronomy that, six years later, Audradus would articulate in a more pointed warning to Charles in his *Book of Revelations*. And, depicting Paul as a Roman soldier transformed into an apostle preaching Christ's law to the pagans, he underscored the king's obligation to promote and maintain Christianity throughout his realm.

In the depiction of the canons delivering the book to the young king at the end of the book, Audradus and Master C translocated the whole Bible into the Turonian present. As a likeness of David, John the Evangelist, the enthroned elder, and even Christ himself, Charles was presented as Scripture's ultimate agent in the Carolingian present.

Audradus had worked from first to last to remind King Charles that he must not simply learn the lessons of the Bible, but should transform them into action. Thus, in the opening lines of the first dedicatory poem (I.3–4), the king was told that the Bible contained not only what he should love and believe in, but also what he should do *(agas)*. The Bible itself brings together contem-

---

2. On the Bible as the *praesentia Dei,* see Hrabanus Maurus, *Allegoria, PL* 112:987.

3. On the connection between the Jerome pages and dedication portraits in Carolingian manuscripts, see Staubach, *Rex christianus,* 2:252–53.

plation and action (*actus;* I.7), and the words *opus,* in the sense of labor, and *actio* run throughout the verses. The theme of the king achieving consistency in "speech and deeds" (see I.60, VI.21, 26, X.14–15) was important to Audradus because he and his fellow canons wanted to move the king to consistently Christian action; this he characterized as the pure action of God (X.16). This rhetoric may be less pronounced in the last poem because by then it was hoped that the king would have been transformed into a more perfect vessel of religious and moral action. Charles should have become the perfect patron of the church, and a continuing comfort to the clergy and his people (X.17).

Indeed, the presentation portrait depicts Charles as this perfected ruler. God now speaks through this divinely trained monarch as consistently as he does in the Bible itself; the divine Hand that had issued the law to Moses and transformed Saint Paul from a worldly and persecuting Roman soldier into a complete Christian now cast light directly onto the governor of the Carolingian kingdom. In this way, the final portrait and accompanying poems brought biblical history into the present through their subject matter and a mise-en-scène referring explicitly to current politics and living people. Thus, the action and voices of the imagined presentation ceremony fused into a more perfect present.

But when Charles received the volume, he was not yet the transformed king imagined by Audradus; and the Bible had not yet done its work on him. The poet used his poems not only to situate the king as he read the Bible from the first book to the last, but to tell him what he was reading and why it was important. The poet intended his verses, however cursory (I.88), to guide the young king through his biblical education; and Audradus and the painters had become the king's constant companions while he read and reread his new Bible. Thus, in the first dedicatory verse the poet laid out the whole scheme of the Bible (I.63–114), but in poem VI he returned to tell the king that he had now finished reading the Old Testament and should turn his attention to its fulfillment in the New (VI.5–6). The last two dedicatory verses did not recapitulate the Bible, but personated it in the form of a remade king and his perfect circle of religious and lay supporters.

At this point Audradus also supplied the king with an education in aesthetics.[4] If the first and second (VI) dedicatory verses had not explicitly referred to paintings, both of the last two poems did. The first dedicatory verse had begun with "haec biblioteca," but the last begins with "haec pictura" (XI.1), thus

---

4. Sigilaus, again deeply influenced by the First Bible and its verses, attempted something of the same in his dedicatory verse to the emperor Lothar in the Lothar Gospels: see "Carmina Varia" 25.23–25, ed. Dümmler, *MGH PLAC* 2:671.

marking a change in referents as the royal reader and his poet and painters stepped beyond the living Bible to its perfected agent. The poet here and in the previous poem tried to guide the king's gaze as he studied the paintings, not just with a description of the miniatures as he had done on some of the brief, but important *tituli,* but with a theory about how he ought to regard the presentation portrait. In verses X and XI he demonstratively invited the king to look at the painting and described, in titular mode, some of its complex details, but he did so with both panegyrical purpose and poetic deference. The king might have noticed, for instance, that the poet talked exclusively about his portrait in poem X on a folio that did not face the painting, but described the other people and the scene itself in the poem (XI) that faced the miniature. Thus, poem X deals more with the viewed and XI more with the viewers, those who are filled with joy as they look at the enthroned king (X.10). This separation of persons had the effect of removing Charles from the realm of the others, just as the painter had set him apart from them and closest to the hand of God in a cloudy, ethereal layer in the painting.

By confining the discussion of the king's portrait to folio 422r, the poet also reinforced the panegyrical conceit that the king could never be equaled or fully captured in painting (X.5–9). The king was superior to all images and, indeed, to all poems, and the poet admitted that all representation of him would fail (X.6) and that no one could fully measure Charles's greatness (X.31–32). Only God himself, however, was truly beyond even the highest poetry (I.188), Audradus said. Thus, the poet with all his poetic talk effectively privileged the descriptive power of words, just as Theodulf had in the *Libri Carolini,* where writing was presented as a truer form of expression than art;[5] and he was quick to acknowledge that the portrait might fail to capture the fullness of the king or his features (X.8–9). His apologetic tone here may have been intended to anticipate and counter any criticism from the subject himself. The Presentation miniature is, after all, the first extant portrait of Charles the Bald, and it may not have been clear to the canons of Tours how the young king would react. Audradus was quick to point out that where the portrait succeeded, because of the exceptional power of art, it did so only because it had captured a true aspect of the king, and general joy among the people assembled in the painting was the evident result (X.4–10). Thus, when art succeeded it did so because it was truthful, but when it failed it did so because people could never

---

5. On the *Libri Carolini,* see Thomas F. X. Noble, "Tradition and Learning in Search of Ideology: The *Libri Carolini,*" in Sullivan, *Gentle Voices of Teachers,* pp. 227–60; and Celia M. Chazelle, "Matter, Spirit, and Image in the *Libri Carolini,*" *Recherches augustiniennes* 21 (1986): 163–84, and "Not in Painting but in Writing: Augustine and the Supremacy of the Word in the *Libri Carolini,*" in *Reading and Wisdom: The "De doctrina christiana" of Augustine in the Middle Ages* (Notre Dame, Ind., 1995), pp. 1–22.

know everything about so great a king (X.9). Again all of this was part of the poet's education of the king, and, in this regard, we need to remember how interested and supportive of royal art and his own image this king was to become. Behind Audradus's bold assertion of art's power (X.4) and his apologetic defense (X.5–9) lay the Carolingian struggle with iconoclastic or, rather, iconodulic thought that had troubled the court of Charlemagne and continued to interest some members of Charles the Bald's.[6] Audradus needed to balance the arguments for and against art and not overreach.

Audradus especially wanted to teach the king how to look and regard[7] because, we might suspect, he may have thought that the king would begin the First Bible at the end with the Presentation miniature. He probably did not imagine, in other words, that Charles would receive the Bible and immediately begin to read it from first to last. Rather, the king may have been invited to look at the magnificent final portrait of himself first, even during the ceremonial presentation or soon afterward. The collective song in the final lines of poems X and XI may belong, as suggested, to moments in that actual or imagined ceremony and may mark the place where Audradus thought the king would begin. With the final pages of the First Bible, Charles Bald would have begun in the present with an imaginary snapshot composed of real people such as Vivian, the named canons, and himself, of ideal types such as the Davidian guards and his own retainers, and of the idealized ceremony of the presentation itself. The events and issues that the final poems raise—the restless Bretons, the theft of church property, and the granting of immunities to Saint-Martin—all grounded the king in the present, where he, of necessity, needed to be. But Audradus also knew that at that moment the king would not yet be a transformed man and that the church was not yet restored to a state of pristine purity; what he needed to do was to send Charles back to the beginning of the codex, to his poems, and to the paintings that would bring him slowly back to the Presentation miniature a changed king. The final word of poem XI is, in fact, "Ave," which is, in some ways, more suitable as a greeting than as a final valediction. The poet was almost, one might suppose, greeting the king before sending him off to begin his marvelous double journey through the Bible. In order to achieve biblical transformation, the poet urged Charles not only to read the Bible, but to reread it constantly.[8] Only when he

---

6. See Ann Freeman, "Carolingian Orthodoxy and the Fate of the *Libri Carolini*," *Viator* 16 (1985): 65–108.

7. Jerome in his letter to Paulinus, which is the first written document of the First Bible, distinguished between different kinds of seeing: see Jerome, "Ad Paulinum Presbyterum," ed. De Bruyne, *Préfaces,* p. 2, and *epistola* 53.4, ed. J. Labourt, in *Saint Jérôme, Lettres* (Paris, 1953), 3:13.

8. See "relegenda" (I.2); "lector" in the vocative case (I.132); "legit" (I.172); "relegit" (I.172); "relecta" (I.172); "lecta series" (VI.5); and "nova ista legenda" (VI.6).

had read and reread and finally understood the reread Bible (I.172), would his transformation be accomplished. Only then would he truly understand what he had become by the end of the Bible and in the Presentation miniature; for the king seen at the end is one already transformed by the Bible and not the young and earthly king who rode into Tours in December 845.

The polarities of words and action, promise and fulfillment, that follow the reader Charles through the verses should not be surprising, because doubling is the predominant pattern expressed by the poetry and paintings of the First Bible. The poet had called this the *iter duplex* (I.115) of the Bible, whose essential nature was shaped by the presence and confluence of the Old and New Testaments. Both the poet and painters play with double images, some of them of great subtlety, such as the doubled *primi* in the Presentation miniature; some of them more obvious, as the poet played at X.33–34 with binary images of higher and lower things. The Majestas Domini painting by Master C (fig. 10), which had belonged to the original codex, already deployed the doubling of prophets and evangelist symbols cornered by the evangelists themselves as the pivotal connection between the two Testaments. Audradus's poem VI, as suggested earlier, in part responded to and drew out the implications of that illumination for the remade codex. Together the Majestas Domini picture and poem VI lie at the fault line of the entire plan, as the king turned from the Old to the New Testament.

With its prophets and transitional poem, folio 329 was a model of the doubling manifested throughout the First Bible, one that reminded the king to be alert to the presence of these double meanings. Moses and Paul, for instance, both of whom speak in basilicas in the bottom registers of their frontispieces, are typological doubles. David and Charles, for both Master C and Audradus, are types of the same royal figure: David is a name for the king himself; the two kings share Virgilian guardians and should share the virtue of humility. Another obvious doubling is that of Jerome and his assistants at the start (fig. 5) and the *pater* and his canons, the *grex Martini*—all of them Bible preparers—at the end (figs. 17 and IV). Thus in the first and last paintings of the First Bible the viewer encounters a *traditio legis,* as the Bible is prepared and presented. Jerome himself underwent personal transformation by translating the Bible; he departed from Rome, with all its symbolic reference to the world and to the possession of power, in order to know the Bible. Similarly Saul, again a symbol of Rome and worldly power, was blinded and once transformed truly began to see. The Jerome frontispiece, another composition by Master C, immediately confronted its royal reader with an image of transformation by means of the Bible, which was the very theme the poet constantly preached to the king. The last painting and the first thus speak to each other in complex and intertwined ways, for Charles was being reminded in both of the transformative powers of the Bible. If in both the Apocalypse and Presentation miniatures the book is shown closed, thereby achieving another fusion of biblical and historical moments, at the point at which Charles opened the First Bible to gaze upon the Presentation miniature, the book had been opened. This king, this new *agnus* (I.47), had now undone the clasps of closed revelation and stood ready like the king on the white horse to achieve victory and to bring about a new justice on earth. Thus, there is a powerful sense in which the last painting of the First Bible was designed to be both the first and last image in the book, for it demanded a double consultation; at the start so that the king could begin his personal and public journey of transformation, and at the end when, transformed by the Bible, he would finally understand what he had become, the greatest man in all the world (X.11–12).

Audradus may have imagined that the king after first viewing the final painting would return to it again in the end after reading the whole codex. Then and only then would the singularity of a transformed king be manifest. Unlike the *primi,* who are shown presenting the book and then singing the king's praises, the doubled and nameless courtiers, guards, and book-bearers, the unnamed *pater* and the historical Vivian, the king dominates the final scene by his singularity. The real and portrayed Bible had worked to set him apart from all others (X.11–12). The living monarch, however, would only become the majestic king portrayed in the miniature after he had been been fully educated by the Bible and his poetic and painterly guides; thus, only at his next return to the Presentation illumination, after reading and rereading the Bible, could he finally hope to equal its hopes and fulfill its deeper design. Then the two paths toward the same goal, one in verse and the other in paint, would yield to the transformed Christian ruler himself. Of the numerous doublings that construct meaning in the First Bible of Charles the Bald—Old Testament and New, text and picture, sacred history and contemporary politics, court and monastery—this last one, this fusion of royal images and royal realities, was the most desired. For just as Christ had fulfilled Old Testament prophecies and visions, providing unity in the whole Bible, so too the living legislator would achieve unity by instituting and enacting God's law among a new Chosen People. Poems and pictures would then fade away as mere outlines, and the changed king would be the effect.

The result of this change was noted by the poet. For, while at I.137–38 it had been the *Bible* that had ordered just things, prohibited the unjust, and rejected evil, in the end it was the *king* himself who, in this reworked line, ordered just things, prohibited the unjust, and cut away all evils (X.13–14). Moreover, the two testaments as *series* (I.113, VI.5–6, VIII.6) or laws had finally fused with the justice of Charles's own *series* (XI.30) or grant of immunities to Saint-Martin. Indeed, this fusion goes further, since at XI.34 when the poet addressed justice as a nearby presence, he was identifying the king with justice itself; Charles transformed by the Bible and with scepter in hand was now the law's very personification. Thus, the final imperative of the First Bible verses was once again addressed to Charles, who was now the exact opposite of the crime of the theft of church property. This opposition of crime and justice, of stolen church property and a just king, becomes the final double of the First Bible. The royal reissuing and protection of its immunities was seen by the canons as a necessary bulwark against the lay spoliation of Saint-Martin; it was this assurance that the canons had sought in 845 as they awaited the king's imposition of a new lay abbot. XI.31–32 was a call for Charles as Justice to fend off all those, like Vivian, who might dare to violate the rights, privileges, and property of the monastery. If the First Bible was a thank-offering for anything, to use Wallace-Hadrill's happy phrase,[9] it was for the renewal of Saint-Martin's perpetual and ancient immunities. A new contract was publicly sealed between the king and his canons the day the immunities were granted and the First Bible became its new testament (*series,* XI.30) or testamentary witness.

Image and verse were to yield finally to a perfect unity, to a single identification and identity after Charles's education and biblical transformation from a young and religiously untrained king into the monumental monarch we see at the end of the First Bible, who governs the perfect circle of a Christian polity according to the sacred law. Charles was now truly King David and the *primi* were his four musicians, singing psalms and praises to their just king with lyre and song (XI.35–38). Then, in this perfect paradise of right order, Charles the Bald would be all action and justice, the mother and father, and the food and drink for all his people, especially for the beleaguered canons of Saint-Martin of Tours, with whom he had had some very earthly dealings in 845.

These themes preoccupied Audradus and Master C, in particular, theirs being the creative doubling that shaped and informed the final construction of the codex. Master C painted the most politically important and artful of the miniatures: the Jerome and David frontispieces, the Majestas Domini and the Presentation miniatures. Audradus wrote all of the new poems and worked with Master C to capture in painting the subtle, but forceful, messages they wished to convey. The familiarity of their shared ideas is suggestive of a special bond of understanding. It seems, however, unlikely that Audradus was himself Master C, since the poet left Saint-Martin in 847 to become the suf-

---

9. Wallace-Hadrill, "A Carolingian Renaissance Prince," p. 162.

fragan bishop of Sens and the painter was still to be found at the monastery in 849 hard at work illuminating the Lothar Gospels (fig. 34).[10] Moreover, Audradus also worked closely with the other painters, including Koehler's Master A, who painted the Apocalypse frontispiece. That miniature's final vignette (fig. 21), in particular, expressed in paint the very themes that he had embodied in his poetry. One can almost imagine Audradus directing the painter of those vignettes to put the straight stick of justice in John's hand and a book in his mouth. And the dancing figure of naked David is pure Audradus Modicus, a visual expression of the theme of humility that he would entertain in passionate dream a short six years later. The very fact that several painters brought to fruition miniatures that expressed the poet's themes is powerful evidence, we believe, that the poet was the architect and main force behind the creation of the First Bible.

The dramatic joining of painters and poet in a daring design of the sort found in the First Bible was not, of course, without risks. In 853, Audradus would be summoned before a then more confident Charles the Bald to explain and defend his visionary prophecy of Charles's appearance before Christ, Vivian's slaughter, and Lothar's overthrow. But in 845, Audradus may have hoped that his sophisticated and panegyrical approach would win him an attentive reader in the king; and he was trying to sway only him, for the book, as he said, was made for no one else (XI.9–10). Vivian was neither the sender nor receiver of this message. He was at most an onlooker and stood furthest away from the depicted Bible, and the assembled *primi* have turned their backs upon him and look toward their true *pater*.

But we need also to measure the changing tone of both the poems and the paintings. Poems X and XI, where Audradus may have hoped the king would begin, are the least filled with singular imperatives in all of the First Bible. The first poem contains a surprisingly imperative tone, as the poet hammered insistently at the young and unreformed king. But as the poet came closer and closer to the end and to a reformed king, he achieved new distance and more respect, for this final Charles was fully Davidian and fully just. Master C's work, in particular, expresses the same dynamic states of transformation, since the subtlety of the Presentation miniature, with its circular simplicity and interpretive complexity, is offset by the directness of the message conveyed by the image of naked David dancing in triumphant humility. Indeed, there is a sense in which the Presentation miniature, with its David, Davidian guards, and four new psalm-singers set in a circular composition, is the David miniature transposed and refigured.

---

10. Koehler, *Die karolingische Miniaturen*, 1:2, pp. 71–85.

The final set of dedicatory verses, the one that faces the Presentation miniature, does not in fact call the king "Charles," but only "David" (XI.7, 35, 42) and "Caesar" (XI.15). The fusion of Carolingian and Old Testament kings that had been announced by the medallion portraits of DAVID REX IMPERATOR + and KAROLVS REX FRANCO<RVM> at the start of the First Bible, in its first full opening (fols. 1v–2r, figs. 2–3 and I, and frontispiece), had finally been achieved at the end, in the last opening of the manuscript (fols. 422v–423r, figs. 16–17 and IV). Indeed, it is not implausible to suppose that as Audradus refined the details of the First Bible's message late in 845 he returned to fol. 1v and either added the inscriptions to the two portrait medallions or directed their addition (fig. 37).[11] This would go some way toward explaining the rather cramped and irregular appearance of those inscriptions:[12] the truncation FRANCO on the Charles medallion, for instance, lacks an expansion sign and ends at an unusual place in the word. Moreover, some of the letters that form REX IMPERATOR in the upper medallion seem squashed and are scattered almost whimsically around the medallion. The *E* of *imperator,* for instance, is tucked behind David's neck, a placement reminiscent of the way Audradus buried his name in the angles of the *Liber Comitis* (fig. 22).

The unusual character of the medallion inscriptions suggests that they were probably lacking when the page was first made but were added like so much else—poem VI, the Apocalypse page vignettes, and the Presentation miniature itself—late in the hurried preparation of the precious volume. Once again the inspired inventions of the First Bible and Audradus broke new ground for Turonian illuminators, since the inscriptions of fol. 1v were imitated not long afterward in the Prüm Gospels (Berlin, Preußischer Kulturbesitz, theol. lat. fol. 733, fol. 23v). Those nearly identical medallions (fig. 37)[13] were most likely the product of the same painter but had been planned in advance with ample space left for inscription. Their more careful construction testifies to the ad hoc character of the inscriptions in the First Bible. The medallion portraits in the Prüm Gospels adorn the genealogy of Christ's descent from David that is described at the start of Matthew (Matt. 1). They decorate a page containing the words LIBER GENERATIONIS IHV XPI FILII D<AVI>D FILII

---

11. The rustic-capital letters of the inscriptions are not inconsistent with the letter forms of Audradus's signature on fol. 2r of the *Liber comitis* of Chartres (see fig. 22), but the evidence is too thin to allow us to conclude that the same hand inscribed both.

12. See chapter 2 n. 103 above. The arguments of Kahsnitz, "Ein Bildnis der Theophanau?," p. 120 and Diebold, "Nos quoque morem," p. 287 n. 57 may, therefore, be reconcilable, since the inscriptions may have been added after the pages were first prepared, but within the same general campaign of preparation.

13. See Koehler, *Die karolingischen Miniaturen,* 1:1, pp. 402–3; Schramm and Mütherich, *Denkmale der deutschen Könige und Kaiser,* p. 125; and Kahsnitz, "Ein Bildnis der Theophanau?," pp. 120–24 and plate 15.

ABRAHAM written in large gold letters. As in the First Bible two of the medallions in the Prüm Gospels have labels and two do not.[14] One bears the inscription DAVID REX IMPERATOR A<V>G<VSTVS>, which is almost identical to the First Bible's, and another, D<AVI>D IMPERATOR A<V>GVSTVS +, that is similar. The medallions in these two books, both produced at Saint-Martin at about the same time, served to highlight the royal lineage of their main subjects, in one case that of Charles the Bald and in the other that of Christ. Thus, David, in both cases, marked the royal beginning of great kings to come.

The inscription on the David medallion in the First Bible was also another example of the poet's epithetic extravagance. For David was all at once both king and emperor or, more properly, king-emperor. With this powerful inscription Audradus alerted his young royal reader, another KAROLVS REX FRANCO<RVM>, of the profound transformation that awaited him at the end of the First Bible. At the start of that book Charles was truly a young David in training, an emperor *in potentia,* a "spe induperator ovans" as the first poem called him (I.196). In the middle of the codex, he was exposed to and educated by the example of the divine humility of DAVID REX ET PROPHETA (figs. 8 and II), the very ideal the critical Synod of Ver had recommended to the king late in 844. But by the end of the great book, in the final dedicatory verse and in the Presentation miniature (figs. 17 and IV), he had finally become DAVID REX IMPERATOR. Charles the Bald was now none other than David himself.

The few short years after the Treaty of Verdun had ushered in, for Charles the Bald, a season of unending struggle and strident advice. Lupus of Ferrières was busily sending the king hortatory letters and importuning him about his own property losses, the synods of Thionville, Ver, and Meaux-Paris criticized royal inaction and abuse, and the Northmen sacked Paris in March 845 while Charles looked helplessly on. The message of the First Bible, seen in this light, was not particularly exceptional, for it matched the tenor of an anxious and critical age, but the vehicle for carrying that message certainly was. The canons' advice to Charles was put together in an extraordinarily stunning package; nothing quite like it had previously been seen by the Carolingians. That too would fit with what we know of the genius of Master C and the driving discontent of Audradus Modicus. Without the palpable dissatisfaction of both the poet and painters, the First Bible would have been a much less interesting book, had it been made at all.

---

14. Berlin, Staatsbibliothek Preußischer Kulturbesitz, theol. lat. fol. 733, fol. 80r, possesses other unlabeled medallions. See Kahsnitz, "Ein Bildnis der Theophanau?," plate 16. The medallion portraits on fol. 2r of the First Bible also remained without inscriptions: see figs. 3 and I.

But we would be naive if, in the end, we imagined that the twenty-two-year-old king would have understood all or even much of the deeper message of his magnificent new Bible. Its poetry and paintings are complex and difficult, indeed almost too clever, which was the result of a strategy of studied subtlety and indirection on the part of the painters and poet. The young king certainly cannot have understood it all. Moreover, the poet's pleas about proper appointments and the painter's depiction of Vivian and the back of the *pater* served as a commentary on a set of events that the canons had come at some level to accept, however unhappily. Charles had his own problems in 845, and he thought the promotion of Vivian would assist him in dealing with some of them,[15] and so at Christmas he proceeded with his plan to appoint Vivian the lay abbot of Saint-Martin. The negotiations that led to the renewal of the monastery's immunities and Vivian's appointment would probably have led him to believe that some of the canons, at least, would remain displeased with his action. But the king had also learned rather quickly in the early 840s how to deal with clerical disappointment by simply bypassing and disregarding the complaints of the aggrieved. Throughout these years, for instance, he successfully postponed answering Lupus's persistent call for the return of the alienated property of Ferrières.[16] In the wake of the sack of Paris in March 845 and the rout he had suffered at Ballon in November, Charles may not have been in the best of moods to heed the canons' loaded Bible when he arrived at Saint-Martin.

The special and exaggerated pleading of Audradus and the canons was in part a reflection of their great distance from him. How else could they reach Charles? Carolingian court protocol would not normally have allowed people such as Audradus to approach the king and plead a special case.[17] Only a present as sumptuous as the First Bible, the canons may have thought, could catch and hold the king's attention. And the poet essentially offered the king a contractual promise: if he learned and wisely followed the Bible and its divine guidance, he would not only achieve more in this life (I.53–54), as had Solomon (I.179–82), but he would secure repose with the saints (VI.30) and an everlasting reward in heaven (X.43–44). Moreover, the First Bible was a present that the king would carry away with him, so that its message stood some chance of achieving a longer-lasting effect. The canons' gift, therefore, was not just a Bible, but with its poems and paintings a very special vehicle for carrying the particular pleas of Saint-Martin straight to the king's heart.

---

15. See Nelson, *Charles the Bald,* pp. 142–49.

16. See Dutton, *Politics of Dreaming,* pp. 160–67.

17. See Stuart Airlie, "Bonds of Power and Bonds of Association in the Court Circle of Louis the Pious," in Godman and Collins, *Charlemagne's Heir,* pp. 194–95.

But Charles may, in the end, have paid little attention. He appointed Vivian, renewed the monastery's immunities, received the Bible, and then rode off to deal with other crises. Perhaps he even unloaded the First Bible on the cathedral of Metz in 869 not just because it had been replaced by other precious Bibles, but because its message was by then too particular and its hectoring tone unwelcome to a more mature king.[18]

For Audradus himself, 845 was something of a turning point in his career. He had feverishly worried over the Norse sacking of Paris and had received his prophetic vision from God of a penitential timetable for Carolingian society. He had labored over the First Bible throughout the summer and fall in the hope that there might be some way of leading a young king to his right and royal path. He had seen that unreformed king appoint a soon-to-be despised lay abbot. And he had watched the royal party ride away with the codex that carried his dreams of a biblically based royal reform. No wonder then that Audradus, frustrated in his efforts to transform a king and unable to become a bishop himself, soon took to full-blown prophetic dream and was consoled by angels and by Christ himself about the obduracy of wayward kings like Charles. Within six years of completing the First Bible, Audradus's prophecies of coming cataclysm for the Carolingians and their kings broke forth with a fury.

But behind him lay the First Bible of Charles the Bald; a book with a pronounced Audradan attitude, a program of royal education and reform, a set of poems that are richer and more revealing than normally supposed, and a set of sumptuous paintings that brought those themes to life. Audradus and the master painters of Saint-Martin of Tours had outdone themselves in creating the codex, but they had so fixed its message in time and place that it has not always spoken to us as fully as it should—but then we were never its intended audience.

---

18. See chapter 5 n. 50 above.

APPENDIX

A Reedition and First Translation of the Dedicatory Verses and *Tituli* of the First Bible of Charles the Bald

Commentary and Notes

I

Rex benedicte, tibi haec placeat biblioteca, Carle,
    Testamenta duo quod relegenda gerit.
Fert quod amas, quod amare velis, quod discere prosit,
    Quod capias, teneas quodque frequenter agas.
5   Corrigit, hortatur, reficit, castigat, honestat,
    Arguit, obsecrat, increpat, ornat, alit.
Eloquium, mores, studium componit et actus
    Estque cibus, potus, norma, via, arma, salus.
Interiora hominis promit, caelestia pandit,
10   Aptat utrumque sibi munere plena dei.
Et praesens transacta canit praesentia monstrans,
    Singula iura silet, singula sed resonat.
Instabilem quamvis stabilem post reddet amantem
    Se, si sit fassis deditus ille suis,
15   <Dedit>us ut verum credat quod continet omne,
    Inde sequens veri spes fiat aequa pii.
Dulcis amor nimium mox rite duobus in ollis
    Tertius incedat, iungat et ipse tria.
Iam subeant menti, fuerint quae noxia culpae,
20   Per lacrimas gemitus perque doloris opus.
Sic sic cum precibus quaeratur gratia Christi,
    Muneris est cuius quicquid in orbe boni.
Quid volumus, petimus, facimus, quid scimus, habemus,
    Inde datur, nostris, utile, non meritis.
25   Aut vanum aut vacuum aut nil aut laudabile nusquam,
    Spiritus auctor agens cui nisi sanctus eat:
Quo duce res adaperta patet, quae clausa latebat
    Antea, eo nutu hanc reserante suo;
Cum quo mens pollet, sine quo tenebrascit in umbris,
30   Ceu careat luce vel rationis ope.
Praeterea corpus minuant ieiunia digne
    Casta atque excubiae noctis ubique bene,
Quatinus ingenium concrescat acumine sensus,
    Cum caro putris abit, cum tenuata perit:
35   Carne fatigata, pedetemptim gliscit acumen
    Cordis et initium sumit habere datum.
Cos acuit ferrum, mihi crede, secare capillum,
    Radere seu pariter absque labore caput.
Nec minus afflictum iusto moderamine corpus
40   Intellectum effert, sanat et auget eum.
Denique dum superent gazae, dum larga facultas,
    Dum maiora inhies, dum utiliora roges,
Da quod egent miseris, miserum defensio fito:
    Pauper egenus inops te miserante boet.

I

O blessed King Charles, may this Bible please you,
    For it contains the two Testaments that should be read again and again.
It conveys what you love, what you should want to love, what it would be good to learn,
    What you should take up, believe in, and frequently do.
5   It corrects, admonishes, repairs, chastises, dignifies,
    Blames, implores, rebukes, adorns, nourishes.
It brings together eloquence, morals, study, and action;
    It is [our] sustenance, drink, rule, way, arms, and salvation.
It reveals the inner side of human beings, it discloses heavenly things,
10   [And], filled with God's gift, it adapts both to itself.
Being present here, it sings the past and shows the present;
    It says nothing about individual laws, but resonates with them.
He will make himself, however unsteady, a steady lover afterwards,
    If he is devoted to his confessions,
15   Devoted to believing the truth that contains everything,
    That from it should come the just hope of holy truth.
May the third, the sweetest love, soon advance as it should in those two,
    And may it bind the three together.
Now let those things, which were the pernicious parts of the crime, come to mind
20   Through the tears of lamentation and through the work of sorrow.
And so let the grace of Christ be sought with prayers,
    [For] whatever good there is in the world is his gift.
What we want, seek, do, what we know [and] have,
    Is, thus, something useful that is granted, not deserved.
25   The creator of life, to whom only the holy man may proceed,
    Never does anything vain or empty, or anything that is unpraiseworthy.
What was previously hidden is [now] opened up [and] revealed by him,
    Whose own will is unlocking this thing;
With him the mind is strong, without him it clouds over in shadows,
30   As if lacking light or the power of reason.
Let strict fasting henceforth appropriately weaken the body,
    And let vigilance keep careful check on it everywhere at night,
So that intelligence may, as far as possible, grow in the sharpness of its understanding,
    While rotting flesh passes away, while weakened flesh dies.
35   When the flesh is tired, the sharpness of the heart gradually increases
    And it strives to hold onto the opportunity it was given.
Believe me, a grindstone sharpens a sword [so that it can] divide a hair
    Or, likewise, easily shave a head.
Not less does a body beaten down with just control
40   Lift up, restore, and enrich understanding.
In fact, while riches and bountiful resources abound,
    While you covet greater things and while you ask for better things,
Give to the wretched what they need, become the protector of the wretched:
    Let the needy and defenseless poor proclaim that you are merciful.

45 Te miserante boet, vivat quicumque misellus:
        Te auxilium vitae postulat esse suae.
     Esto pater, frater, mater, soror, agnus utrinque,
        Debilibus spes, res gloria, summa dies.
     Dilige iustitiam: callis comitetur amicus
50   Iustitiae tecum primus ad omne bonum.
     Exalta, muni, custodi, collige, lauda,
        Sublima clerum seu venerare tuum.
     Aedibus et sacris meritos sic defer honores,
        Sedibus in sanctis ut merearis opem.
55 Tempore manduca, bibe, dormi, surge, labora:
        Sunt facienda suis omnia temporibus.
     His habitis aliisque bonis in nomine trino
        Cunctipotentis eri cum deitate sui,
     Huius ab initio thomi scrutarier oro
60   Eius scripta pia mente, opere, ore, fide.
     Hic fons, hic doctrina potens, hic flumina opima
        Eclesiae sanctae candidiora nive.
     Scilicet alticanori quinque volumina Moysi
        Iuncta nitent, mortem illius usque canant.
65 Iosue dux ducens consurgit fortis in armis
        In patriam populum, iure tenente locum.
     Septimus ecce liber censorum nomina fatur,
        Quorum Hebrea fuit sub ditione manus.
     Horum facta, genus, tempus, loca, bella, triumphi
70   Sunt inserta sibi debito honore sui.
     Femina quis sociata sedet Ruth nobilis una,
        Quam Iob eximiae consequitur fidei.
     Hunc imitare libens, quoniam patientia pura
        Extitit ac nobis magna figura fuit.
75 Quattuor et Regum libri bis octo Prophetas
        Ante, quibus David iungitur hymnificus:
     Hymnica psalmorum cecinit qui carmina David
        Plurima de Christo mystica saepe loquens.
     Prodiit ex cuius regali virgo Maria
80   Semine, quae peperit virgo beata deum.
     Pacificus Salomon nec non Sapientia iuxta,
        Tertius est Iesus continuatus eis.
     Post Paralypomenon, Ezras quoque sive Nemias,
        Hinc Hester, Iudith, et Tobias recinit.
85 Inclita bella deinde tonant Machabea quondam
        Pro lege ac patria proque salute data.
     Haec scriptura quidem breviter memorata vetusta
        Stat, quanquam modico rusticuloque stilo.
     Initiant testamenti praecepta novelli
90   Bis duo concordi famine sanctivomi:

45 Let every little wretch live [and] proclaim that you are merciful:
      He wants you to be the sustainer of his life.
    Be a father, brother, mother, sister, a lamb on both sides,
      [Be] the hope, glorious presence, [and] supreme day for the frail.
    Love justice: let the foremost friend of the path of justice
50   Accompany you to everything good.
    Exalt, protect, guard, unite, praise,
      Lift up and venerate your clergy.
    Confer deserved honors upon sacred churches,
      So that you might be worthy of help in holy places.
55 At the [appropriate] times eat, drink, sleep, rise up, [and] work:
      All things ought to be done in their own time.
    With these and other good things having been done in the threefold name
      Of the almighty master with his divine nature,
    I pray that his Scriptures [will] be examined from the start of this volume
60   With a pious mind, with effort, with speech, [and] with faith.
    For here is the fount, here the powerful teaching, here the overflowing streams
      Of the holy church [that are] whiter than snow.
    That is, the five joined volumes of high-singing Moses shine;
      They sing up until the death of that man.
65 The leader Joshua rises up mighty in arms, leads the people
      Into [their] homeland, [and] the law takes hold of that place.
    Behold, the seventh book proclaims the names of the judges,
      Under whose power the Hebrew host lived.
    The deeds, descent, times, places, wars, and victories of these people
70   Were inserted in it with their deserved distinction.
    There was one noble woman, Ruth, associated with them,
      Whom Job, a man of outstanding faith, follows.
    [It] is pleasing to imitate this man, since he possessed
      Outstanding patience and was a great model for us.
75 Four books of Kings [come] before sixteen [books of] Prophets,
      To which the hymnifier David is joined:
    David, who sang the rhythmical songs of the Psalms,
      Often speaks of the many mysteries of Christ.
    From his royal seed the Virgin Mary came forth;
80   This blessed Virgin gave birth to God.
    Peaceful Solomon [comes next] and then [the Book of] Wisdom,
      The third [book] following them is Jesus.
    After [comes] Chronicles, then Ezra or Nehemiah,
      And at this point Esther, Judith, and Tobit also sing.
85 Then the renowned Maccabean battles on behalf of the law,
      The land, and the salvation given [them] thunder forth.
    Indeed, this old Scripture stands briefly recalled [here],
      Although in a meager and rather rustic style.
    The teachings of the New Testament begin
90   With the fourfold harmonious speech of holy proclamation:

Mattheus, Marcus, Lucas, celsusque Iohannes
   In sensu parili dogma tonando dei.
Personae quorum variae, doctrina sed una,
   Unus utrisque tenor, una sequenda via.
95   Hi, quid vel quae, quanta seu vel qualiter egit
   A patre descendens natus, ubique docent.
Hinc hominis primo facies asscribitur, orsus
   Est quia sat domini caelitus ex genesi.
Forma leonis inest pulchre formata secundo,
100   Quod tetigit rura devia voce sua.
Rebus ait sacris siquidem quia tertius, inde
   Nunc olli species imprimitur vituli.
More aquilae quoniam transcendit sidera quartus,
   Eius ob id specimen sthematis ipse gerit.
105   Quis et apostolicos Lucas, quos edidit, actus
   Subdit, ubi totus instruitur populus.
Catholicae hinc septem redolent mirabile cartae,
   Format apostolicus quas operando stilus.
His haerent bis septem Pauli scripta deinde,
110   Ante lupina cui vox modo ovina micat.
Hoc concludit opus iam visio sancta Iohannis,
   Visio sancta satis ac memoranda nimis.
Haec nova rite cluit series subiuncta priori,
   Umbra prior quarum causaque posterior.
115   Ergo iter est duplex, utriusque effectus in uno,
   Quo tribuente datur scansio celsa poli.
Hic, quia divitiae aeternae vitalia mensae
   Implent omnino nectare perpetuo,
Hic, paradyse, tuus nitida ratione patescit
120   Multimodus fructus melliferaxque locus.
Hic sitiens potum, esuriens panem, anxius aeque
   Laetitiam inveniet, laetus et inde fiet.
Haec tamen in hoc mortali dum corpore quisque
   Degit habetque magis, plus ab amore velit.
125   Sic si ligna magis dentur, magis aestuat ignis,
   Sic mage vina sitit, prout mage quisque bibit.
Cum vero spes res fuerit, tunc pleniter horum
   Plenus amator erit, iam saciatus ero.
Ad quod haec domus, haec doctrina, haec semita tantum;
130   Mens instet vere sub deitatis ope.
In phisicis, logicis, etiam moralibus istic
   Omnia sunt, lector, in brevitate tibi.
Hic hic argentum, aurum, gemmae, vascula, vestes
   Et quicquid terrae carius esse valet.
135   Hic et lex preciosa—nihil preciosius illa
   Aut est aut viget, aut ridet oletve sacre—

Matthew, Mark, Luke, and heavenly John,
    In thundering forth the teachings of God, [speak] with the same meaning.
[They are] different persons, but [there is only] one teaching;
    The course in each [is] one, the way to be pursued is one.
95   These [evangelists] everywhere teach why or what, how much or in what way
    The one born and descending from [God] the Father acted.
Hence, the likeness of a man is applied to the first [evangelist],
    Because he properly began with the heavenly birth of the Lord.
The beautifully formed shape of the lion belongs to the second [evangelist],
100   Because he struck unfrequented fields with his own voice.
Indeed, because the third [evangelist] speaks of sacred things,
    The image of a calf is now assigned to that one.
The fourth [evangelist], since he rises above the stars like an eagle,
    On account of that bears the token of that theme.
105 And to these Luke adds the acts of the apostles, which he related,
    In which all peoples are taught.
At this point the seven Catholic letters, which the apostles
    Wrote with care, are wonderfully fragrant.
To these then adhere the fourteen letters of Paul,
110   From whom formerly a wolf's voice and now a sheep's voice flashes forth.
The holy vision of John now ends this work,
    A holy vision which is full and very memorable.
This New Testament, which is added to the earlier one, is rightly esteemed,
    [For] the earlier of the [Testaments] is a shadow, the later one its reason.
115 Thus the journey is double, [but] the achievement of both is in one,
    By means of its gift a heavenly ascent toward the stars is granted.
Here, because the riches of the eternal table fill [our] vital parts
    Completely with everlasting nectar,
Here, O paradise, your various fruits and honey-producing place
120   Are made manifest by shining reason.
Here the parched will find drink, the hungry will find bread,
    And the troubled too will find happiness, and after that will become happy.
Nevertheless, while each of us lingers in this mortal body
    And has more [material things], he should wish [to have] more from love.
125 For just as a fire grows larger if more wood is supplied,
    So one who drinks more wine will thirst for it that much more.
But when the hope [of salvation] is the thing [sought], then he will completely be
    The complete lover of these things, [and] I shall then be satisfied.
[To achieve] so great a thing this is the house, this is the teaching, this is the path;
130   Let the mind move forward with the assistance of the deity.
All things, O reader, in physics, logic, and even morals,
    Are in this [Bible] in summary form for you.
Right here there is silver, gold, precious gems, dishes, clothes
    And whatever else is held to be dearer to the world.
135 And here is the precious law, for nothing more precious than that law
    Either exists or flourishes, either ridicules or betrays the holy.

Iusta iubens, iniusta vetans, mala cuncta repellens,
    Omnibus inque bonis nobilitate potens.
Discidium, furor, ira, dolus, discordia, rixa
140   Consilio legis huius obire queunt.
Erudit indoctos, quosdam sapientibus aequans,
    Contribuit mediis dogma salutis ita.
Magna pluit, magnis disponit parvula, parvis,
    Est in utroque stilus iustitiae validus.
145 Notitiam Iesu praebet confessio munda,
    Extat ea en homini lex veneranda sibi.
Extat ea en homini lumen per compita mundi,
    Terribili voce lux et origo sui.
Artibus ingenuis praecellit dignius ista
150   Ars genere, eloquio, vi, ratione, vice.
Utile sive decens nec non perstringit honestum,
    Imbuit, exornat, instruit, armat, amat.
Haec aperit, totus postquam mutaverit orbis;
    Quid sit ibi eclesia mox reditura citim.
155 Terret ibi plures, quosdam demulcet et illic,
    Fixa futura notans nec dubitata quidem.
Ante tamen reserat clare primordia cosmi
    Et per quam illius esse fuit sophiam:
In primis caeli terraeque marisque creator,
160   Ipsius et natus, spiritus atque agius.
Huius ab amne fluit divina scientia late,
    Mundum pestiferis expolians tenebris:
Quoque modo quisquis caveat munitus ab armis
    Hostis perversi tela inimica nimis.
165 Quadrivium gignit virtutis nobile sane,
    Terrigenum mittit per quod in astra genus.
Haec quam multiplici sermone salubria semper
    Attrahit atque monet sive monendo iubet.
Haec iubet, atra fugat, dehinc fallacia pellit,
170   Vera superna cupit: haec facit, illa fugit.
Exul ab exilio dapibus solatur opimis,
    Cum legit aut relegit cumque relecta sapit.
Haec mala vile vehit coeuntia temporis huius
    Nec digna aeternis aestimat esse bonis
175 Aut ea, cerne, timet: tantum formidat amare,
    Quantum, ne non sit coetibus in superis.
Hic dominus loquitur, hic nos ei corde loquamur,
    Quo nil maius adit, nil vel adire potest.
Quisquis es instructus mundanis usibus hisce,
180   Quis Salomone opibus ditior emicuit?
Hoc concessa cui dives sapientia fecit,
    Regibus ac cunctis hunc ea praeposuit.

It orders just things, prohibits the unjust, drives away all evils,
 And rules with nobility in all good things.
Discord, madness, anger, sorrow, disagreement, quarrels,
140 [All these] can, with the counsel of this law, cease.
The law instructs the unlearned, making some equal to the wise,
 And so it imparts the teaching of salvation to all.
It rains great things upon the small [and] lays small things upon the great;
 For both it is the mighty pen of justice.
145 Pure confession supplies knowledge of Jesus,
 And, indeed, that law, to be venerated for itself, is visible to humans.
Indeed, that [law] is visible to humans, [it is] the light at the world's crossroads,
 With awesome voice, [it is] the light and beginning of itself.
That art in its origin, eloquence, force, reason, [and] fortune
150 Surpasses the liberal arts in worthiness.
[The Bible] draws together [everything] useful, proper, and virtuous;
 It inspires, adorns, teaches, defends, [and] loves.
It [will] reveal these things, as soon as the whole world will have changed;
 What the church should be will quickly return then.
155 [The Bible] then terrifies many people and thus it soothes some,
 Noting, indeed, things that will surely come to pass.
Nevertheless, it first clearly discloses the beginnings of the universe,
 And through whose wisdom it came to be.
In the beginning [there was] the creator of heaven, and earth, and sea,
160 And the one born of that one, and the Holy Spirit.
Divine knowledge flows far and wide from the river of this one [God],
 Freeing the world from destructive darkness.
Let anyone who is only protected by arms also beware
 The extremely hostile weapons of the wicked enemy.
165 [The Bible] truly begets a noble quadrivium of virtue,
 Through which it sends the earthborn race to the stars.
With rich and varied speech it always incites and advises,
 Or, by advising, commands these healthy things.
It commands these things, it banishes the darkness, then it drives away false things,
170 It desires heavenly truths: it causes these things, it spurns those.
An exile is consoled [on his return] from exile with rich feasts
 When he reads or rereads, and when he understands what he has reread.
He holds as cheap the gathering evils of this age
 And does not think them worthy [to be counted] among the eternal goods,
175 And notice that he fears those things: he is terrified to love such a thing,
 Lest he not be [placed] in the heavenly assembly.
Here the Lord speaks, here let us speak to him from the heart,
 Where one approaches nothing greater and can approach nothing greater.
You have been trained in these very worldly practices, [but]
180 Who was richer in glittering wealth than Solomon?
The rich wisdom granted to him brought this about,
 And that [wisdom] placed him before all kings.

Tu quoque, qui es humilis, prudens—intentio sancta—
    Se propter sophiam dilige, posce, cape.
185 An non plus id pro quo aliud fit, quam actio quae fit?
    Se tamen haec sophia plus nec habere quiit.
Ergo deus trinus pax seu sapientia vera:
    Ultra non laus nec versificalis apex.
Huic operi magno magnis te nisibus aptas,
190   Inclite rex Carole, lumine care mage.
Es splendor populi, lux mundi, gloria regni,
    Et bonitate prior nec pietate minor,
Nunc etiam cunctis praelatus iustius, alme,
    In genere humano nisu, opere, arte, fide:
195 Vi David, intellectu Salomon benedicto,
    In specie Ioseph, spe induperator ovans.
Qui mare, qui terram, qui totum continet orbem,
    Te conservet, amet, ducat adusque polum.
Sit tibi honor, pax, ordo, decus, patientia, regnum,
200   Prosperitas omnis et sine fine. Vale.

II

Exit Hieronimus Roma condiscere verba
    Hierusalem Hebraeae legis honorificae.

Eustochio nec non Paulae divina salutis
    Iura dat altithrono fultus ubique deo.

5 Hieronimus translata sui, quae transtulit, almus
    Ollis hic tribuit, quis ea conposuit.

III

Adam primus uti fingitur istic,
Cuius costa sacrae carpitur Evae.

    Christus Evam ducit Adae,
    Quam vocat viraginem.
5   Ast edant ne poma vitae,
    Prohibet ipse conditor.

    Suadet nuper creatae
    Anguis dolo puellae.
    Post haec amoena lustrans
10   Adam vocat redemptor.

Uterque ab umbris pellitur inde sacris
Et iam labori rura colunt habiti.

You also, you who are humble and prudent, and whose purpose is holy,
    Love, seek, and grasp wisdom for its own sake.
185 [But] is not that for which something is done greater than the action itself?
    Yet this wisdom was [still] not able to contain more than itself.
  Therefore, the threefold God [is] peace or true wisdom,
    Beyond which there is no praise or perfect poetry.
  You are, with great effort, adapting yourself to this great work,
190   O glorious King Charles, more precious than light.
  You are the brilliance of the people, the light of the world, the glory of the kingdom,
    First in goodness [and] the same in devotion,
  O dear one, even now, you are a more just ruler than all other humans
    In [your] effort, work, skill, and faith:
195 In power you are a David, in blessed intelligence a Solomon,
    In likeness a Joseph, in hope a triumphant emperor.
  Let him who encompasses the sea, the earth, and the entire world
    Preserve, love, and lead you to the heavens.
  May you have distinction, peace, order, adornment, patience, a kingdom,
200   And all prosperity without end. Farewell.

II

Jerome leaves Rome for Jerusalem to learn well
    The words of the honorable Hebrew law.

Strengthened everywhere by God, [who is] enthroned on high, he gives
    The divine laws of salvation to Eustochium and also to Paula.

5 Here bountiful Jerome himself bestows on these men the words passed down,
    Which he translated, [and] with them those he composed.

III

Adam, the first man, is fashioned there to thrive;
His rib is removed for the sacred Eve.

  To Adam Christ brings Eve,
  Whom [Adam] calls Woman.
5 But the creator himself prohibits them
  From eating the fruit [of the tree] of life.

  With deceit the serpent beguiles
  The newly created girl.
  After wandering around this delightful place,
10 The redeemer summons Adam.

Both of them are driven out of the sacred shelter
And now, accustomed to work, they farm the fields.

IV

Suscipit legem Moyses corusca
Regis e dextra superi, sed infra
Iam docet Christi populum repletus
    Nectare sancto.

V

Psalmificus David resplendet et ordo peritus
    Eius opus canere musica ab arte bene.

VI

Exulta, laetare satis, rex inclite David,
    Egregii voti compos ubique tui.
Carle, decus regni, fax cosmi, gloria cleri,
    Eclesiae fautor militiaeque decor,
5   En iam lecta tibi series transacta vetusta,
    Sed nova rite sequens ista legenda patet.
Cuius in initio clare primordia clara
    Mattheus domini concinit ex genesi.
Ceu leo per deserta fremit deserta minando
10   Vox tua, Marce, suo fulta perenne deo.
Mystica sacra sacre partes per quattuor orbis
    Fert studium Lucae lucis ab arce piae.
Ad genitum patris super aethera, celse Iohannes,
    Scandis et ex verbo verba colenda canis.
15   Eximii hi iaciunt late mysteria Christi,
    In sensu parili conveniuntque sibi,
Plusve minusve, vel aequa boant sua, sicque dehiscunt,
    Attamen effectus unus utrinque novus.
Hoc euangelium sanat, blanditur, honorat,
20   Castigat, reficit, munit, honestat, alit.
Hic modus effandi, hic virtus, hic actio munda,
    Hic cibus, hic potus, hic benedicta salus,
Hic vita, caritas, via, spes, verumque fidesque
    Seu bona cuncta simul consociata vigent:
25   His assuesce, diu haec meditare, haec dilige sive
    In sermone, opere haec habitare stude.
Rex bone, rex sapiens, rex prudens, rex venerande,
    Rex Carole alme, vale cum pietatis ope.
Det tibi sceptra patris Iesus, confirmet, adunet,
30   Proemia sanctorum ut merearis. Amen.

IV

Moses takes up the law
From the shimmering right hand of the heavenly king.
But below, now filled to the brim with the holy nectar,
    He teaches the people of Christ.

V

The psalm maker David shines brilliantly, and the company is
    Well trained in the art of music to sing his work.

VI

Rejoice, glorious King David, be completely happy,
    Having everywhere obtained your surpassing wish.
O Charles, glory of the kingdom, light of the universe, pride of the clergy,
    Patron of the church and adornment of the army,
5   Behold you have now read the Old Testament prepared for you,
    But the New one that rightly follows [it] reveals things fit to be read.
At the start of it Matthew clearly recites the clear beginnings
    From the birth of the Lord.
As the lion in threatening deserted places roars in deserted places,
10   Your voice, O Mark, is forever strengthened by its God.
The zeal of Luke from the pinnacle of pious light sacredly carries forth
    The sacred mysteries throughout the four parts of the world.
O celestial John, you climb above the ethereal heights to the one born of the Father,
    And from the Word you sing words fit to be cherished.
15 These exceptional [evangelists] lay out the mysteries of Christ far and wide,
    And with the same understanding they agree with each other,
More or less, or else they exclaim their own important things and so divide,
    Nevertheless, there is one result, [though] distinct in each.
This gospel cures, pleases, honors,
20   Chastises, repairs, protects, dignifies, nourishes.
Here is a way of speaking, here a virtue, here pure action,
    Here sustenance, here drink, here blessed salvation,
Here is life, charity, the way, hope, truth, and faith,
    Or all good things joined together [and] flourishing at once:
25 Become familiar with these things, ponder them for a long time, love them,
    And strive in speech and work to live them.
Good king, wise king, prudent king, venerable king,
    Kind King Charles, remain strong in the power of [your] devotion.
Let Jesus give to you, strengthen, and unite the scepters of [your] father,
30   So that you may merit the rewards of the saints.   Amen.

VII

Rex micat aethereus condigne sive prophetae
    Hic, euangelicae quattuor atque tubae.

VIII

Hic Saulum dominus caecat, hinc fundit in imam
    Terram, post trahitur caecus, ut ire queat.

Alloquitur Sabaoth Ananiam quaerere Saulum,
    Reddit et en olli lumina adempta sibi.

5   Quam bene, sancte, doces vitalia dogmata, Paule,
    Ex serie prisca caelitus atque nova.

IX

Septem sigillis agnus innocens modis
Signata miris iura disserit patris.

Leges e veteris sinu novellae
Almis pectoribus liquantur ecce,
5   Quae lucem populis dedere multis.

X

O decus, o veneranda salus, o splendide David,
    Rex Carole alme, vige cunctipotentis ope.
Gloria, laus, honor, omne decens, miseratio clemens,
    Pictus es hic studio artis ab eximio.
5   Sed quia tam haec rutilans species it, non nisi fecit
    Vera tui, omnis cui cedit imago viri;
Es prior effigie, sensu prior, artibus, odis
    His prior aut illis. Restat in ambiguis
En bene grata tuis haec ignoratio, David.
10   Fulget ubique locus laetitiae nimius.
Fert et eis manifeste, quod sis maior utrinque
    Magnis in cunctis, omnibus orbe viris.
Iusta iubes, iniusta vetas, mala cuncta recidis:
    Dictis seu factis is via sancta tuis.
15   Quae canis, ipse facis neque in his reprehensio sordet:
    Haut in utroque, nisi actio pura dei.
Eclesiae fotor, cleris populisque levamen,
    Ordinibusque sacris quam sacer ordo satis.
Per te pontifices pueros cum chrismate sancto

VII

The heavenly king gleams worthily, and the prophets [also shine]
  Here, and the four evangelical heralds.

VIII

Here the Lord blinds Saul, hence he lies on the low ground;
  Next the blind man is led, in order to go forward.

The Lord of hosts tells Ananias to seek out Saul,
  And, behold, he restores to that one the vision he had taken away.

5 How well, Saint Paul, you teach the vital lessons of life
  From the heavenly Old and New Testaments.

IX

The innocent lamb examines the laws of the Father
Sealed with seven seals by remarkable means.

Behold, new laws from the bosom of the old
Are clarified by nourishing spirits,
5 Which have given light to many peoples.

X

O glory, O venerable salvation, O brilliant David,
  Kind King Charles, flourish with the power of the Almighty.
Fame, praise, honor, everything fine, gentle mercy,
  You are depicted here by means of an exceptional application of art.
5 Coloring these things so, an outline emerges, but not unless it represents
  True aspects of you, to whom every image of a man is inferior.
You are superior to the portrait and to the perception,
  Superior to those arts or to these poems. Notice well, David,
That this understandable ignorance [of you] persists in your unclear [features].
10 Everywhere a state of exceeding joy shines forth.
And it is abundantly clear to them that you are, on both sides, greater
  Than the great in all things and greater than all the men in the world.
You order just things, you prohibit the unjust, you cut away all evils:
  You proceed along a holy way in your speech and deeds.
15 What you sing, you yourself do, and in these things blame does not arise;
  Nor is there in either anything except the pure action of God.
[You are] the patron of the church, a solace to the clergy and people,
  And to the sacred orders what [each] sacred order [needs].
Through you bishops are rightly able to renew children

20   Nomine de Christi rite novare queunt.
     Quis tribuis meritos merito deitatis honores,
         Dum te subdis eis corde, opere, ore, fide.
     Scis, ideo servas, quod portio debeat ire
         Prima tui domini, qui dedit esse tibi.
25   Pauper, egenus, inops, vidua, orfanus, anxius, orbus,
         His aliisque datus es pater atque cibus.
     Iudicii volvis totiens extrema diei
         Quodque putris caro sis ac periturus homo.
     Propterea es iustus, prudens, fortis, moderatus,
30   Semper larga manus et pietatis opus.
     Quis pluviae guttas, numerum quis novit harenae?
         Te laudare potest pleniter aut merite?
     Ceu plumbum argento, aes auro, rus sidere distat,
         Gemma vitro, scandit plus tua fama modo.
35   Ante Brito stabilis fiet vel musio muri
         Pax bona, quam nomen desit honosque tuum.
     Iam iam pro tanto, pro tali rege profusas
         Orbis agat mecum totus abunde preces:
     Ut valeat, vigeat, vivat per saecula felix,
40   Utatur pace prosperitate fruens,
     Regnum habeat, teneat, dilatet, fulciat, ornet,
         Addat ei iura legis ab arce pia,
     Insuper his habitis praeclare in tempore mortis
         Perpetuam requiem hic mereatur. Amen.

XI

     Haec etiam pictura recludit, qualiter heros
         Offert Vivianus cum grege nunc hoc opus,
     Ante ubi post patrem primi: Tesmundus amandus,
         Sigualdus iustus, summus Aregarius.
5   Quis tribus est probitas, pietas, verumque fidesque,
         Cetera honesta quoque consociata simul;
     Quartus his iunctus haeret, sanctissime David,
         Qui te vi tota mentis amore colit.
     Hi proni tibimet domino de parte beati
10   Martini ac fratrum ecce librum tribuunt.
     Cuius honore rogant: placeat, laudetur, ametur,
         Scrutetur, prosit, auxilietur, alat.
     In quo nil aliud quam fratrum sola voluntas
         Ex, tua quas, villis, iussio reddiderat.
15   Reddis eas, Caesar, Martini pro veneratu
         Domni ceu precibus semper amabilibus
     Perpetui nec non Briccii tutamine sancti
         Proque aliis reliquis, o paradise, tuis,

20   With holy oil in the name of Christ.
    On them you worthily bestow honors as deserved because of God,
        While you submit yourself to them in your heart, labor, speech, [and] faith.
    You know [and] thus maintain that first fruits of your Lord,
        Who gave being to you, ought to go [to them].
25 The poor, destitute, weak, widowed, orphaned, troubled, [and] blind,
        To these and to others you were set up as father and sustenance.
    You very often ponder the last things of judgment day
        And that you are [but] rotting flesh and a human soon to die.
    Thus you are just, prudent, strong, and moderate,
30   Always a generous giver and an example of devotion.
    Who has counted the drops of rain [or] the grains of sand [on the sea-shore]?
        Can [anyone] praise you fully or as you deserve?
    As lead is far from silver, bronze from gold, earth from sky,
        [And] gem from glass, your fame now rises even more.
35 The Bretons will become settled, or the cat peaceful toward the mouse,
        Before your renown and honor fail.
    At this very time, for such a great man and a king of such excellence,
        Let the whole world join with me in abundantly offering up overflowing prayers:
    That he may live happily, powerfully, and vigorously throughout the ages,
40   That he may possess and enjoy peace and prosperity,
    That he may hold, contain, extend, strengthen, and embellish the kingdom,
        That he may lay the heavenly rules of the law upon it,
    And, besides obtaining these things, that at the moment of death
        He may win certain and everlasting rest.   Amen.

XI

This painting actually shows how the noble warrior
    Vivian with the company now presents this book,
In which the most eminent [brothers] are before [and] after the father:
    Beloved Tesmundus, just Sigualdus, supreme Aregarius.
5   In those three there is wisdom, devotion, truth, and faith,
    And also the other virtues joined together at the same time.
A fourth one, O most holy David, is joined to and follows them;
    He cherishes you with all the power [and] love of his mind.
Behold, these humble ones are bestowing the book upon you alone, lord,
10   On behalf of blessed Martin and the brethren.
In his honor they ask: may it please, be praised, be loved,
    Be examined, be beneficial, aid, [and] nourish.
In which [book] there is nothing other than the good-will alone of the brothers,
    Over the lands which your command had returned.
15 You are returning them, Caesar, in veneration of Lord Martin,
    As if [in answer] to the constant and loving prayers of Perpetuus
And also in defense of Saint Brice,
    And on behalf of your other saints, O paradise,

Immo magis pro te, Iesu salvator amate,
20   Sis ut ei vita denique perpetua.
Pro famulis nobis etiam oratoribus aptis,
    Quos sitis obruerat, frigus et atra fames,
O rex, o reverende, fiat renovatio fixa
    A mercede data sive salute tua.
25 Praevaleat regale decus superetque potestas
    Regum de more, qui coluere bonum.
Praeceptum genitoris, avi, proavi renovasti:
    Hoc stet, hoc maneat, hoc nec obire queat.
Quod tua sancta manus nuper firmavit honeste
30   Praecepti serie, prorsus eat stabile.
Quid facient alii, regis mutatio tanti
    In facto hoc fuerit si hoste vigente malo?
I procul atque procul, scelus, hoc crudele per omne:
    Tu prope, iustitia, vince nociva fuga.
35 Quas laudes tibi, quas grates, quae carmina, David,
    Quod par dulce melos vox, lira, corda canet?
Nos, siquidem psalmos, missas, speciale precamur,
    Psallemus pro te, coniuge, prole pie.
Sic nostri vere post nos quicunque futuri
40   Assiduas fundent multiplicesque preces.
Sint tibi spes, virtus, lumen, victoria, Christus,
    Pax, laus continue, rex bone David. Ave.

But rather more for you, Jesus, [our] beloved savior,
20   So that you may in the end be everlasting life to him.
On behalf of the servants bound to us and also for [our] suppliants,
        Over whom thirst, cold, and foul hunger had fallen,
Let this renewal, O king, O venerable one, given in reward
        Or for your own salvation, become permanent.
25   May royal glory dominate and may the power of kings,
        Who have cherished the good, as usual prevail.
You have renewed the charter of [your] father, grandfather, [and] great-grandfather:
        Let this stand, let this remain, let this have the power to endure.
Your holy hand has newly and publicly confirmed that [renewal]
30   In the sequence of the charter; let it remain absolutely firm.
What will others be able to do, [even] with an evil enemy flourishing,
        If the agreement of so great a king was expressed in this act?
Keep off, far off, crime, this cruel thing [found] everywhere:
        You, O justice, being so near, drive it into harmful flight.
35   What praises, what thanks, what songs, O David,
        Will [this] sweet tune, sweet voice, lyre, and strings sing for you?
Since we pray specially in psalms and in masses,
        We shall devoutly sing psalms for you, [your] wife, [and your] child.
In this way those of us who will come afterwards
40   Will bring forth constant and bountiful prayers [for you].
May there be hope, virtue, light, victory, Christ,
        Peace, and praise for you without end, good King David. Be well!

Commentary and Notes

I

1   *biblioteca,* that is, a Bible that might contain the Old Testament, the New Testament, or both. See Du Cange, *Glossarium mediae et infimae Latinitatis,* 1:650. Both Alcuin, *carmen* 65.1.3, ed. Dümmler, *MGH PLAC* 1:283 and Theodulf, *carmen* 42.1, ed. Dümmler, *MGH PLAC* 1:540, called pandects "bibliothecae."

9   *interiora hominis,* cf. Rom. 7:22.

15   *<dedit>us,* Traube's expansion based on earlier readings. Only *-us* is visible in the manuscript today.

15–18   Since "spes" is found at I.16, it is likely that the trinitarian imagery suggested by the "tertius" at I.18 is "fides," implied by "credat" at I.15, "spes" at I.16, and "caritas" at I.17–18. See 1 Cor. 13:13. Charity as the highest of the three virtues mentioned by Paul fits the thematic purpose of the poet and is repeated at VI.23.

17   *dulcis amor,* see Alcuin, *carmen* 46.3, ed. Dümmler, *MGH PLAC* 1:259, "dulcis amor patris" and 55.1.1, p. 266, "dulcis amor"; Audradus 9.234, ed. Traube, *MGH PLAC* 3:97 "dulcis amor patris."

19–20   Cf. Gen. 3–4, fig. 6, and First Bible III.

20   *gemitus* in the codex. Traube, without comment, printed "genitus."

        per lacrimas gemitus, cf. Virgil, *Aeneid* 10.465: "gemitum lacrimasque."

24   *non meritis,* Audradus 5.113, ed. Traube, *MGH PLAC* 3:76 and 8.*prol.*26, p. 89.

26   *spiritus auctor,* Audradus 1.36, ed. Traube, *MGH PLAC* 3:742.

        eat, a letter after *e* in the codex was painted over.

32   *excubiae noctis,* in the Turonian Virgil (Bern, Burgerbibliothek 165, p. 95) at *Aeneid* 4.201, "excubias" was glossed as "vigiliae nocturnae." Audradus 12 (*Liber revelationum*).6, ed. Traube, "Roma nobilis," p. 381, noted that he had himself suffered from "illusiones nocturnas." Cf. 2 Kings 11:7.

34   *caro putris,* cf. X.28.

37   *mihi crede,* Ovid, *Ars amatoria* 2.259, 3.653.

37–38   See Prov. 27:17. See also Traube's rethinking of this sentence at *MGH PLAC* 3:752.

39   *Nec minus,* Audradus 9.184, ed. Traube, *MGH PLAC* 3:96 and 11.341, p. 117.

40   *effert* in the codex. Traube, without remark, printed "offert."

        eum, that is, "intellectum."

43   *fito* is a future imperative for *fio* formed on the model of *sum,* thus *esto.* See *Thesaurus Linguae Latinae,* vol. 6 (Leipzig, 1912–1926), col. 84.

47   *agnus,* that is, savior. Cf. IX.1. The lamb here may be a reference to the Lamb of God shown in the Apocalypse miniature; this was a christological connection also made in the Codex Aureus of Saint-Emmeram in which Charles (on fol. 5v) sits across from the Lamb of God (fol. 6r).

        utrinque would seem to refer to the two paired sexes in the line: "pater, frater" and "mater, soror."

48   *summa dies,* Virgil, *Aeneid* 2.324; Lucan, *Bellum civile* 7.195.

49–50   *amicus primus,* that is, Christ.

50   *primus ad omne bonum,* Theodulf, *carmen* 28.102, ed. Dümmler, *MGH PLAC* 1:496.

56   Cf. Eccles. 3:1–14.

57   *nomine trino,* Alcuin, *carmen* 65.4a.17, ed. Dümmler, *MGH PLAC* 1:284; Audradus, *Proemium.* 3, ed. Traube, *MGH PLAC* 3:741; and Hincmar, *carmen* 2.23, ed. Traube, *MGH PLAC* 3:410.

58   *eri,* an *h* before "eri" was painted over in the codex. Traube, without remark, printed "heri."

59   *scrutarier,* a paragogic expansion of *scrutari.* See Virgil, *Aeneid* 11.242, "farier," and Horace, *Ep.* 2.2.148, "faterier," for similar usages.

60   *ore,* that is, with assent or praise.

61   *Hic fons,* cf. Alcuin, *carmen* 66.3, ed. Dümmler, *MGH PLAC* 1:285: "Hic est fons vitae"; I.161; and also "Sigilai Versus ad Hlotharium imperatorem," ed. Dümmler, *MGH PLAC* 2:671: "Quattuor hic rutilant uno de fonte fluentes."

62   *eclesiae sanctae,* Theodulf, *carmen* 76.27, ed. Traube, *MGH PLAC* 3:577.

65   *fortis in armis,* Lucan, *Bellum civile* 5.345; Alcuin, *carmen* 9.159, ed. Dümmler, *MGH PLAC* 1:233 and 62.117, p. 279.

69   Cf. Alcuin, *carmen* 69.103, ed. Dümmler, *MGH PLAC* 1:290.

71–72   For a similar linking of Ruth and Job at this point, see Alcuin, *carmen* 68.3, ed. Dümmler, *MGH PLAC* 1:287 and 69.106–7, p. 290.

73–74   *patientia pura . . . magna figura,* see Jerome, "Ad Paulinum Presbyterum," ed. De Bruyne, *Préfaces,* p. 3, and *epistola* 53, ed. Labourt, *Saint Jérôme, Lettres,* 3:17.7: "Iob exemplar patientiae."

76   *David hymnificus,* cf. V.1: "Psalmificus David."

77   *hymnica psalmorum cecinit qui carmina David,* cf. Alcuin, *carmen* 69.112–13, ed. Dümmler, *MGH PLAC* 1:290, "David, Ymnica qui cecinit psalmorum carmina vatis."

81   *Salomon* here includes Proverbs, Ecclesiastes, and the Song of Songs.

82   *Iesus,* that is Jesus, son of Eleazar, son of Sirach, the putative author of the Book of Sirach or Ecclesiasticus.

83   *quoque sive,* the poet here means to include Nehemiah as part of the book of Ezra, as it is in the First Bible and the Turonian tradition.

84   Judith and Tobit actually occur in reverse order in the First Bible at fols. 301ra–305rb and fols. 297vb–300vb respectively. Fischer thought this reversal of order in the poem should not be taken as a description of the actual order of contents in the Bible, but merely as a poetic device: see Fischer, *Lateinische Bibelhandschriften,* pp. 281–82. For an even more scrambled order of books in a poetic list, see Alcuin, *carmen* 69.143–44, ed. Dümmler, *MGH PLAC* 1:291.

85   *inclita belli,* cf. Alcuin, *carmen* 9.67, ed. Dümmler, *MGH PLAC* 1:230.

90   *sanctivomi,* cf. Audradus 5.173, ed. Traube, *MGH PLAC* 3:78, "carcere flammivomo."

91   Cf. Theodulf, *carmen* 41.87, ed. Dümmler, *MGH PLAC* 1:534.

96   *a patre descendens natus,* cf. Audradus 1.38, ed. Traube, *MGH PLAC* 3:742, "A patre procedens et nato."

97–98   See Matt. 1. The theme is repeated at First Bible VI.7–8. Cf. also Theodulf, *carmen* 41.89–90, ed. Dümmler, *MGH PLAC* 1:535.

99   Cf. VI.9–10.

100   *rura devia,* cf. Audradus 5.192, ed. Traube, *MGH PLAC* 3:78, "per devia vallis." See also Mark 1:3, Luke 3:4; John 1:23: "Vox clamantis in deserto."

103   See VI.13–14.

104   *sthematis,* that is "themas, -tis."

105   *quos* in the codex. Traube, without remark, printed "quod."

107–8   *cartae* refers to the seven Catholic letters, which in the First Bible (fols. 378r–382v) precede the letters of Paul (fols. 383r–415r).

110   The poet here combines two images: both the transformation of Saul the rapacious persecutor into Paul the pious Christian and, with the verb "micat," the flash of blinding light that brought about his conversion. See Acts 9:3–30, 22:6–21, 26:12–18.

114   The poet's image here may be that just as the sun, a christological symbol, casts a shadow, so Christ causes and accounts for the shadow or outline of the Old Testament.

118   *nectare,* cf. IV.4.

119   *paradyse,* see XI.18.

124   *ab amore,* cf. I.17.

125–26   Cf. Theodulf, *carmen* 28.347–52, ed. Dümmler, *MGH PLAC* 1:502.

127   *spes,* that is, "spes salutis."

128   *saciatus,* that is, "satiatus."

133   Cf. 1 Cor. 3:12 and Zach. 14:14.

135   *lex preciosa . . . illa,* cf. Theodulf, *carmen* 41.151, ed. Dümmler, *MGH PLAC* 1:536.

137   *iusta . . . cuncta,* cf. X.13 and Theodulf, *carmen* 41.149, ed. Dümmler, *MGH PLAC* 1:536.

138   *nobilitate potens,* Ovid, *Metamorphoses* 13.22 and Venantius Fortunatus, *carmen* 6.1a.38, ed. F. Leo, *MGH Auctores Antiquissimi* (Berlin, 1881), 4:1, p. 130.

142   *dogma salutis,* cf. Audradus 5.11 and 233, ed. Traube, *MGH PLAC* 3:73 and 79, "dona salutis" and "verba salutis."

143   Cf. Theodulf, *carmen* 41.167, ed. Dümmler, *MGH PLAC* 1:536.

144   *stilus,* literally a stylus or straight stick used to write on wax tablets: cf. also I.108. See Richard H. Rouse and Mary A. Rouse, "The Vocabulary of Wax Tablets," *Harvard Library Bulletin,* new series 1 (1990): 15–16. The word might also stand for "style" or "composition," as the poet seems to have used it at I.88.

145   *confessio munda,* cf. Audradus 10.119, ed. Traube, *MGH PLAC* 3:104, "confessio pura." Cf. also Heb. 3:1.

147   *per compita mundi,* that is, the cross. See also Theodulf, *carmen* 41.143, ed. Dümmler, *MGH PLAC* 1:536.

148   *lux et origo sui,* cf. Theodulf, *carmen* 41.152, ed. Dümmler, *MGH PLAC* 1:536: "lux et origo boni."

149   *artibus ingenuis,* cf. Ovid, *Fasti* 3.6, "ingenuis artibus"; Theodulf, *carmen* 36.24, ed. Dümmler, *MGH PLAC* 1:528.

155   *quosdam* in the codex. Traube, without remark, printed "quodam."

159   *in primis,* cf. Gen. 1:1.
           caeli terraeque marisque, Audradus 9.204, ed. Traube, *MGH PLAC* 3:97; 11.187, p. 113; 10.148, p. 105; Virgil, *Aeneid* 1.598: "terraeque marisque."

162   *expolians* in the codex. Traube, without remark, expanded to "exspolians," but in the Vulgate *expolians* and *spolians* are the standard forms. There is, in fact, no use of *exspolians* in the Vulgate. Normally, as in 1 Sam. 18:4 and elsewhere, *expoliare* means "to rob," but in Col. 2:15 and 3:9 Paul speaks of Christ and Christians removing the forces of darkness.

163   *ab armis,* Virgil, *Aeneid* 10.46, 12.844.

164   *hostis perversi,* cf. XI.32, "hostis malus."
           tela inimica, Virgil, *Aeneid* 11.809.

166   *terrigenum,* cf. Audradus 5.235, ed. Traube, *MGH PLAC* 3:79 and 5.358, ed. Traube, *MGH PLAC* 3:83.

168   *monet* in the codex. Traube, without remark, printed "movet."

170   *cupit* in the codex. Traube, without remark, printed "capit."
           haec . . . illa, for a similar construction, see X.7–8.

182   *praeposuit* in the codex. Traube, without remark, printed "proposuit."

187   *pax,* cf. Eph. 2:14.
           sapientia vera, Alcuin *carmen* 37.17, ed. Dümmler, *MGH PLAC* 1:252 and 69.31, p. 288.

191   *splendor populi,* cf. Ps. 89:17 and Isa. 60:3.
           lux mundi, John 8:12, 9:5; Matt. 5:14, all references to Christ; cf. "fax cosmi" at VI.3 below.
           gloria regni, Audradus 11.366, ed. Traube, *MGH PLAC* 3:118. Cf. also Ps. 144:11 in which the psalmist speaks of the "gloria regni" of the Lord and 1 Par. 29:25 in which God grants the "gloria regni" to Solomon.

192   *nec pietate minor,* Venantius Fortunatus, *carmen* 4.26.24, ed. Leo, *MGH Auctores Antiquissimi* 4.1:95.

195–96   See Theodulf, *carmen* 25.29–30, "Ad Karolum regem," ed. Dümmler, *MGH PLAC* 1:484:

> Nomine reddis avum, Salomonem stemmate sensus,
>   Viribus et David, sive Ioseph specie.

See also *carmen* 76.13–14, p. 577, which contains a variation on the above, but which is probably not a poem by Theodulf.

196   *Ioseph,* see Gen. 37:3–4. On Joseph as young and the victim of fraternal hostility, see *Carmen de Timone comite* 39–40, ed. Dümmler, *MGH PLAC* 2:121; Milo, *De sobrietate* 1.450–52, ed. Traube, *MGH PLAC* 3:629; Hrabanus Maurus, *epistola* 15, ed. Dümmler, *MGH Epistolae* 5:406.23–26. *ovans,* cf. Audradus 5.72, ed. Traube, *MGH PLAC* 3:75.

198   *te conservet,* Alcuin, *carmen* 110.18.12, ed. Dümmler, *MGH PLAC* 1:343.

200   *et sine fine vale,* cf. Audradus 5.61, ed. Traube, *MGH PLAC* 3:75, "et sine fine valeto."

II

2   *honorificae,* see Traube, *MGH PLAC* 3:752 on this reading. The codex has an E-caudata, which is partially obscured by a wrinkle in the parchment.

3   *Eustochio nec non Paulae,* see the preface of Jerome to the Book of Daniel, ed. De Bruyne, *Préfaces,* p. 126.24–26: "Vnde obsecro uos, O Paula et Eustochium, fundatis pro me preces ad dominum: ut quamdiu in hoc corpusculo sum, scribam aliquid gratum uobis, utile ecclesiae, dignum posteris"; Jerome, preface to the minor prophets, ed. De Bruyne, p. 135: "O Paula et Eustochium"; and *epistola* 54, ed. Labourt, *Saint Jérôme, Lettres,* 3:25.18–19: "Taceo de Paula et Eustochio, stirpis uestrae floribus . . ."

5   *translata·s ui,* thus in the codex, with a dot placed after "translata" to indicate proper word separation. Traube printed "translata sibi," which is an easier and perhaps preferred reading, but in his later corrections, *MGH PLAC* 3:752, noted the codex reading.

5   *translata* the implied referent is "uerba," but here the poet plays with the double sense of "transfero" as the Scriptures are physically passed to him and which he then translates and physically hands over to others.

6   *conposuit* in the codex. Traube, without remark, printed "composuit."
      quis, that is, "quibus."

III

The same set of verses is to be found in the Moutier-Grandval Bible, London, British Library, Addit. 10546, fol. 5v.

3–4   See Gen. 2:22–23.

IV

The same set of verses is to be found in the Moutier-Grandval Bible, London, British Library, Addit. 10546, fol. 25v.

V

1   *ordo,* that is, as labeled in the illumination, the musicians ASAPH, AEMAN, HEMAN, IDITHVN, and the guards CERETHI ET PHELETHI. Asaph, Aeman, Aethan, and Idithun are named as David's musicians and singers at 1 Par. 15:19, 16:7, 16:42, 25:6; 2 Par. 35:15. For the two

families of guards, the Cerethi and Phelethi, see 2 Sam. 8:18, 15:18, and 20:7. Above David occurs the inscription DAVID REX ET PROP<HETA>. The four virtues PRVDENTIA, IVSTITIA, FORTITVDO, and TEMPERANTIA are so labeled in the corners of the illumination.

VI

3   *fax cosmi* can be taken as the equivalent of "lux mundi" at I.191. For another instance of "cosmi," see I.157.
        gloria cleri, Alcuin, *carmen* 43.7, ed. Dümmler, *MGH PLAC* 1:254.

5   *series,* that is, Testament. Cf. also I.113 and VIII.6.

7–8   Matt. 1–2.

7–14   Cf. I.97–104.

9   *per deserta,* see Mark 1:3: "Vox clamantis in deserto."

11   *mystica sacra,* Ovid, *Heroides* 2.42.
        partes emended here from "partis," which occurs in the codex and in Traube's edition.
        partes per quattuor orbis may refer to Luke's commitment to spread the Gospel as revealed in his two prologues at Luke 1:1–4 and Acts 1:1–2 and the history of the diffusion of the faith related in the Acts of the Apostles.

12   *lucis ab arce piae,* cf. X.42: "ab arce pia."

13   *super aethera,* Virgil, *Aeneid* 1.379; Ovid, *Fasti* 3.347; Lucan 1.678; Theodulf, *carmen* 12.31, ed. Dümmler, *MGH PLAC* 1:467; Audradus 9.94, ed. Traube, *MGH PLAC* 3:93 and 9.330, p. 100.

16–18   Cf. I.91–94.

17   *plusve minusve,* cf. Ovid, *Fasti* 5.110, 6.274.

18   *effectus unus,* Ovid *Amores* 1.8.54.

21   *actio munda,* cf. X.16: "actio pura" and I.185, "actio."

23   *Hic vita caritas,* but in the codex the scribe wrote and corrected with diacritical marks: HICCA"VITA RITAS.
        Two sets of theological threes are interspersed in this line: "vita," "via," "veritas" of John 14:6 and "caritas," "spes," "fides" of 1 Cor. 13:13. For the latter triad, see also I.15–18.

24   *bona cuncta simul consociata vigent,* cf. Theodulf, *carmen* 71.22, ed. Dümmler, *MGH PLAC* 1:561, "bona cuncta simul consociata manent."
        simul consociata, cf. XI.6.

27   *rex sapiens,* Charles the Bald, student of Walahfrid Strabo and soon to be the patron of Eriugena and a court school, was especially styled a wise king by his poets and clerics. In Baltimore, Walters Art Gallery, Ms. 2, fol. 60v, one encounters, for instance, the elegiac couplet:

     Perlege, rex sapiens, sophiae pia dogmata sanctae
        Sicque fidem firma pectore et ore tuo.

     The reference to *rex sapiens* may well refer to Charles: see Édouard Jeauneau, "Un 'dossier' carolingien sur la création de l'homme (Genèse I,26–III,24)," *Revue des Études augustiniennes* 28 (1982): 119–20, rpt. in Jeauneau, *Études érigéniennes,* pp. 567–68.

28   *cum pietatis ope,* cf. X.30: "pietatis opus."

29   *sceptra patris,* that is, Louis the Pious. Although royal portraits almost always show the king holding but one rod, either the long or short scepter, the poets almost always speak of *sceptra*. These plural *sceptra* were probably meant to represent the many kingdoms a king held. See the verses of the Codex Aureus of Saint-Emmeram IV.8 "sceptra tenendo sua," ed. Traube, *MGH PLAC* 3:252 and ed. Dutton and Jeauneau, "Verses of the 'Codex Aureus,'" p. 92, and rpt. in Jeauneau, *Études érigéniennes,* p. 610.

VII

The same set of verses is to be found in the Moutier-Grandval Bible, London, British Library, Addit. 10546, fol.352v.

2   *tubae,* on these instruments and the meaning of the word in the ninth century, see Bullough, *Carolingian Renewal,* pp. 242–44. See also Ps. 46:6 and Theodulf, *carmen* 41.143, ed. Dümmler, *MGH PLAC* 1:536, "Haec tuba terribilis mugit per compita mundi," which reflects Virgil, *Aeneid* 9.503.

VIII

1–2   Cf. Acts 9:1–9.

2   *post trahitur caecus,* see Acts 9:8: "Ad manus autem illum trahentes, introduxerunt Damascum." *ut ire queat,* that is, for the blind man to be led through the doorway seen in the illumination. See also John 10:2: "qui autem intrat per ostium, pastor est ovium."

3   Cf. Acts 9:10–18.
       Sabaoth, also used by Audradus at 11.472, ed. Traube, *MGH PLAC* 3:121.
       Ananiam corrected in the codex from ANNANIAM when the second *N* was painted over.

4   *lumina adempta,* cf. Virgil, *Aeneid* 3.658 and Ovid, *Tristia* 4.4.45.

6   *serie prisca atque nova,* as in I.113 and VI.5, *series* here is a synonym for Testament.

IX

The same set of verses is to be found in the Moutier-Grandval Bible, London, British Library, Addit. 10546, fol. 449r. For a close analysis of this poem, see Jean Croquison, "Une vision eschatologique carolingienne," *Cahiers archéologiques* 4 (1949): 120–26.

1–2   *septem sigillis . . .signata,* cf. Rev. 5:1; Jerome, "Ad Paulinum Presbyterum," ed. De Bruyne, *Préfaces,* p. 2, and *epistola* 53, ed. Labourt, in *Saint Jérôme, Lettres,* 3:13.28: "Liber in apocalypsi septem sigillis signatus ostenditur."

2   *iura* in the codex. Traube, without remark, printed "iussa."

5   *quae,* the antecedent would seem to be "leges" rather than "pectora."

X

1   *O decus,* Virgil, *Georgics* 2.40 and *Aeneid* 11.508; Ovid, *Fasti* 6.810, *Tristia* 5.2.49; Alcuin, *carmen* 7.21, ed. Dümmler, *MGH PLAC* 1:226; Theodulf, *carmen* 13.1, ed. Dümmler, *MGH PLAC* 1:467.

3   *gloria, laus, honor,* cf. 2 Pet. 1:17; Theodulf, *carmen* 69.1, ed. Dümmler, *MGH PLAC* 1:558; Alcuin, *carmen* 45.26, ed. Dümmler, *MGH PLAC* 1:257, "laus, honor, atque decus"; Audradus 5.147, ed. Traube, *MGH PLAC* 3:77: "Sit regi domino virtus, laus, gloria semper."

5   *rutilans,* although literally meaning "coloring red," may be reduced to "coloring." For other uses, see the third of the Lothar Gospel verses, ed. Dümmler, *MGH PLAC* 2, p. 671.1: "species rutilat." Also see the use of the the the word by Audradus 7.16, ed. Traube, *MGH PLAC* 3:86 and 9.324, *MGH PLAC* 3:100.

6   *imago viri,* cf. Isa. 44:13.

8   *his . . . illis,* for a related construction, see I.170.

10   *locus* seems to refer to the assembled people as they regard the king.

11   *eis,* that is, the assembled people.

13   *Iusta . . . cuncta,* cf. I.137 and Theodulf, *carmen* 41.149, ed. Dümmler, *MGH PLAC* 1:536.

15   *canis,* that is, since Charles is David and sings songs.

16   *Haut* as emended by Traube from "aut" in the codex.
       actio pura, cf. VI.21, "actio munda," and I.185, "actio."

17   *fotor,* that is, "fautor"; cf. VI.4 "eclesiae fautor."

20   *novare,* that is, to renew or confirm.

21   *merito deitatis honores,* cf. Audradus 1.1, ed. Traube, *MGH PLAC* 3:741, "summo deitatis honore."

28   *putris caro,* cf. I.34.

29   Cf. I.165.

30   *pietatis opus,* Audradus 3.8, ed. Traube, *MGH PLAC* 3:745 and 11.468, p. 121; cf. VI.28.

31   Cf. Ecclus. 1:2: "Arenam maris, et pluviae guttas, / Et dies saeculi quis dinumeravit?" Cf. also Theodulf, *carmen* 41.203–4, ed. Dümmler, *MGH PLAC* 1:537 and 71.66, p. 562.

32   *merite,* for "merito."

34   *gemma vitro,* here the poet seems to reverse the order of comparisons found in X.33, which moves from lower to higher things, for gems would seem to have been more highly prized than glass in the Carolingian world. See Genevra Kornbluth, *Engraved Gems of the Carolingian Empire* (University Park, Pennsylvania, 1995), pp. 1– 18.

35   *musio muri,* Theodulf twice refered to the *musio:* in *carmen* 28.442, ed. Dümmler, *MGH PLAC* 1:505, "musio mure facit," and 25.164, p. 487, "aut timido muri musio terga dabit."

37   *iam iam,* Audradus 9.214, ed. Traube, *MGH PLAC* 3:97 and 10.130, p. 104.

39   Cf. Audradus 5.374, ed. Traube, *MGH PLAC* 3:83, "felix per saecula vivat."

39–40   Cf. Lothar Gospels lines 7–9, ed. Dümmler, *MGH PLAC* 2:671:

Imperium ut teneat, dilatet, firmet, adunet,
Utatur bene pace fruens et prosperitate
Ac valeat, vigeat, vivat per secula felix.

42   *ab arce pia,* cf. VI.12.

43   *Insuper his,* Virgil, *Aeneid* 9.274.
        in tempore mortis, thus the poet prays that the king at the moment of death will immediately be received by Christ. On the purgatorial sufferings of Charlemagne and Louis the Pious, see Dutton, *Politics of Dreaming,* pp. 50–80, 219–21.

XI

1   *heros,* cf. "maximus heros," Virgil, *Aeneid* 6.192 and Audradus 9.116, ed. Traube, *MGH PLAC* 3:94. Audradus was speaking of a martyr, which was one of the uses for the epithet in the ninth century. For some applications of the word to living Carolingian kings, see *Karolus Magnus et Leo Papa* 149, ed. Dümmler, *MGH PLAC* 1:369 and 464, 1:378, "venerabilis heros," in both cases applied to Charlemagne; "Versus libris saeculi octavi adiecti," 8.2, ed. Dümmler, *MGH PLAC* 1:89, "fortissimus heros / Rex Carolus," a reference to Charlemagne; Eriugena, *Aulae sidereae* 101, ed. Traube, *MGH PLAC* 3:552, "Heros magnanimus longaevus," a reference to Charles the Bald. For references to noble warriors in the ninth century, see Sedulius Scottus, *carmen* 39.16 and 37, ed. Traube, *MGH PLAC* 3:203.

2   *Vivianus,* count of Tours, 845–51.

3   *ante ubi post patrem,* "ubi" can be taken here as "where" or "in which," that is, in the facing painting. For a similar use of "ubi," see I.106. But "ante" and "post" serve as prepositions governing the accusative "patrem." Lauer, "Iconographie carolingienne," pp. 192–93, placed a comma after "ubi," which would be one solution to the presence of parallel prepositions; another solution would be to understand *et* after "ubi" or the enclictic *-que* after "post." The poet's awkward phrase was an attempt to describe the double depiction of the four "primi."
        primi may be taken as meaning foremost or most eminent.
        primi Tesmundus amandus. This was the reading of Du Cange in the late seventeenth century: *Glossarium mediae et infimae Latinitatis,* 1:393. Some scholars have read this as "primites, mundus Amandus." See Berger, *Histoire de la Vulgate,* p. 217; Rand and Howe, "Vatican Livy," p. 30 and n.

7; Koehler, *Die karolingische Miniaturen,* 1:1, p. 227. Rand and Howe, "Vatican Livy," p. 31 and n. 1, however, discuss "the meaningless 'primites'" and preferred to emend to "primates." The scribe, however, left a discernible space between "primi" and "Tesmundus," thus seeming to indicate where he thought the division between the words should fall. In the first edition of *MGH PLAC* 3 in 1886 Traube printed "primi Tesmundus amandus" but later changed his mind. In "Untersuchungen zur Überlieferungsgeschichte römischer Schriftsteller, I: Zu Valerius Maximus. Zur Chorographie des Augustus. Zu Cornelis Nepos. Zu Livius," in *Sitzungsberichte der philosophisch-philologischen und historischen Klasse der königlich bayerischen Akademie der Wissenschaften zu München* (Munich, 1892), p. 428, rpt. in Traube, *Kleine Schriften,* p. 33, he changed the reading to "primnites mundus Amandus," reasoning, in part, that Tesmundus was a ridiculous name. In his afterthoughts or *Praeterita* to the 1896 edition of *MGH PLAC* 3:752 he referred his readers to the 1892 correction. It should, however, be noted that Tesmundus may not be as ridiculous a name as Traube supposed, since a Tesmunnus appears in an early-tenth-century document from Saint-Martin: see Mabille, *Pancarte Noire,* p. 216 and charter LXII, fol. 69, p. 98 and chronological index no. 123.

4   *Sigualdus,* Rand and Howe, "Vatican Livy," p. 31, suggest that he may have been "the dean Siwaldus mentioned in the testament of 841." See Mabille, *Pancarte Noire,* p. 81 (charter 35, fol. 40r) and p. 129 (charter 117, fol. 129r). Rand and Howe also suspected that Sigualdus might be the same person named Sigilau on the list of names of the brothers of Saint-Martin of Tours found in the Saint-Gall list: *Libri Confraternitatum Sancti Galli Augiensis Fabariensis, MGH Necrologia Germaniae, Supplementband,* ed. Piper, pp. 13–14, 77–78. Some have thought that person might be the Sigilaus who supervised the preparation of the Lothar Gospels (see *MGH PLAC* 2, ed. Dümmler, p. 671.16–17), but there is no clear indication that these were the same individual, and the substantial differences in the forms of their names suggest that they were not.
        summus in the codex. Traube, without remark, printed "primus."
        Aregarius, this monk is quite likely the *Haregarius* named in the Saint-Gall list: see *Libri Confraternitatum Sancti Galli Augiensis Fabariensis, MGH Necrologia Germaniae, Supplementband,* ed. Piper, p. 13, col. 14, no. 74 and p. 77, col. 236, no. 77.

6   *consociata simul,* cf. VI.24.
7   *iunctus haeret,* on "haereo" as physically "follows," see I.109; "iunctus" reinforces that description.
8   *amore colit,* Alcuin, *carmen* 3.34.64, ed. Dümmler, *MGH PLAC* 1:220.
11   *cuius honore,* that is, Saint Martin's.
        laudetur, ametur, Alcuin, *carmen* 69.9, ed. Dümmler, *MGH PLAC* 1:288.
13   *sola voluntas,* Venantius Fortunatus, *carmen* 9.7.64, ed. Leo, *MGH Auctores Antiquissimi* 4.1:214.
14   *Ex, tua quas, villis, iussio reddiderat,* this probably refers to the king's confirmation of a series of *villae* first given by Louis the Pious in the time of Abbot Fridugis to Saint-Martin: see Charles the Bald, charter 61, *Recueil des actes de Charles,* ed. Tessier, 1:174–77.
15   *Caesar,* on the other imperial appellations in the First Bible, see "induperator" at I.196 and the medallion inscription of "David Rex Imperator" on fol. 1v.
17   *Perpetui,* that is Perpetuus, archbishop of Tours (461–91).
        Sanctus Briccius, that is Brice, archbishop of Tours (398–444).
18   *aliis reliquis,* for *aliis reliquiis.* These relics are the other saints of Tours.
        o paradise, cf. I.119.
23   *fiat* in the codex. Traube, without remark, printed "fiet."
        renouatio, that is, the renewal of Saint-Martin's immunities on 27 December 845: see Charles the Bald, charter 80, *Recueil des actes de Charles,* ed. Tessier, 1:224–26.
25   *regale decus,* Ovid, *Metamorphoses* 9.690.
27   *Praeceptum genitoris, avi, proavi renovasti,* that is, the charter of his father, grandfather, and great-grandfather. In Charlemagne's first grant of immunity to Saint-Martin issued at Quierzy in April 782 he refers to an earlier act of his father Pepin: see charter 141, ed. E. Mühlbacher, *Die Urkunden der Karolinger, MGH Diplomata Karolinorum* 1 (Munich, 1979), p. 192.5–17. The grant of

immunity to Saint-Martin during the first part of Alcuin's abbacy repeated that charter and the reference to Pepin: ed. Mühlbacher, *MGH Diplomata Karolinorum* 1:262–63.

29   *quod tua sancta manus,* cf. Audradus 6.42, ed. Traube, *MGH PLAC* 3:85, "Quos tua, Petre, manus sacro." At XI.29 the poet notes Charles's actual signing of the renewal of immunities.

30   *praecepti serie,* the word "series" used at I.113, VI.5, and VIII.6 to refer to a Testament, is here employed in its strictly legal sense as "relation" or "document": see Charles the Bald, charter 81, *Recueil des actes de Charles,* ed. Tessier, 1:228.26–27: "in serie donationis."

32   *hoste vigente malo.* that is, the devil. Cf. I.164, "hostis perversus."

33   *I procul atque procul,* cf. Virgil, *Aeneid* 6.258, "Procul, o procul este, profani."

38   *coniuge,* that is, Queen Ermintrude (m. 842, d. 869).

38   *prole,* a daughter Judith was born in 844.

42   *Ave,* cf. 2 John 1:10–11.

Index

PLATES

1. Poem I.1–50; Paris, BN lat. 1, fol. 1r

2. Poem I.51–100, with medallion portraits of DAVID REX IMPERATOR +, *top*, and KAROLVS REX FRANCO<RVM>, *bottom;* Paris, BN lat. 1, fol. 1v

REBVS ALT SACRIS QVEDAM QVIA TERTIVS INDE
NVNC OLIM VOVO INTERIMITVR VITVLI
MORE MYSTAL OMNIA TRANSCENDIT SIDERA QVARTVS
IN SVBLIME SPECIEM STIGMATIS IPSE GERIT
QVATER APOSTOLICOS LVCAS QVOS EDIDIT ALTVS
SVBDIT VBI TOTVS INSTRVIT ET POPVLVS
CATHOLICAE HINC SEPTIMA IDOLIS MIRABILE DICTV
FORMAT APOSTOLICVS VAS OPERANDO STYLVS
HIS HAERENT BIS SEPTEM PAVLI SCRIPTA DEINDE
RITE LVENS CVI VOX MODO QVINA MICAT
OCCONCLVDIT OPVS IAM VISIO SCA IOHANNIS
VISIOS EA SATIS AC MEMORANDA NIMIS
HAEC NOVA RITE CLVIT SERIES SVBIVNCTA PRIORI
VMBRA PRIOR QVARVM CAVSA Q: POSTERIOR
COETERE DVPLEX VTRIVSQ: EFFICTVS INVN
QVO TRIBVENTE DATVR SCAN CIO CELIS POLI
HIC QVIA DIVITIAE AETERNAE VELVT ALIA MENSAE
IMPLENT OMNINO SECTARE PERPETVO
HIC TABA DYS ET VVS NITIDA RATIONE ET ESCIT
MVLTIMODVS FRVCTVS MELLIFERAXQ: LOCVS
HIC SITIENS POTVM ESVRIENS PANEM ANXIVS AEQ:
LAETITIAM INVENIET LAETVS ET INDE FLET
HAEC TAMEN IN HOC MORTALI DV CORPORE QVISQ:
DEGIT HABET Q: MAGIS ELVS ABAMORE VELLIT
...ISSA MAGIS...IS....MAGIS ESTORATIONIS

S...QVI...ILLA...VT MAGE QVISQ: BIT
CVM VERO SE RIS AVERIT TVNC ELIGIT HORVM
ILLVS AMATOR ERIT TRI...AC IXTVS... PRO
ADQVO PHILOSOLVS HAEC DOCTRINA HAEC SEMITA TANTVM
MENS ENS SIBI ... RE SVBDIT TA TES DEI
...STIAM MORALIBVS ISTIC
OMNI...VVLT LECTOR IN BREVITATE TIBI
HIC HARGENTVM AVRVM GEMMAE VARIAE...ESTES
...QVI...QVIDVLI...RAT ONER VSE...QVE...
HIC ET LEX PRECIOSA NIHIL PRECIOSIVS ILLA
AVTEM AVT VOCE AVENDIT OLET VI SACRE
IVSTA IVBENS INIVSTA VITANS MALA CVNCTA REPELLEN
O...QVIS...QVI BONIS IVS RIS ITATE TOTIVS
D...DINAM FVLGOR GRADI OLVS DISCORDIA IRERA
CONSILIO LEGIS HVIVS OBIRE QVE ON.
R...DEBIT IN NOCTO QVOS SIM SAPIENTIA ALEO...IS
CONTERIT ET MEDIIS DOGMA... VS TESTA...
MAGNA PLVIT MAGNIS DISPONIT PARQ: TA PARVIS
...RVTROQ: STILVS IVSTITIAE CALIDVS
...OTI EX MIH V PRAEBET CONFESSA CVSTOR
IN ETIA IN HOMON LEX VINI EN IN DX...BI
...SEX VALIS HOMINI LVMIN TER COMITA MVNDI
...TERTIS...QVOL LVX E IORIGO SVI
...A..DVS INGENVIS PERABELLI TIQVO IVS IS TA
...SSE...TER...LOQVID VIR ATIONIS IVICE

4. Poem I.151–200; Paris, BN lat. 1, fol. 2v

5. Jerome frontispiece; Paris, BN lat. 1, fol. 3v

ADAM PRIMVS VTI FIN / CVIVS COSTA SACRAE / XPS EVA DVSIT ADAE · / QVAM VOCAT VIR AGSSII ·
GITVR ISTIC · / CARPITVR EVAE / AST EDANT NSPMAVITAS PROIMT IPSE CON SPITOS

SVA IT NVPER CREATAE ANGVIS DOLO PVELLAI / POSTH ECA MOENA LVSTRAM · ADA IVOCAT REDEMPTOR ·

VTERQ ABVMBRIS PELLITVR INDE SACRIS · / STIAC LABORI RVRA COLVIT HABITI ·

6. Genesis frontispiece; Paris, BN lat. 1, fol. 10v

7. Exodus frontispiece; Paris, BN lat. 1, fol. 27v

8. Psalms frontispiece; Paris, BN lat. 1, fol. 215v

EXVLTA LAETARE SATIS REX INCLITE DAVID · INSENSV PARILI CONVENIVNT QVE SIBI

EGREGII VOTI COMPOS VBIQVE TVI PLVS VE MINVS VE VEL AEQVA BOANT SVA SICQ DEHISCVN

CARLE DICVS REGNI SAX COSMI GLORIA CLERI ATTAMEN EFFECTVS VNVS VTRINQ NOVVS

ECLESIAE FAVTOR MILITIAEQ DECOR HOC EVANGELIV SAHAT BLANDITVR HONORAT

ENIAM LECTA TIBI SERIES TRANSACTA VETVSTA · CASTIGAT REFICIT MVNIT HONESTAT ALIT

SED NOVA RITE SEQVENS ISTI LEGENDA PATET HIC MODVS EFFANDI HIC VIRTVS HIC ACTIO MVNDA

CVIVS EN INITIO CLARE PRIMORDIA CLARA HIC CIBVS HIC POTVS HIC BENEDICTA SALVS

MATTHEVS DNI CONCINIT EX GENESI HIC CARITAS VIA SPES VERVMQ FIDESQ

CVI LAETVS LAETERIA FREMIT DE SERTAMINANDO SEV BONA CVNCTA SIMVL CONSOCIATA VIGEN

VOX TVA MARCE SVO FVLTA PERENNI DO HIS ASSVESCE DIV HAEC MEDITARE HAEC DILIGE SIVE

MYSTICA SACRA SACRE PARTIS PER OVAT MOR ORBIS IN SERMONE OPERE HAEC HABITARE STVDE

FERT STVDIVM LVCAE LVCIS A BARCE PIAE REX BONE REX SAPIENS REX PRVDENS REX VENERANDE

GENITVM PATRIS SVPER AETHERA CELSE IOHANNES REX CAROLE ALME VALE CVM PIETATIS OPE

SCANDIS ET EX VERBO VERBA COLENDA CANIS DET TIBI SCEPTRA PATRIS IHS CONFIRMET ADVNET

EXIMII HI IACVNT LATE MYSTERIA XPI PROEMIA SCORVM VT MEREARIS AMEN

9. Poem VI; Paris, BN lat. 1, fol. 329r

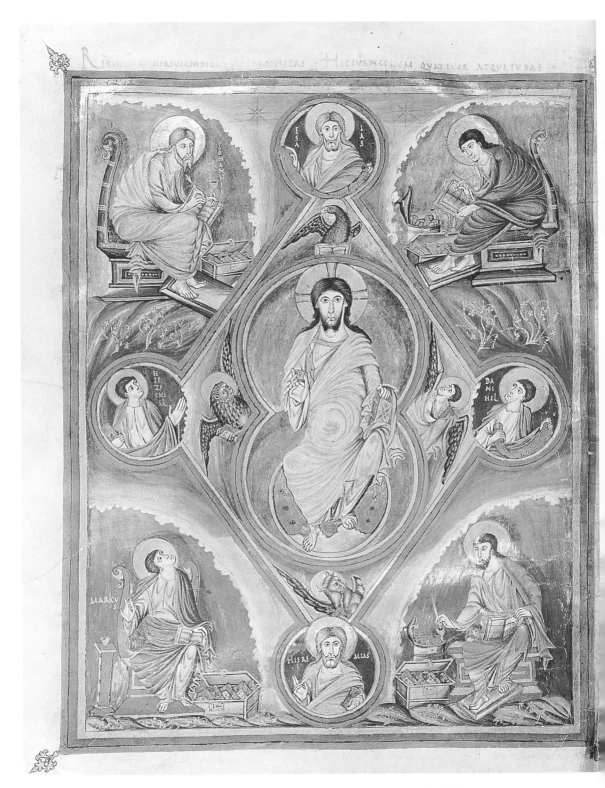

10. Majestas Domini, the Gospels frontispiece; Paris, BN lat. 1, fol. 329v

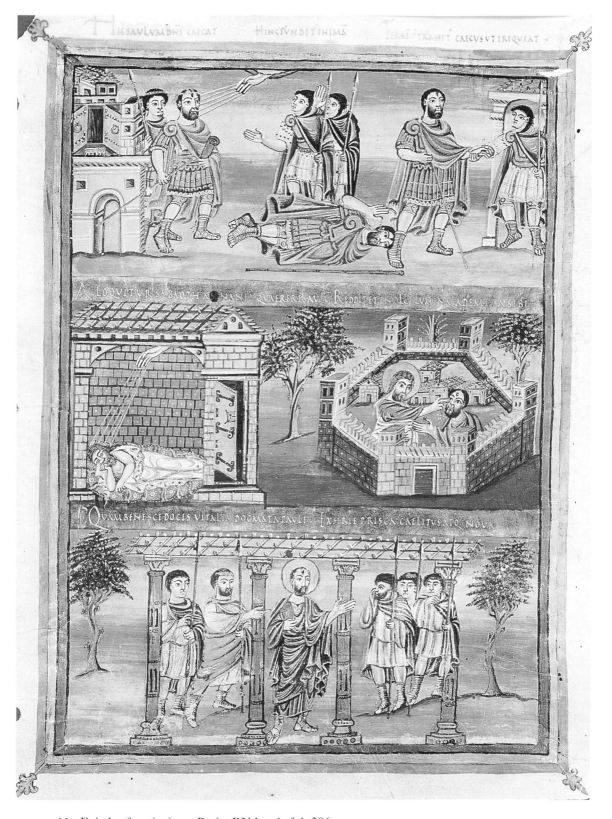

11. Epistles frontispiece; Paris, BN lat. 1, fol. 386v

exeamus igitur ad eum extra castra Improperium eius
portantes Non enim habemus hic manentem ciuitatem
sed futuram inquirimus per ipsum ergo offeramus
hostia laudis semp do Id e fructu labiorum confitentium
nomini eius Beneficentiae aut et communionis nolite
obliuisci talib: enim hostiis promeretur ds

O boedite ppositis uris et subiacete eis Ipsi enim peruigi
lant quasi rationem pro animab: uris reddituri ut cum
gaudio hoc faciant et non gementes hoc enim non expedit
uobis Orate pro nobis Confidimus eni qui a bonam
conscientiam habemus In omnib: beneuolenter conuer
sari Amplius aut depcor uos hoc facere quo celerius
restituar uobis

D s aut pacis qui eduxit de mortuis pastorem magnum
ouium in sanguine testamenti aeterni dnm nrm ihm
xpm Aptet uos in omni bono ut faciatis uoluntatem eius
faciens in uobis quod placeat cora se per ihm xpm
cui e gloria in saecula saeculorum am

R ogo aut uos frs ut sufferatis uerbum solaci et eni
per paucas scripsi uobis Cognoscite fratrem nrm
timotheum dimissum Cum quo si celerius uenerit uide
bo uos Salutate omnes ppositos uros Et omnes scos
Salutant uos de italia gratia cum omnib: uobis am

E x p l i e p l a a d h e b r a e o s

12. End of the Letter to the Hebrews; Paris, BN lat. 1, fol. 415r

13. Apocalypse frontispiece; Paris, BN lat. 1, fol. 415v

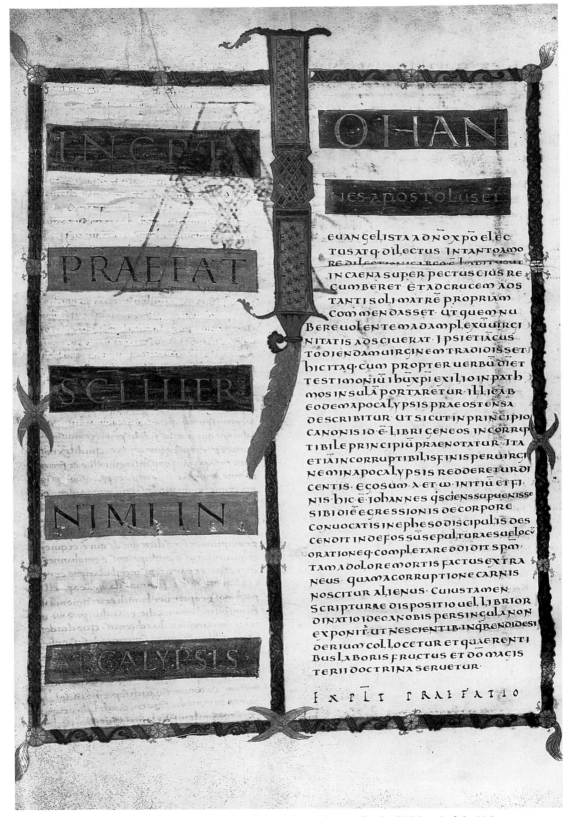

INCPIT

PRAEFAT

S CI LIER

NIMI IN

APCALYPSIS

IOHAN
NES APOSTOLUS ET

euangelista a dno xpo elec
tus atq dilectus intanto amo
re dilectionis a rcus habitus ut
in caena super pectus ejus re
cumberet et ad crucem a os
tanti soli matre propriam
commendasset ut quem nu
bere uolentem adamplexu uirgi
nitatis adsciuerat ipsi et iam cus
todiendam uirginem tradidisset
hic itaq cum propter uerbu diet
testimoniu ibu xpi exilio in path
mos insula portaretur illic ab
eo dem apocalypsis praeostensa
describitur ut sicut in principio
canonis io e libri geneos in corrup
tibile principiu praenotatur ita
etia incorruptibilis finis per uirci
nem in apocalypsis redderetur di
centis ego sum a et w initiu et fi
nis hic e iohannes qsciens sup uenisse
sibi die egressionis de corpore
conuocatis inepheso discipulis des
cendit in de fos sa se pulturae se loc
orationeq completa re ddidit spm
tam a dolore mortis factus extra
neus qua m a corruptione carnis
noscitur alienus cuius tamen
scripturae dispositio uel librior
dinatio ideo a nobis per singula non
exponit ut nescienti b ingrendi desi
derium col locetur et qu erenti
bus laboris fructus et do magis
terii doctrina seruetur

EXPLIT PRAEFATIO

14. *Incipit* and Text of Jerome's Preface to Apocalypse; Paris, BN lat. 1, fol. 416r

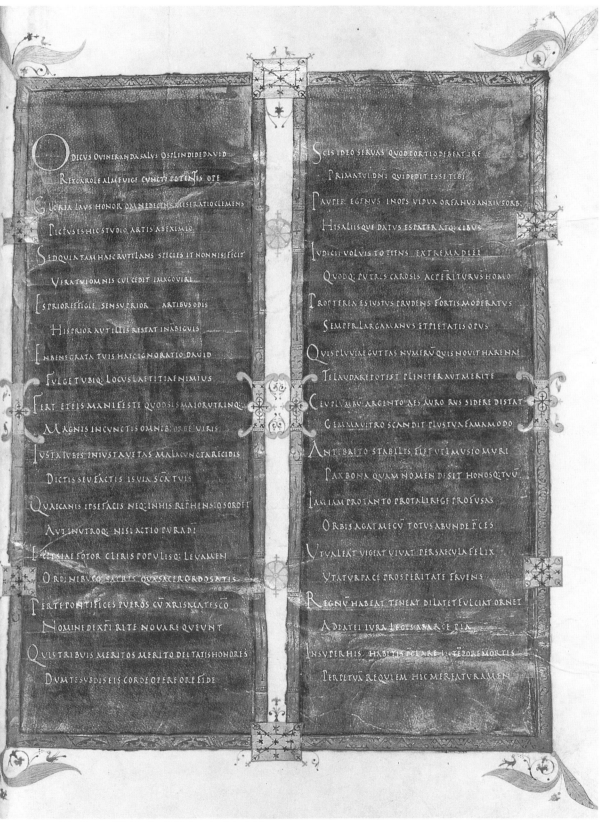

O DECVS O VENERANDA SALVS O SPLENDIDE DAVID
REX CAROLE ALME VIGE CVNCTI POTENTIS OPE
GLORIA LAVS HONOR OMNE DECENS RESERATIO CLEMENS
PICTVS ES HIC STVDIO ARTIS AB EXIMIO
SED QVIA TAM HAEC RVTILANS SPECIES ET NON NISI FECIT
VERA TVI OMNIS CVI CEDIT IMAGO VIRI
ES PRIOR EFFIGIE SENSV PRIOR ARTIBVS ODIS
HIS PRIOR AVT ILLIS RESTAT IN ABICVIS
IN BENE GRATA TVIS HAEC IGNORATIO DAVID
FVLGET VBIQ; LOCVS LAETITIAE NIMIVS
FERT ET EIS MANIFESTE QVOD SIS MAIOR VTRINQ;
MAGNIS IN CVNCTIS OMNIB; ORBE VIRIS
IVSTA IVBES INIVSTA VETAS MALA CVNCTA RECIDIS
DICTIS SEV FACTIS IS VIA SCA TVIS
QVAE CANIS IPSE FACIS NEQ; IN HIS REPREHENSIO SORDET
AVT IN VTROQ; NISI LACTIO PVRA DI
ECLESIAE FOTOR CLERIS POPVLISQ; LEVAMEN
ORDINIB; VSQ; SACRIS QVA SACER ORDO SATIS
PER TE PONTIFICES PVEROS CV XRISMATE SCO
NOMINE DEXTRA RITE NOVARE QVEVNT
QVIS TRIBVIS MERITOS MERITO DEITATIS HONORES
DVM TE SVBDIS EIS CORDE OPERE ORE FIDE

SCIS IDEO SERVAS QVOD PORTIO DEBEAT IRE
PRIMATVI DNI QVI DEDIT ESSE TIBI
PAVPER EGENVS INOPS VIDVA ORFANVS ANXIVS ORB;
HIS ALIISQVE DATVS ES PATER ATQ; CIBVS
IVDICII VOLVIS TOTIENS EXTREMA DIEI
QVODQ; PVTRIS CAROSIS AC PERITVRVS HOMO
PROPTEREA ES IVSTVS PRVDENS FORTIS MODERATVS
SEMPER LARGA MANVS ET PIETATIS OPVS
QVIS PLVVIAE GVTTAS NVMERV QVIS NOVIT HARENAE
TE LAVDARE POTEST PLENITER AVT MERITE
CEV PLVMBV ARGENTO AES AVRO RVS SIDERE DISTAT
GEMMA VITRO SCANDIT PLVS TVA FAMA MODO
ANT; BRITO STABILIS FIET VEL MVSIO MVRI
PAX BONA QVAM NOMEN DESIT HONOSQ; TVV
IAM IAM PRO TANTO PRO TALI REGE PROFVSAS
ORBIS AGAT MECV TOTVS ABVNDE PCES
VT VALEAT VIGEAT VIVAT PER SAECVLA FELIX
VT ATVR PACE PROSPERITATE FRVENS
REGNV HABEAT TENEAT DILATET FVLCIAT ORNET
ADDAT EI IVRA LEGES A PARTE PIA
IN SVPER HIS HABITIS PCLARE IN TEPORE MORTIS
PERPETVA REQVIEM HIC MEREATVR AMEN

15. Poem X; Paris, BN lat. 1, fol. 422r

16. Poem XI; Paris, BN lat. 1, fol. 422v

17. The Presentation miniature; Paris, BN lat. 1, fol. 423r

INCIPIT
EPISTOLA
ADROMAN

PAVLVS
seruus ihū
xpi uocatus
apostolus se
crecatus in eu
angeliū di quod
ante promiserat·

PER PHETAS SUOS IN SCRIPTURIS
SCIS DE FILIO SUO· QUI FACTUS·E·
ET EX SEMINE DAUID SECUNDŪ
CARNEM· QUI DESTINATUS·E·
FILIUS DI IN UIRTUTE· SECUNDŪ
SPM SCIFICATIONIS EX RESURREC
TIONE MORTUORŪ IHU XPI DNI NI·
Per quem accepimus gratiam et aposto
latum ad oboediendū fidei in omnib; gen
tib; pro nomine eius. In quib; esas et uos
uocati ihu xpi· Omnib; qui sunt romae
dilectis di uocatis sais· gratia uobis et pax
a do patre nostro et dno ihu xpo·
Primum quidem gratias ago do meo per
ihm xpm pro omnib; uobis· quia fides ura
annuntiatur in uniuerso mundo· Testis eni

omni credenti· Iudaeo prir
enim di in eo reuelatur ex
tum·e· Iustus aut ex fideu
Reuelatur enim ira di de ca
tem et iniustitiam homine
di iniustitia detinent·
manifestum·e· in illis· D
Inuisibilia enim ipsius a cr
facta sunt intellecta consp
quoq; eius uirtus et diuin
les· quia cum cognouis sen
ficauerunt aut gratias eg
in cogitationib; suis· et obi
eorum· Dicentes enim se
et mutauerunt gloria inc
dinem imaginis corrupt il
et quadrupedum et serpe
didit illos dns in desideria
diciam ut contumelius af
metipsis· qui commutar
mendacium· et coluer e
us quam creatori qui·e· b
Propterea tradidit illos e
nam feminae eorum imm
usum in eum usum qui·e·
ter aut et masculi relicto
arserunt in desideriis su
masculos turpitudinem o
quam oportuit erroris su
et sicut non probauerum
tradidit illos dns in repro b
quae non conueniunt· r
malitia fornicatione a
inuidia homicidio conten
susurrones detractores d
superbos elatos inuentor

18. Beginning of the Letter to the Romans, detail; Paris, BN lat. 1, fol. 387r

19. The first vignette from the Apocalypse frontispiece, middle left; Paris, BN lat. 1, fol. 415v

20. The second vignette from the Apocalypse frontispiece, top middle; Paris, BN lat. 1, fol. 415v

21. The third vignette from the Apocalypse frontispiece, middle right; Paris, BN lat. 1, fol. 415v

22. The *Liber comitis* of Saint-Père of Chartres, with AVDRADVS inscribed in the interlaced angles of the page; and rearranged above: Chartres, Bibliothèque municipale 24 (32), fol. 2r. (after Wilmart)

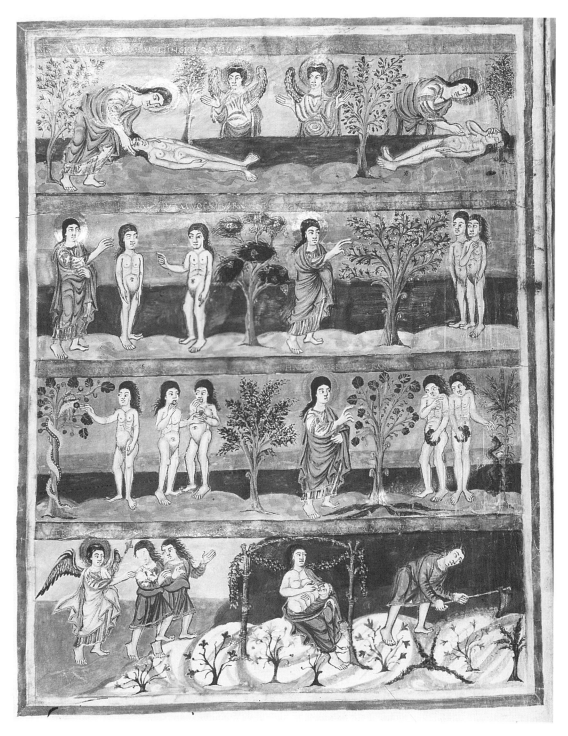

23. Genesis frontispiece; London, BL, Add. MS 10546, fol. 5v

24. Exodus frontispiece: London, BL, Add. MS 10546, fol. 25v

25. Majestas Domini, the Gospels frontispiece: London, BL, Add. MS 10546, fol. 352v

26. Apocalypse tailpiece: London, BL, Add. MS 10546, fol. 449r

27. The Trojans sail from burning Troy; Vatican, Bib. Apos., Cod. lat. 3225, pict. 17.

28. Aeneas and the Trojans in Thrace; Vatican, Bib. Apos., Cod. lat. 3225, pict. 18

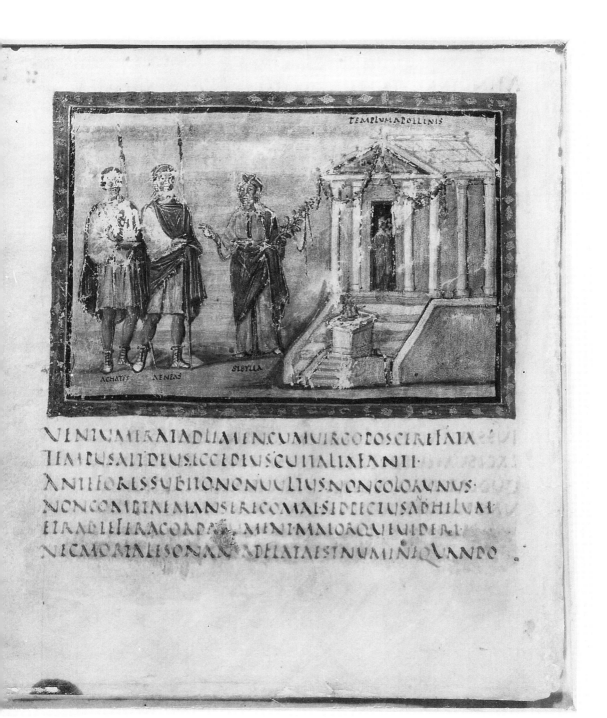

29. Achates and Aeneas consult the Sibyl; Vatican, Bib. Apos., Cod. lat. 3225, pict. 31.

DICITAEDARDANIDAINEQ·ENIMINISCIMUSHURBEM
IICINUSAUDITIQ·ADUERTITISAEQUORECUASUM
QUIDEETITISQUAECAUSARATESAUTCUIUSICENTIS
IIUSADAUSONIUM·TOTPERUADACAERUIAUEXIT
SIUEIRRORIUAISIUIEMPESTATIBUSACTI
QUALIAMUITAMARINAUIAIPATIUNTURINALTO·

30. King Latinus and the Trojan envoys; Vatican, Bib. Apos., Cod. lat.
3225, pict. 41

IIAECIEEAIOSIQUOSNUMEROPATERELLICITOMNE
SIABANTIEACENTUMNITIDIINERAISEDIBUSALTIS
OMNIBUSEXTEMPIOTEUCRISIUBEIORDINEDUCI
INSTRATOSOSTROALIPEDESPICTISQUEIATENTIS
AURTAPICTORIIDEMUSSAMONITIAENUIEE
TECTIAUROTUINUMMAX·UNISUBDINTISAURUM
ABSITIAENIAEGUR·UITEMAINOS·UEIIUCAELIS

31. King Latinus gives gifts to the Trojans; Vatican, Bib. Apos., Cod.
lat. 3225, pict. 42.

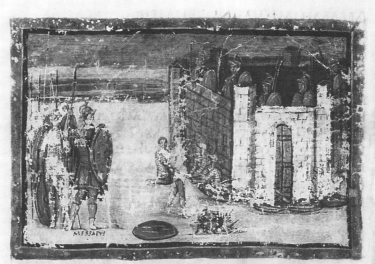

32. Messapus and the Rutulians lay siege to the Trojan camp; Vatican,
Bib. Apos., Cod. lat. 3225, pict. 48.

33. Ascanius chairs the Trojan war council at which Nisus and
Euryalus speak; Vatican, Bib. Apos., Cod. lat. 3225, pict. 49.

34. Lothar I; Paris, BN lat. 266, fol. 1v

35. Ivory panel; Cambridge,
FitzWilliam Museum (McClean
Bequest M.12/1904)

36. Judith frontispiece; Rome, Monastery of San Paolo fuori le mura, Bible, fol. 234v

37. Medallion portraits with inscriptions. Top left: First Bible, fol. 1v, DAVID REX IMPERATOR +; bottom left, KAROLVS REX FRANCO<RVM>. Top right, Berlin, Staatsbibliothek Preußischer Kulturbesitz, theol. lat. fol. 733, fol. 23v, DAVID REX IMPERATOR A<V>G<VSTVS>; bottom right, D<AVI>D IMPERATOR A<V>GVSTVS +